SEASONS of
FAITH
AND
CONSCIENCE

Seasons of Faith and Conscience

Kairos, Confession, Liturgy

Bill Wylie Kellermann

The Catholic Foreign Mission Society of America (Maryknoll) recruits and trains people for overseas missionary service. Through Orbis Books, Maryknoll aims to foster the international dialogue that is essential to mission. The books published, however, reflect the opinions of their authors and are not meant to represent the official position of the society.

An earlier form of Chapter 2 appeared in *Sojourners* August/September 1989. Chapters 6, 7, 9, 13 and 14 were previously published, also in *Sojourners,* as the series, Seasons of Faith and Conscience, beginning in January 1985.

Library of Congress Cataloging-in-Publication Data

Kellermann, Bill Wylie.
    Seasons of faith and conscience: Kairos, confession, liturgy /
  Bill Wylie Kellermann.
      p. cm.
    Includes bibliographical references and index.
    ISBN 0-88344-726-6
    1. Liturgics.   2. Christianity and international affairs.
  3. Sociology, Christian.   4. Christianity and politics.   I. Title.
  BV178.K45   1991
  264 — dc20   91-7262
                                                       CIP

for Bill Stringfellow

If, then, we can see the theater of Christian beginnings in terms of a "war of myths," one can identify it even better as one of liturgy against liturgy or liturgies, with the understanding that liturgy involves the whole life style, action and ethic as well as recital.

Amos Wilder
Jesus' Parables and the War of Myths

Because there are competing and conflicting programs of resymbolization available to us, we are engaged in a battle for the mind, heart, and imagination of our society. It is not yet clear which liturgy will prevail in the postindustrial, post-Christian West, but it is clear that the outcome of the liturgical conflict will be decisive for policy formation and public values in our society as concerns politics, economics, and law.

Walter Brueggemann
Israel's Praise

The social orders created by liberalism and socialism have generated fears of a future impoverished of meaning, if not indeed devastated by pollution, poverty, depletion of basic resources, and war. Religion, whose demise as a vehicle of meaning and truth has so long been announced, has reemerged as a vehicle of protest and a tool for envisioning new possibilities.

Rosemary Radford Ruether
Women-Church

All the same, the deep social commitment of some Christian groups is often inspired by a more meaningful celebration of the Eucharist. This is generally in small groups, among youth, workers, women, religious, priests, and the like. They are, not infrequently, marginalized by the official church authorities. Eucharistic life pulsates among them.

Tissa Balasuriya
The Eucharist and Human Liberation

CONTENTS

FOREWORD
by Jim Wallis

Two decades ago, I was a student at Trinity Evangelical Divinity School, just north of Chicago. A small group of young seminarians began to meet regularly for intense discussion, prayer, and Bible study. Though we were studying in one of the bastions of conservative evangelicalism, biblical discourse and discernment had lost its vitality and integrity, being almost thoroughly shackled by the conformities of cultural and civil religion. Biblical faith, we were told, had virtually nothing to do with the burning questions tearing American society apart — racism, poverty, and the war in Vietnam. Or, if anything, evangelical religion placed the churches firmly on the side of the government and the majority culture, as far as such social and political issues were concerned.

We heard a different word from the Scriptures, and what we were hearing set our hearts ablaze. Our little band would gather almost every day to wrestle with the imperatives of faith and the crisis of our historical circumstances. We met often until late at night in one of our dormitory rooms, talking and praying, laughing and crying, and, most importantly, studying the Bible. It changed our lives and created a community. From those early days, Sojourners community and magazine was born.

About the same time, but further east, another group of seminarians had started a Bible study. This one met in the boiler room at Union Seminary in New York City. At this citadel of liberal Protestantism, the Bible had also been emptied of its lively relevance and political immediacy. Academic scrutiny had all but replaced biblical discernment and devotion. Bill Kellermann and the other boiler room Bible students were making similar discoveries about the presence and power of the word of God in history, indeed, in our history.

Looking back now, one can discern the beginnings of new movements in the churches from those two experiences and many others. Those new movements are profoundly ecumenical, deeply biblical, and creatively liturgical. They are neither conservative nor liberal and defy catagorization into the old polarities that have defined and stifled the churches for so long. If any word fits, it is "radical"—not in the sense of left-wing ideology and politics but rather in their "rootedness" in historic biblical faith. The consequences of such rootedness have been radical indeed, creating a whole new dimension of American political dissent and alternative social vision which has confronted the established rulers of both church and state.

Looking back, on a more personal note, I see the beginnings of my deep friendship with Bill Kellermann, the author of this remarkable book. He is a rare biblical theologian and Christian, combining theology and action the way the Bible does, the one always informing the other. Bill represents the new kind of theologian the new movements in the church are producing. He not only articulates the faith experience, he experiments with it. He is and does what he says.

The Bible is central to the reformulation of faith and action now occurring throughout the churches. A new generation of biblical theologians is emerging: reinterpreting Scripture in the light of social and political realities, breaking out of old patterns and categories, transcending the entrenched theological camps that constricted and controlled biblical discussion for so long, opening up the word of God to the world and the world to the word, and empowering ordinary people to biblical thinking, discernment, and action. Among the new generation of biblical expositors, there is none more creative, clear, and compelling than Bill Kellermann.

A great deal of the inspiration for the new generation of biblical theologians came from the person to whom this book is dedicated, William Stringfellow. His role as elder, mentor, and spiritual father to a number of us, including Bill Kellermann and myself, was and remains pivotal. The many hours and days Bill and I spent around Stringfellow's table, often with priest and poet Daniel Berrigan, were instrumental in shaping both biblical and personal discernment.

In my view, William Stringfellow is the most significant twentieth-century American theologian, though the Harvard-trained and Harlem-based lawyer never had formal theological education. He understood the Bible and the meaning of the word of God for modern America more than any of the theological giants of his day.

In his Block Island retreat, he passed on to us not only biblical knowledge and interpretation, but a passion for the word and a determination to give it incarnational reality in our own lives and circumstances. William Stringfellow also passed on his own well-worn Bible to Bill Kellermann when he died. It was, I always thought, a fitting gesture to a young Bible scholar and activist who would undoubtedly help open up the world to a whole new generation of Christians who desire to live and act as biblical people.

That is exactly what this extraordinary book will do. It is exemplary of the kind of biblical work that is reshaping the church and transforming biblical scholarship itself. And it will help to explain to the politicians, military leaders, and magistrates, wise enough to read it, why the cycle of political resistance has begun to coincide with the church's liturgical calendar!

It was an honor to be able to publish parts of this book in earlier form in *Sojourners* magazine. And I am grateful beyond measure to have such a friend and companion as Bill Kellermann.

This book has been a long time in coming. But it was worth the wait. William Stringfellow would have been very proud. The rest of us are very fortunate.

Acknowledgments

The thanks of my heart:

To Jeanie Wylie Kellermann, author in her own right, co-con-
spirator, jailhouse romance, spouse, and best friend; to
whom this book might also rightly be dedicated. For sleepless
nights, for encouragements and critiques and goadings, and
space to get it done. You have not only my thanks but my
heart.

To the Detroit Peace Community and the Michigan Faith and
Resistance Circle; and before them to Greenwood and Great
Lakes Life; to Covenant for Peace, Sojourners, Jonah House
and Atlantic Life, Ground Zero, NDE, the Catholic Workers — a host of communities too many to name — experi-
menters all with the truth of liturgical direct action.

To Joyce Hollyday and Jim Wallis for originally conceiving this
book and setting magazine deadlines for its earliest pieces.

To Ched Myers for lighting my fire about the project when once
it had gone out, and for thoughtful criticism and suggestions
which have influenced both structure and content of the
book.

To Walter Wink for instructing me, even as we were taken away
in a White House bust, on the rebuke of inner demons whose
craft it is to suppress our writing.

To several bishops, rare and uncommonly good, who have directly or indirectly supported this book and the ministries behind
it: my own (United Methodist), Judith Craig, and before her
Edsel Ammons. Also two Episcopal bishops, H. Coleman
McGehee and R. Stewart Wood.

To the faculty and staff of the Whitaker School of Theology for
welcoming material such as this into its diaconal curriculum,
and especially to Whitaker students for joining me in the

struggle with this material and its public practice.

To friends who provided space for reflection or writing: Vic and
Keira for the "chicken coop," the monks of Gethsemani for
silence.

To John Bach for "Leafletwriting 101."

To Deb Ferris for liberating these words from hard-disk captiv-
ity.

To Rick Cassidy for his boundless enthusiasm for almost everything, including this project and Orbis Books.

To Robert Ellsberg for being such an editor and becoming such
a friend.

To other friends who read the manuscript and commented: Liz
Walters during a six-month jail bit, John Zettner, Tom Jones,
Bea Wylie, Carol Gilbert, Ardeth Platte.

To my parents; may they recognize in these pages the faith and
tradition they have shared with me.

To Lydia and Lucia for being so full of life. May your baptisms
into Christ bear the fruits of service and justice as right worship.

To Daniel Berrigan for calling my name once down a long hall
of Union Seminary and asking if I prayed; for the liturgy and
poetry of his life.

I pray every one of them will find this reading faithful and true.

INTRODUCTION

At the beginning of this decade the unmaking of the Berlin Wall has been an astonishing feature of our history. The image of ordinary people from both sides chipping away at it with hammers has become iconic in the international media. Imaginations have been touched and a common store of anger and hope ritually released in this spontaneous outpouring of popular direct action.

A South African pastor working in Soweto recounted to me his own act of solidarity, common among the international community, of taking the opportunity on a Berlin stopover to level a few blows of his own at the Wall and all it betokens. It occurred to me just then to wonder: What if in the years preceding, Christians East and West had gone regularly to the Wall, prayerbooks in one hand and hammers in the other, to pray and begin symbolically to dismantle the wall, suffering perhaps arrest or other untoward consequences. What if?

Shortly thereafter a reply formed within me: They did. For the last decade or more Christians all over North America and Europe, indeed all over the world, have been cutting fences, crossing lines, and wielding hammers in worship, all of which take aim more or less at that very wall. I begin with a personal story.

It was Holy Saturday 1983. We had gathered, a group of friends, in the woods of northern Michigan. Darkness settled in about our cabin and with it the cold of night.

Less than a mile up the blacktop road was Wurtsmith Air Force Base, home of the 379th Bombardment Wing of the Strategic Air Command. Sixteen B-52s with nuclear mission targets in the Soviet Union sat on the runway. They were being further armed with cruise missiles, a nuclear weapon of pinpoint accuracy, that extended the bombers' range and capacity to fight in a first-strike nuclear attack. The arrival of the missiles and the arrival of Easter occasioned our presence there. Together they defined a moment of historic and personal import.

For months we had been gathering periodically in retreat for Bible study, prayer, and discernment. Each of us—a Methodist pastor, several members of the Catholic Worker movement, a handful of Catholic priests with experience in third-world or inner-city ministry—had come to the point of considering a direct action with more risk than we had undertaken before. Given the times, where were we called? Hence the topic of our prayer.

Because the cruise was raising opposition in Europe that we wished to support, and because of its role in first-strike scenarios, we had settled on Wurtsmith as the focus of our action. All of us had long ago concluded that such weapons were not only illegal by international standards and immoral by ethical ones, but also theologically blasphemous, the power of death writ large. In the course of discussion one of my friends said, "You know what I'd like to do? Celebrate the Easter Vigil liturgy walking onto the base." In that moment I recall a nearly audible thump in my own heart, an immediate confirmation of personal certainty. Quickly, almost effortlessly, after months of uncertainty, we all agreed. Of course there was more agonizing over details and risks, but the direction of things was set.

So here it was the eve of resurrection. And we were gathered to act.

At 2:00 A.M. we began the liturgy of the Word. Those who know the Easter Vigil will recall that there is in Christian liturgy no finer collection of readings from the Hebrew scriptures: the story of creation, the flood, Abraham's sacrifice of Isaac, the Red Sea crossing, Ezekiel's new heart and spirit, the valley of dry bones called to live, and the like. A feast of faithfulness, passage, and hope.

There in the cabin we also made intercession, marking names and peoples upon a sheet subsequently to be used as an altar cloth: children (by name), the poor, friends in prison, soup kitchen guests, the dead and disappeared of Central America, peace-campers at Greenham Common, members of parishes

back home, families. A communion of the living. A solidarity of
the spirit, this prayer for passage, this claim upon the future.

After singing a hymn, we exited into the night. Against our
expectations, it had begun to snow, heavy and wet. Single file
from the road through the woods to the extreme end of the
runway, the snow fell about us like a dense silence. It felt for
all the world like setting out for an action from Thomas Merton's
monastic hermitage in the Kentucky hills.

At the barbed-wire fence we paused and circled in preparation for two symbolic deeds. The first was to light the Paschal
candle. Into these, our dark times, enter the light of Christ. So
we prayed, flame in hand. The second, indeed one with the
other, was to cut the fence. From our Bible study we were mindful how the seal on the stone of the tomb is against tampering,
a legal barrier backed up, by one account, with the force of an
armed guard. Twang! The security of death guarding death was
broken in liturgy. The wall was breached.

Thereupon seven of us began our three-and-a-half-mile trek
toward the high-security area, the loaded B-52s. It had been our
intention to paint at the foot of the runway, in six-foot high
letters legible from a landing plane, CHRIST IS RISEN! DIS-
ARM! We had toted along supplies sufficient: buckets of yellow
paint, brushes, rollers. The wet and freezing snow, however,
foreclosed that plan.

We walked on mostly in silence, lying down periodically in a
fumbling comedy, to avoid the view of patrolling security cars.
As the nuclear storage bunkers came into sight, we arrived at a
small building, the enclosure for some sort of electronic equip-
ment. Here on the walls we inscribed our message, paint con-
gealing in the freezing drizzle. And here we carried the vigil
liturgy another step forward: we renewed our baptismal vows.

I had not foreseen the personal power of that moment: to
look down the runway toward the machines and their cargo, and
there to "renounce Satan and all his works." There I promised
in a way not fully understood before to "persevere in resisting
evil, and, whenever I fall into sin, repent and return to the
Lord." A life may be called back to such moments, indeed may
turn on them.

The sky had begun to lighten. Birds were rousing. Shivering, we conferred and decided we had had enough of the dodging and weaving. We would proceed upright with dignity, in the manner of right worship. Here an astonishing phenomenon occurred, one reportedly not uncommon in such undertakings. We passed unseen! On one side were the bunkers, encircled with barbed-wire, lit like perpetual noon-day, driven roundabout by a constant patrol of vehicles, and observed from above by watchtowers, beneath which we processed. On the other side, parked for maintenance or refueling, huge bombers stood in a line equally well-lit. It was as though the waters had parted. We walked unhindered to the open entrance of the high-security area where planes on alert stood ready to fly.

There, measured by a sudden flurry of activity within, we were finally noticed. Armored vehicles and pickup trucks rushed to surround us. We spread our altar cloth of intercessions on the runway. About it we scattered blood, brought in small bottles, to signify the blood of the innocents, the blood of the Lamb. Producing the elements of the eucharist, we completed the service at gunpoint, surrounded by young airmen armed with automatic weapons.

We were a dishevelled band. Bedraggled, dressed in plastic garbage bags as makeshift protection against the unexpected weather, we were soaked nonetheless and cold to the bone. In weakness and exhaustion, we suffered a sense of our own foolishness.

The airmen held us in their sights but did not approach. Extending the service, we sang plaintive gospel songs and hymns of resurrection. At long last an officer approached us.

"Are you," he asked tentatively, "base personnel?"

"No."

"Do you work on the base?"

"No."

Then surveying the scene yet again, "Well, would you pick up your trash and leave?"

It was clear almost immediately that our breach of security was so severe an embarrassment that should we simply depart quietly, no record or mention need come to the attention of community public or even military higher-ups. We consulted among ourselves and declined. The liturgy was complete in its own right, but it had momentum and direction we did not intend to abandon. Herded into a bus, strip-searched, interrogated by various agencies military and civil, we were in the end dumped unceremoniously at the front gate without charges.

Our friends awaited us with leaflets in hand. At the gate to the base and the doors to the churches in town we distributed the news. The leaflets described the cruise and its meaning for policy. They described our pilgrimage. And they offered this simple confession of faith:

> We believe that God has already intervened in this dark history of ours.
>
> We believe there is hope. Many people have yielded to despair. They can already hear the terrible sound of the door slamming shut on human history. But we are here to say otherwise. Someone is hidden at the heart of things, breaking in to break out, on behalf of human life.
>
> We believe that God rules our common history. Not the Soviet Union. Not the United States. Not the NATO or Warsaw Pact forces. Despite their big and competing claims.
>
> We believe that human beings (so says Easter) are free from the power of death in all its forms and delivery systems. We are not stuck with the balance of terror arrangements. We're not in bondage to these weapons. We are truly and fully free to unmake them. Now. Not tomorrow or next week or next year. But this very morning.
>
> We believe that God who raised Christ from the dead will also quicken our imaginations, and thereby our bodies and lives.
>
> We believe this is the meaning of the resurrection. And we've come to say so.

Was anything actually accomplished? In a certain sense that is the central question of this book. Oh, that Easter Vigil was the first in a long series of actions and leafletings, trespasses and arrests, an ongoing campaign of presence and resistance at that air base. As I write this, a friend sits in jail, a six-month sentence, for a subsequent entrance to distribute leaflets at

Wurtsmith. But the fact of the ensuing campaign does not fully answer the question. Is such action a proper and effective form in the struggle against these weapons and the system of which they are emblems?

I have told the story in detail because through it my growing sense of what I call liturgical direct action was further formed. I tell it not because it is so remarkable and rare, but contrariwise, because such actions in this last decade have become commonplace in the faith-based nonviolent movement of resistance to the arms race, to third-world intervention, and even to ecological destruction. Examples abound. I name these almost arbitrarily.

Advent 1986. An Episcopal bishop celebrates the eucharist outside Williams International, a Michigan cruise missile engine manufacturer which is the focus for a series of Christian civil disobedience actions. Several hundred people participate. The service is right out of the Book of Common Prayer, but the context magnifies certain meanings, certain hopes, certain calls to repentance. Its significance is not lost on the diocese.

Epiphany 1987. Four people enter the Willow Grove Naval Air Station outside Philadelphia. With hammers they damage a P-3 Orion anti-submarine nuclear-capable aircraft (with a role in Pentagon first-strike scenarios) and two military helicopters of the sort employed in third-world intervention. They celebrate the feast day of Christ's appearance by enacting Isaiah's prophecy that "swords will be beaten into plowshares." Since the first one in 1980, over one hundred people have participated in such "plowshares" actions, disarmament at once prayerful, symbolic, and concrete.

Lent 1989. Beginning Ash Wednesday and continuing through Holy Week a series of groups gather in Las Vegas to enter the desert. They go to the Nevada Test Site, where nuclear weapons tests (for upgraded warheads, stockpile maintenance, and new systems such as Star Wars) are carried out approximately once every three weeks. The groups pray together, consider the meaning of temptation and repentance, and conclude by entering the property, where they are arrested. The continuing witness, called the Nevada Desert Experience, was begun by a group of Franciscans a decade ago and is now facilitated by a team of organizers year-round in Las Vegas. Just inside the main gate to the site two permanent large barbed-wire holding pens have been constructed for the processing of "demonstrators."

Good Friday 1989. As every year for the last decade, and in a manner similar to many other communities, the Stations of the Cross are walked in Detroit in a public and political way. Seeing the crucifixion of Christ in the suffering of victims, three hundred people process through the streets of Detroit, pausing to pray at places where suffering is manifest (neighborhoods neglected and destroyed, the county jail, the site of a handgun shooting), where needs are ministered to (a soup kitchen, free health clinic, shelter for runaways), or decisions made (city-county building, the Federal building). The meditation booklet from which they read specifies the connection of this suffering to the arms race. In addition, this year the day coincides with the anniversary of Oscar Romero's assassination. His memory and the suffering of the Salvadoran people are prominent in the litany.

Pentecost 1989. It is a "Faith and Resistance Retreat." These have become common, especially throughout the Midwest. As with others, this one is ecumenically called by Episcopal, Roman Catholic, and United Methodist bishops, and by the Presbyterian Church. In the course of the weekend there is Bible study given to the lections of the season, political analysis, nonviolence training, and some guided instruction in personal discernment. The Spirit is invoked and wrestled. On Pentecost proper there is a brief service outside the gate of a military contractor, whereupon a smaller group of people climb over the fence to plant a tree, nurturing hope. They are arrested and sentenced to thirty days in jail.

These instances are exemplary and typical. The sites vary from the Pentagon to its missile silos, from nuclear labs and think-tanks to Trident submarine bases, from corporate headquarters to SAC Headquarters, from manufacturing facilities to the arms bazaars where the weapons are marketed. The list goes on, covering the continental map.

In 1989 there were some fifty-five hundred arrests at seventy-four different sites in the United States and Canada for actions of resistance to nuclearism.[1] In a year which properly touted the nonviolent resistance of movements in China and Central Europe, this record number went nearly unnoticed in the American media. Add arrests for resistance to homelessness, third-world intervention, and environmental degradation, and the figures would nearly double. I hazard to suggest that the vast majority of those arrested were Christians, and that many of the actions were of the sort I have described.

This book is an attempt from within that movement to make biblical, theological, political, and even liturgical sense of these actions. It is on the one hand addressed to that same wide community in hopes of clarifying what we have been instinctively about for the last decade or more. (The instincts have been right and good.) It reflects on our common experience and is written in hopes of nourishing our movement further.

It is also addressed to the church. I am convinced that these actions constitute a virtual liturgical renewal movement in the streets. They are a gift to the life and faith of the church. They illuminate the simple fact that every act of worship, every occasion where the sovereignty of the Word of God is celebrated, every instance where the realm of God is acknowledged, is always and everywhere expressly political.

For this reason the book begins biblically, with an analysis of the constructive (*and subversive*) social function of worship in Hebrew scripture. The political import of liturgy is found rooted there and in the public ministry of Jesus, whose liturgical politics are rarely noticed in the gospels. Issues of allegiance and sovereignty are everywhere and always central to worship; these are invariably quite political issues.

Since these acts of prayer and conscience are flagrantly ecumenical there has been a natural if unanticipated fusion of liturgical sensibility brought from Catholic quarters and the confessional impulse of certain Protestant traditions. Chapter 2 takes up confessional politics, especially from the notorious example of the church in Nazi Germany. How did confession of faith in the Lordship of Christ define the church struggle and nourish political resistance?

Chapter 2 also sets before us several of the important "kairos documents," which are raising, from various third-world contexts, the question of whether this is a decisive moment of truth and grace for the North American church. Are we being called to conversion and action by the Word of God in this shifting present moment of history, which is so dangerous and exciting?

Some readers will be familiar with the material in Chapter 3, which focuses on the religious and mythic dimension of nuclear imperialism. Others will count it dated or of only passing pertinence in the light of Cold War thaws and disarmament talk. However, I give it this attention for several reasons. First, it is the context of myth and history in which these current experiments with liturgical action have largely arisen. Second, imperial nuclearism, I believe, may be recognized as spiritually and politically entangled, even seminal, in the emergence of other crises we face, namely, ecological degradation, the injustice of the global economy, the perfection of low-intensity warfare, and the like. Third, even as freedom is celebrated and geopolitical shifts take place, these are being acclaimed as triumphs for the West, a vindication of military and political policy. If some weapons systems are foresworn and others dismantled, the same cannot be said of their mythic meanings. These remain imprinted on psyches and culture. If they now go less high profile, perhaps it is merely that they are driven underground, where their motive power is only the stronger.

Something similar may be said for Chapter 4 on the principalities. The biblical material draws from recent exegetical work on the powers as social entities both material and spiritual. It leads toward the approach of liturgical direct action as an essential tactic in naming and exposing and engaging the powers that be in common history. It, too, draws on the example of nuclear imperialism, and for similar reasons. Specifically, it offers a biblically realistic assessment of how nuclearism, its technologies and institutions, may tenaciously survive the fresh breeze of sentiment for global disarmament.

The last chapter turns current and concrete with abundant examples of liturgical direct action. The depth structure of the church year gets some consideration as the rubric for discernment and public witness which it has become. Temptations to confusion and abuse, also abundant, are reflected upon. All in all, the chapter rounds out a churchly apologetic for this variety of action.

The seasonal meditations which comprise the second half of the book were, in fact, written first. They arose from and for particular actions in a particular season. They are perhaps the most confessional material in the book. Each in its way is a statement of faith.

It is inevitable, I suppose, that some will complain that this book reduces worship to an instrument or a tactic of social struggle. I can only testify to the faith of those who undertake these actions, and my own. I fear and delight to place my life in the hands of the Living God. Prayers and praise arise from the depths of my heart. I understand, however, that this is also a choice, call it Christian discipleship if you will. That choice implies much, including many things still hidden from me, but I comprehend at least that it is a choice to stand under the sovereignty of God, in actuality to declare that sovereignty in history. It is a choice for that community, for that social world commonly called the kingdom of God. It is a Reality I bet my life upon. Liturgically put, Yahweh reigns! and Christ is risen!

Eastertide, 1990

PART I

LITURGY
AND
TRANSFORMATION

CHAPTER 1

CONFESSION AND COMBAT: LITURGY IN SCRIPTURE

*After this I looked, and behold, a great number, from every
nation, from all tribes and peoples and tongues, standing
before the throne and before the Lamb, clothed in white robes,
with palm branches in their hands, and crying out with a loud
voice, "Salvation belongs to our God who sits upon the throne,
and to the Lamb!" And all the angels stood round the throne
and round the elders and the four living creatures, and they
fell on their faces before the throne and worshiped God, saying
"Amen! Blessing and glory and honor and power belong to
our God forever and ever! Amen."*

Revelation 7:9-12

DOXOLOGY AND DOMINION

The heart rises to this. It is like that common moment in the
Great Thanksgiving when we join our voices with all the company of God's people in heaven and on earth, saying "Holy,
holy, holy Lord, God of power and might, Heaven and earth are
full of your glory. Hosanna in the highest. Blessed is the one
who comes in the name of the Lord. Hosanna in the highest."
Before the elements of bread and wine as before the very throne
of heaven, we may know that the vocation of every person,
indeed of all creatures here below, is to praise God. It is deepest
inner urge and delight. Longing and love.

3

Yet, like the last supper or eucharist situated in time and history, the doxologies of Revelation (1:5-6; 4:1-11; 5:8-14; 7:9-17; 12:10-12; 15:1-5; 19:1-8) go up amid turmoil, trial, the disorientations of imperial blasphemy, and the crises of allegiance. In this hymn from chapter 7 it is specifically those "clothed in white robes" who announce salvation, who sing it and pray it. We are already alerted (Rv 6:11) that such garb signifies those who are slain for the word of God and for the witness they bear. To underscore the point, lest the symbol escape us or any meaning be lost, an exchange follows:

> Then one of the elders addressed me, saying, "Who are these, clothed in white robes, and whence have they come?" I said to him, "Sir, you know." And he said to me, "These are they who have come out of the great tribulation; they have washed their robes and made them white in the blood of the Lamb" (Rv 7:13-14).

Hence their praise, their confession of faith, is at once the cause and consequence of martyrdom. Praise is no Sunday School pastime. It rises on the raw edge of common history, acknowledging and even affecting it.

Liturgical "moments" of prayer and praise, such as this one, punctuate the book. They simultaneously mark structural shifts in Revelation and turning moments in the saga of history it tells. And, for reflection here, such moments are thoroughly revealing about the nature of worship. Three points will serve to preface our consideration of what we might call liturgical politics.

Worship is a sign of allegiance, and it obviates or mitigates every other claim on the obedience of the faithful. In a period of crisis this implies and identifies a conflict. In Revelation it is the beast and his minions who proclaim their sovereignty and demand obeisance. The famous refrain of wonder, despair, and perverse praise uttered by human beings who follow the beast of empire is found in chapter 13. People "worshiped the dragon, for he had given his authority to the beast, and they worshiped the beast saying, 'Who is like the beast, and who can fight against it?'" This song is seductive. The whole earth, the mass of humanity is taken into the chant. The alternatives are clear; one cannot sit both at the table of the idols and the table of the Lord. Their hymns cannot be uttered in the same breath. There is a conflict of liturgies. The praise of God declares a choice. In that sense, worship, everywhere and always, is political.

Indeed, in one of the most astonishing passages of the book, the collapse of empire and its entire world, which is to say the doom of Babylon (read Rome and its historical surrogates), is occasion for what? Praise in heaven.[1] "Hallelujah! The smoke [of Babylon] goes up forever and ever ... Hallelujah! For the Lord our God the Almighty reigns" (19:3,6). Now the songs of worship contrast with the lamentation of kings and merchants who had cast their lot with the glories and securities of the imperial city. This liturgy signifies and celebrates the end of one world and the beginning of another. In that sense, faithful worship is inherently subversive.

The smoke that rises forever and ever is the parallel of the intercession of the saints, which goes up as one with the incense upon the heavenly altar:

> And another angel came and stood at the altar with a golden censer; and he was given much incense to mingle with the prayers of all the saints upon the golden altar before the throne; and the smoke of the incense rose with the prayers of the saints from the hand of the angel before God. Then the angel took the censer and filled it with fire from the altar and threw it on the earth; and there were peals of thunder, loud noises, flashes of lightning, and an earthquake (8:3-5).

Daniel Berrigan observes of this passage:

> The liturgy is instructive. There is an element of ascent, tranquil prayers go up, incense is offered, then comes the majestic moment: the casting to earth of fire from the altar. As though to say, this is the way with true liturgy; it burns, it shakes the earth, causes thunders, voices, lightnings, tremblings. A passionate will is expressed: to connect the divine with the terrestrial, the human and the heavenly. God is fire and the fire falls to earth.[2]

True liturgy burns and shakes. Can we be so bold as to say that, by the grace of God, liturgy sets things in motion within heaven and upon the earth? I believe we can. Liturgy, everywhere and always, in one way or another, addresses history. It not only celebrates the new world, but gives it a foothold, helps to construct it.

A SOCIOLOGY OF PRAISE: MAKING AND UNMAKING THE WORLD

In a footnote to *Israel's Praise*, Walter Brueggemann cites a 1985 order of the Pretoria regime which prohibited blacks from singing Christmas carols in the townships because they generated such revolutionary energy. A newspaper report quotes a South African police agent: "Carols are too emotional to be sung in a time of unrest. . . . Candles have become revolutionary symbols."[3]

As much as anything, the instance typifies the significance of Brueggemann's sociological reading of the psalms. He is concerned to trace the social function of praise and so sets out to explore the psalms, not merely with respect to their origin, but also their ongoing *use* in the life of Israel. His suggestion, very nearly incendiary, is that they function "characteristically and inevitably in the deployment and legitimation of social power."[4] Because this book is so important to the way I conceive the politics of liturgy and confession, I will consider some of his key points at length.

Brueggemann's point of departure is an attentive rereading of Sigmund Mowinckel's classic study of the psalms, in particular "The Festival of the Enthronement of Yahweh and the Origin of Eschatology."[5] In essence Mowinckel posited an annual festival in the early days of the Jerusalem Temple under the sponsorship of the king, which liturgically enthroned Yahweh as sovereign. The other gods, defeated in combat, pledged their service and obedience for another year, and Yahweh decreed health and *shalom* for Israel.

Because, according to Mowinckel, the king sat in for Yahweh in the ritual proceedings, the Davidic monarchy itself was simultaneously legitimized anew, which is to say, the social world of established Israel was regenerated and defined in the creative symbolism of the cult. At the same time, because the cultic enactment never fully met expectation, because the reality always fell short of the promise, hope was projected into the future and eschatology was born. Hence Mowinckel's title. Notice, Brueggemann urges, that in this way the current administration would be at once endorsed and critiqued.

The point here and in Brueggemann's analysis is that liturgy effects and defines social reality; it "makes" the world in which human beings live. As Mowinckel puts it:

> The cult is not only originally, but everywhere and always, drama. Cult is a holy enterprise, but it is at the same time a holy reality. It is not merely a playful drama, a play, but an effective and reality-generating drama, a drama which actualizes with real power the dramatic event, a reality which shows forth real power, or in other words, a sacrament.[6]

Reality is the operative word here, underscored by emphatic redundancy. Cultic praise is not merely responsive. It constructs the perceived social world.

In this connection Brueggeman points to the influential sociological work of Peter Berger and Thomas Luckmann, who describe how structures and patterns of a given social arrangement are produced and legitimated.[7] Reality, which is first and foremost the reality of everyday life, is experienced as firm and given, almost as though it were the only possible social configuration. It is in fact socially chosen, a "fiction" made to appear plausible and even inevitable by a variety of symbolic legitimations, first by language itself, but also by the rudimentary propositions of common wisdom, proverbs, slogans, the taken-for-granted cultural assumptions, explanatory histories, and so on. The highest and most integrated level of legitimation is the "symbolic universe" where all the diverse provinces of meaning are encompassed and ordered in a totality. Here, "all the sectors of the institutional order are integrated in an all-embracing frame of reference, which now constitutes a universe in the literal sense of the word, because *all* human experience can now be conceived as taking place within it."[8]

In a society religiously integrated this symbolic universe constitutes a kind of "sacred canopy" covering and connecting all of life. It is of course this level of things which is addressed, embraced, and legitimated, sustained or subverted by liturgy. It refers to, implies, and articulates the symbolic order. However, both maintenance and subversion are to be stressed here, for these are the two basic relationships of liturgy to any dominant social order. Berger names one function "world maintenance" and the other "world shaking." Brueggemann says that liturgy involves an aspect of worldmaking or, conversely, unmaking, and demonstrates how this works with respect to the enthronement of Yahweh. He works backward and forward from Mowinckel's proposed festival by means of specific texts.

At the root of the enthronement festival and Yahweh's perennial victory over the gods is Israel's liturgy of liberation: victory over Pharaoh and the exodus from Egypt. The most ancient account is the most simple, that found in the Song of Miriam:

> Sing to the LORD, for he has triumphed gloriously,
> the horse and his rider he has thrown into the sea.
> (Ex 15:21)

Note that in its oldest form the exodus is already liturgy, a doxology on the lips of liberated slave women. It is a refrain to be danced, tambourines in hand. By it the God-given realm of freedom is celebrated and sung again to life in joy. The new "world" is suggested, announced, envisioned, in the same refrain with the demise, God's unmaking, of the old.

The Song of Moses (Ex 15:1-18) begins with Miriam's refrain, but details the journey and specifically joins it to the trembling dismay of the other nations: "Lord, who is like you among the gods?" Says Brueggemann:

> Every retelling makes the members of the ruling junta nervous, because the world is indeed being constructed against them. ... [The nations] tremble not only because of potential loss, but because they are profoundly vulner-

able. The poem culminates with a doxology of enthronement: "The Lord will reign for ever and ever." (v. 18).
Yahweh's enthronement asserts Pharaoh will not reign,
and if Pharaoh will not reign, his brick quotas are obsolete
and his social privilege is terminated. Among the others
who will not reign are the inhabitants of Philistia, the
chiefs of Edom, the leaders of Moab, the inhabitants of
Canaan (vs.14-15).[9]

If the song dates from the twelfth or eleventh century B.C.E.,[10]
in which these feudal nations flourished, it would have functioned then specifically in that context to nullify the myths of
their legitimacy. The liberation story happened in a time past,
but as a "subversive memory" liturgically borne, its claim and
power is asserted now in a new way.

Commenting on these concluding verses, George Pixley
writes:

> Until early in the present century it was thought that Israel
> had not celebrated Yahweh as king until it had organized
> a monarchial state of its own. But today we know that the
> reign of Yahweh was a basic building block of the revo-
> lutionary ideology of Israel's peasant movement [in
> Canaan], and that it was in the name of Yahweh's rule
> that Israel refused to install human rulers. (See Gideon's
> response to the elders of Israel—Judges 8:22-23.)[11]

We begin to see how the fundamental acclamation of the
enthronement psalms, "Yahweh reigns!", functions in a variety
of contexts. Brueggemann imaginatively portrays several distinct
social contexts.[12] It is one thing—an essentially dangerous and
destabilizing assertion—whispered in the slave camps of Egypt.
It is another—a call to distinct identity, a declaration of freedom
which refuses the claims of encroaching neighbors—in the
period of Samuel and the Judges. And, returning to the Jerusalem enthronement festival, yet another under the sponsorship
and patronage of the king. Here, the rule of Yahweh is *equated*
with the dominant order. The God of liberation may be domesticated in the service of monarchial regime and status quo order.

The memory is all but suppressed. Its energy is harnessed and deflected. In the hands of establishment liturgists the proclamation may become idolatry.

This also is a key to understanding liturgy in our own time and place. It is not merely that imperial America constructs a symbolic universe through civic and political liturgies. (We will examine mythic nuclear symbolics as one instance of such a construction.) The church's liturgy, as well, may conform to, endorse, and maintain that universe by such methods as the Jerusalem monarchy employed.

Here's how. When the exodus liturgy moves from slave camps and peasant confederation assemblies into the temple precincts of a capital city, it undergoes another change. Brueggemann sees this as something of an inevitable shift. "This move from the edge of freedom to the temple is a necessary move, for it permits the tales of transformation to become visible and solidified as 'world' — royal world, visible world, ordered world, safe world, new world."[13] Continuity is assured. The story is preserved. The liturgy comes to befit an abiding God and life-world.

It also befits the king who foots the bill.

The tale of liberation in this context becomes hotter to handle. Mechanisms emerge. A shift in weight occurs. A certain drift may be recognized. In psalms under the royal sponsorship, there is a tendency to emphasize the *summons* to praise (Sing to the Lord!), but downplay, mute, or even suppress the *reason* for praise. Why sing? Not because "horse and rider have been thrown into the sea," but because "great is the Lord and greatly to be praised" (Ps 96).[14]

Moreover, a kind of generality presides. There is a subtle shift from the concrete to the abstract, from the "descriptive" to the "declarative," from recounting how God acts for justice in a specific time and place to reciting characteristic actions without mentioning any particulars.[15] (Compare, for example, psalms 136 and 107.) Here even verb forms reflect the kind of language which world maintenance requires. By such methods memory is effectively impaired. "Doxology which robs Israel of its concrete memory yields a god who does not do anything and who is therefore an idol . . . a god who is a pale replica of Israel's God."[16]

It is, of course, this idolatry against which the prophets had

the guts and good sense to rail. Through them the voice of the
living God might still speak, naming the idol, and rebuking the
cultic charade of the temple-state:

> I hate, I despise your feasts,
>   and I take no delight in your solemn assemblies.
> Even though you offer me your burnt offerings
>   and cereal offerings,
>   I will not accept them,
> and the peace offerings of your fatted beasts
>   I will not look upon.
> Take away from me the noise of your songs;
>   to the melody of your harps I will not listen.
> But let justice roll down like waters,
>   and righteousness like an ever-flowing stream.
>   (Am 5:21-24)

The living God shakes the world of idolatry maintained
through the liturgy of royal doxology. Yahweh subverts and even
breaks that world. Jeremiah, who faced a fully advanced version
of this, recognized its big lie, a political-economic system which
saw itself beyond question, whose slogans redundantly hailed
"peace, peace" when there was no peace, which clung to the
altar as an act of deceitful worship. Says the God of Jeremiah:

> You gain nothing by putting your trust in this lie. You steal,
> murder, you commit adultery and perjury, you burn sac-
> rifices to Baal, and you run after other gods whom you
> have not known; will you then come and stand before me
> in this house which bears my name, and say, "We are
> safe"? Safe, you think, to indulge in all these abominations.
> Do you regard this house which bears my name as a den
> of thieves? I warn you, I myself have seen all this, says the
> Lord (Jer 7:8-11).

To make God's world-shaking and world-breaking power and
intention explicit, Jeremiah undertakes a symbolic action, a kind
of counter-liturgy in the streets, by publicly and ritually smashing
to pieces an earthen pot.[17] Would the reign of Yahweh unmake

the world even of Israel? It would. Indeed it did.

   After Nebuchadnezzar's invasion of Judah, siege and destruction of Jerusalem, and the deportation of large elements of the
population (especially the literate elite) to Babylon, there was
a new social and political context in which to sing the song of
Yahweh's victorious reign: exile (fifth century B.C.E.). Only now
the words stick in the throat.

> By the waters of Babylon,
>   there we sat down and wept,
>   when we remembered Zion.
> On the willows there
>   we hung up our lyres,
> For there our captives
>   required of us songs,
> And our tormentors, mirth, saying,
>   "Sing us one of the songs of Zion!"
> How shall we sing the LORD's song
>   in a foreign land? (Ps 137:1-4)

Now the temptation was no longer to the idolatry of a flat and
colorless image of Yahweh, but the new pantheon of Babylonian
deities, who had much to commend themselves (including victory and empire under their belts). Against them, in their home
turf, surrounded by all the signs and trappings of empire, under
the taunts of captors, Yahweh might indeed appear pale and
weak. Yet memory, a subversive memory, was nourished.

> If I forget you, O Jerusalem,
>   let my right hand wither!
> Let my tongue cleave to the roof of my mouth,
>   if I do not remember you,
>   if I do not set Jerusalem
>   above my highest joy. (v. 5-6)

   Israel's world might be remade, but it would require the subversion and deconstruction of the imperial claim. And that must
begin in liturgy. The so-called Priestly[18] creation account of Genesis 1 (literally a world-making text) functioned liturgically in

this very way: to counter and subvert, even satirize, the Babylonian creation myth.[19] Over against the famous combat liturgy
of Babylonian gods Marduk and Tiamat, exiled Israel set its own
primordial story of Yahweh's sovereignty. A liturgy of the word.
Similarly, in the Priestly version of the exodus narrative the
people partake the ritual of passover and unleavened bread as
a single rite precisely at the moment Yahweh effects their freedom from Pharaoh (Ex 12:1-20). And celebration of this meal
in the Babylonian scene is specified on the same day as the
imperial creation liturgy. It becomes expressly a pointed act of
freedom. There is more to be said of this,[20] but that must wait
for the moment.

Brueggemann's key text from the exilic period is from Second
Isaiah:

> How beautiful upon the mountains
>   are the feet of him who brings good tidings,
> who publishes peace, who brings good tidings
>   of good,
>   who publishes salvation,
>   who says to Zion, "Your God reigns."
>   (Is 52:7)

Sound familiar? The messenger bears hot news, right out of the
enthronement psalms, right out of the exodus narrative. Brueggemann makes much of the word *basar*, who "brings good tid-
ings." It is the same word that becomes "gospel" or "good news"
in the New Testament. Originally functioning to report the outcome of a battle, it has been theologically appropriated (liturgically in the enthronement psalms) to report "a victory of God
wrought elsewhere that has decisive effect on the situation in
which the reported outcome is spoken and heard. ... In the
speaking and hearing, the content of the message takes on social
reality."[21]

If the burden of Isaiah is to declare exile ended because
Babylonian power is to be nullified, the poet is up against the
powerful grip of that empire on the heart and mind, the very
imagination of the captive community.

The gospel enacted in Second Isaiah is that Babylon is defeated. It is only a liturgic, poetic event. The imperial armies still march. The imperial media still seduce. The imperial economy still discriminates. But the news breaks out of the liturgy and begins to erode the old world. The liturgy begins to subvert the empire. People begin to notice the cracks in the establishment. Some begin to sense that the truth of the gospel invites the first-time acts of civil disobedience against the empire. Confidence wanes. Support is withdrawn. The observant begin to sense a difference. A new world pushes with determination against the old one.[22]

This is precisely what Berger describes when he suggests that "it is possible to effectively challenge the Leviathan of predefinition."[23] In a situation of revolution or other moment of social transformation, one finds that "outward acts against the old order are invariably preceded by the disintegration of inward allegiance and loyalties."[24]

LITURGY AND ALLEGIANCE

The word *liturgy* is employed throughout this book trusting in the currency of common usage. However, its etymology is interesting. Thomas Merton wrote an essay in the early sixties (it eventually became the first in a collection on the church year) in which he traced the meaning of liturgy in classical Greek to a kind of political activity. "*Leitourgia* was a 'public work,' a contribution made by a free citizen of the *polis* to the celebration and manifestation of the visible life of the *polis*."[25] It was a public work done at a private or personal cost, such as the act of providing for the dithyrambic dance and procession, the production of a drama for the city, or even the building of a bridge or public road. In borrowing this word, originally without any real religious significance, from the political lexicon of the Greek city-states, first the translators of the Hebrew Bible into Greek and then the church by its usage have planted an etymological memory which rises now to the surface.

Richard K. Fenn, a sociologist writing about secularization, picks up the import of this meaning. His book *Liturgies and Trials* is an analysis of the confrontation between religious and secular languages, between religious and secular worlds, in the specific instances of several judicial trials (Catonsville is one of these). He concludes that the political nature of the liturgy arises partly from its claim to define the truly public world:

> The point here is simply that to take part in any liturgy is to signify to oneself and others that one is constituting a community and oneself as a member of that community. So to take part in the Christian liturgy is to take on one's role in a new kingdom: one that "shall have no end." It is the political act of all time and is therefore potentially seditious within the secular politics of a specific time and place. Caesar understood the political nature of the liturgy all too well. . . . Certainly it behooves all Caesars to know what vows are being taken by their subjects and what freedoms are being claimed in the name of kingdoms other than their own.[26]

One of the sources to which liturgical historians turn for clues of early Christian worship is a remarkable correspondence between Pliny the Younger, provincial administrator over Bithynia early in the second century, and his "lord," the Roman Emperor Trajan. It is of such note because the letter describes with a lawyer's care both what he was able to discover concerning the liturgy of the Christians and how he compelled them (or not) to repent. From fallen-away believers and some deaconesses whom he tortured, Pliny ascertained that "they were in the habit of meeting on a certain fixed day before it was light, when they sang in alternate verses a hymn to Christ, as to a god, and bound themselves by a sacred oath [*sacramento*]." Moreover, the Christians regrouped later in the day for a meal. "Even this practice they had abandoned," he says, "after the publication of my edict, by which, according to your orders, I had forbidden political associations."[27]

Pliny was distressed. Attendance in the Roman temples had taken a big downturn. The "sacred festivals" were being neglected. His method of interrogation and enforced Roman evangelism, subsequently to become notorious, was to set before the believers an image of the emperor. Should they curse Christ and worship the image, they were released. If not, the opportunity being twice offered, the obstinate were summarily executed. Trajan's even-handed reply basically concurred and the correspondence, it appears, might just as well have become a policy memo on the topic for some time to come. Caesar understood the political nature of liturgy all too well.[28]

The Acts of the Apostles may have served Pliny's suspects as something of a Christian handbook on this matter of allegiance. Richard Cassidy's *Society and Politics in the Acts of the Apostles* has effectively demonstrated, albeit against the tide of common interpretation, that it offers counsel with regard to appearances before Roman officials and their local surrogates.[29] Just count, he suggests, the number of trials and closely consider the comportment of the Christians. In the final analysis, whatever the outcome might be (whether execution, imprisonment, miraculous liberation, or formal exoneration), the ultimate key to the posture of believers is summed up in the testimony of Peter and John before the Sanhedrin: "We must obey God rather than human beings" (Acts 5:29).[30] In every instance they witness to the sovereignty of God in their lives and indeed in history. It is a public scandal, all but unnoticed in Acts, that Paul, a Roman citizen on trial, incessantly declares Jesus Christ his Lord—*kyrios*—the very title properly reserved by the rites of empire to Caesar. Indeed, he has the pluck to try converting his judges and jailers, his captors and conveyors to this very view. He intercedes on their behalf.

I have been suggesting that this apparently simple matter of allegiance bears with it the power and implication of world formation. Walter Wink puts it perhaps more deeply in seeing the conflict of worlds as simultaneously a conflict of spirits. He points out that when the Roman magistrates ordered the Christians to bow before the image of the emperor, they were in fact being pressed to worship the imperial *genius* or spirit. When instead, in their practice of counter-liturgy, they knelt and offered prayers to God on the emperor's behalf, they undertook an act far more revolutionary than outright rebellion would have been.

Rebellion simply acknowledges the absoluteness and ultimacy of the emperor's power, and attempts to seize it.
Prayer denies that ultimacy altogether by acknowledging a
higher power. Rebellion would have focused solely on the
physical institution and its current incumbents and
attempted to displace them by an act of superior force.
But prayer challenged the very spirituality of the empire
itself and called the empire's "angel," as it were, before
the judgement seat of God.[31]

Rome countered with its own weapon of liturgical combat:
"spectacles" in the "circus," to which the Christians were subjected. On certain days in the civic religious cycle the populace
was provided front-row seats to the ritual execution of criminals,
namely Christians under persecution. Having made their seditious capital offense, believers were thrown to the beasts (bulls,
bears, wild boars, leopards, and, of course, lions). But there, the
martyrs were victorious.

When Christians knelt in the Colosseum to pray as lions
bore down on them, something sullied the audience's thirst
for revenge. Even in death these Christians were not only
challenging the ultimacy of the emperor and the "spirit"
of empire but also demonstrating the emperor's powerlessness to impose his will even by death. The final sanction
had been publicly robbed of its power.[32]

These same issues played out in a variety of ways. Among the
more militant of the early fathers (so-called) was Tertullian. In
a long treatise on idolatry he takes up the question of whether
a Christian might serve in the Roman army. For Tertullian the
issue is not primarily violence but idolatry. Who is sovereign?
Tertullian is utterly strident, legalistic even: "There is no agreement between the divine and human sacrament, the standard of
Christ and the standard of the devil, the camp of light and the
camp of darkness. One cannot serve two masters—God and
Caesar."[33] Here is another edifying etymological coincidence.
Sacrament first meant an oath of loyalty or allegiance, in this
case the oath of *military induction* sworn to the emperor, before

the gods. Indeed, to be a Roman soldier entailed not only making the vow, but submitting to a liturgical cycle of religious observances officially prescribed and enforced.[34]

Among the prescriptive requirements for baptism, Hippolytus
of third-century Rome numbers these:

> A soldier with authority must not kill people. If he is com-
> manded, he must refuse, and he must not take an oath. If
> he will not agree, he must be rejected. Those who have
> the power of the sword, or a civil magistrate who wears
> the purple, must cease or be rejected. If a catechumen, or
> one of the faithful wishes to become a soldier, let him be
> rejected, for he has despised God.[35]

At least until Constantine the church was generally clear about
the choice of ultimate allegiance, whether put forward by God
or Caesar.

JESUS AND LITURGICAL ACTION

For Christians the primary warrant for liturgical direct action,
the place and person where meditation on these questions must
finally come is to Jesus of Nazareth. With respect to his liturgical
practice, perhaps the single most edifying point to be made is
that he was killed in a Roman liturgy of political execution. Ched
Myers recognized this most clearly in his commentary on the
Gospel of Mark:

> When the Roman security forces have completed the
> deeds of the torture-room, Jesus is marched out of the city
> to the place of crucifixion (15:20). The drama of the *via
> dolorosa*, like so many other aspects of the gospel narrative,
> has become in churchly tradition a pious exercise in per-
> sonal anguish, replete with self-flagellation. Gone is its
> true signification: the political theater of imperial tri-
> umph.[36]

He points to Rome's well-documented practice of parading its
defeated military foes through the streets. Josephus describes,

for example, the ceremonial execution of Simon bar Giora, the self-proclaimed king of the Zealot Temple occupation. After the siege and destruction of Jerusalem by Roman legions, Simon was transported to the capital for a formal political humiliation.

> The triumphal procession concluded at the temple of Jupiter Capitolinus. . . . Simon bar Giora, who had just taken part in the procession among the prisoners, and, with a noose put over him, was dragged by force to the proper spot at the forum, all the while being tortured by those who led him. It was at that spot where Roman law required that those sentenced to death for villainy be slain. When his death was announced, it was greeted with universal acclamation, and the sacrifices were begun (*Wars*, VII, v,6).[37]

In Rome the standard procession of a full triumph rolled by in the following order: 1) captured arms and spoils of war; 2) gifts presented by conquered peoples; 3) the white oxen to be sacrificed to Jupiter (as in Josephus's reference); 4) prisoners in chains; 5) lictors in red war dress with laureate *fasces*; 6) magistrates and the senate; 7) *triumphator* in a chariot; 8) Romans liberated from slavery; 9) soldiers wearing laurel-wreaths on their heads and singing.[38]

Out in the occupied provinces such as Judea, the public march to the site of execution served precisely the same ceremonial function and sufficed to convey the same message of imperial omnipotence. The cross, of course, was the standard Roman instrument of this public ritual.

This understanding is reflected in the famous passage from Colossians: "He has cancelled the bond which was outstanding against us with its legal demands; he has set it aside nailing it to the cross. There he disarmed the powers and authorities and made a public spectacle of them, leading them as captives in his triumphal procession" (Col 2:14-15). In a wonderful twist of gospel irony the liturgical procession is alluded to but its meaning is exactly opposite of what the powers intend. In the crucifixion it is the authorities which are paraded, humiliated, exposed, and even rendered powerless. Here we are very near the heart of the entire question of liturgical action.[39] This, of course, is the hidden political meaning of the way of the cross, which has recently been rediscovered. Not pious and private anguish but public exposure and, in truth, victory.

The gospel of John tells the passion narrative with a similar ironic reversal of liturgical and political meaning in mind. In John's eye, the crucifixion is a coronation. It is a New Testament enthronement drama. As in the synoptic trials before Pilate, kingship is the charge, pressed repeatedly in the interrogation here. Jesus in his turn speaks more freely and at length about his kingdom, particularly its relation to truth and nonviolence. Then, specifically as an aspect of his torture and humiliation, Jesus is dressed in the purple robe and the crown of thorns to be given mock homage (19:3). In that same garb he is formally presented to the crowd: Behold the man! Then, by John's reckoning, at the very hour the Passover observance begins, the Jews are asked, "Shall I crucify your King?" to which they reply, "We have no king but Caesar!" (This, it has been pointed out, is a virtual renunciation of Israel's profession to have no king but God, as proclaimed in the Passover hymn *Nishmat kol hay*.[40]) The acclamation of Caesar's ultimate kingship by the crowd is precisely what the mockery and humiliation ritual is designed to endorse and affirm. It is the reality they are manipulated to embrace. Nevertheless, as John sees it, the exact opposite again transpires: Jesus is lifted up as true king, finally upon the cross, with Pilate's own trilingual and international inscription for a title, "Jesus the Nazorean, King of the Jews" (19:19). In the very moment of his death God is glorified, and Jesus reigns in execution. A powerful liturgical conflict is thereby described and a choice of allegiance put not simply once to the crowd but over again to disciples who look on as John's faithful readers.

I do not believe this liturgical combat is simply the overlay of subsequent interpretation, engaged only in John's own time and community. All of the gospels tell the story of Jesus from within a liturgical context and practice.[41] However, it seems to me that the nonviolent struggle employing weapons of liturgy may also be identified in the life and ministry of Jesus. To what extent might he have recognized and enacted the sort of ironies which John, for example, portrays? What forms of liturgical "mythic combat"[42] do the gospels suggest he employed?

In the agony of death, as the object of a Roman crucifixion, Jesus takes public recourse to the psalms. He prays one with a loud voice. By the testimony of two gospels he cries out the opening words of Psalm 22, " 'Eloi, Eloi, lama sabachthani?' which means, 'My God, my God, why hast thou forsaken me?' "(Mk 15:34; cf. Mt 27:46). The cry would be heard, in the manner of Old Testament and rabbinic usage, as an invocation of the psalm in its entirety.[43] The evangelists do, in fact, hear the whole psalm and shape the crucifixion narrative with an eye to its details, in particular:

> All who see me mock at me,
>> they make mouths at me, they wag their
>> heads;
> "He committed his cause to the LORD; let him
>> deliver him,
>> let him rescue him, for he delights in him!"
>> (Ps 22:7-8)

or again,

>> they have pierced my hands and feet—
> I can count all my bones—
>> they stare and gloat over me;
> they divide my garments among them,
> and for my raiment they cast lots.
>> (Ps 22:16-18)

The psalm's lament is truly of the moment. Beyond the details, it prays in the voice of one surrounded by beasts, beset on every side by the powers of death and utterly helpless.

What remains hidden and implied is the psalm's full world and word. The unmitigated cry of abandonment goes up to the One "enthroned on the praises of Israel" (Ps 22:3), and if a dreadful silence reigns in this hour of its utterance, the prayer is offered nevertheless in faith that the Lord hears. What the cry sets in motion is finally a song of hope! Recite it to the end. Where the hymn finally comes to rest is on the sovereignty of

God. "For dominion belongs to the Lord, and he rules over the nations." Indeed in this very moment.

Perhaps because the psalms functioned personally in this same way for him, William Stringfellow has noticed the liturgical depth of Jesus' cry:

> The politics of the Cross delivers a message to the nations, to all regimes and powers, and even unto the ends of the earth, marked by the cry of Jesus that invokes the psalm: *kingly power belongs to the Lord, and dominion over the nations is his* (Psalm 22:28). *That* is truly what the incarnation is all about.

> How can those buried in the earth
> do him homage,
> how can those who go down to the grave
> bow before him?
> But I shall live for his sake,
> my posterity shall serve him.
> This shall be told of the Lord to future
> generations;
> and they shall justify him,
> declaring to a people yet unborn
> that this was his doing. (Psalm 22:29-31)

> In the psalm, the last word in the cry of Jesus from the cross is an assurance of the efficacy of the Resurrection. To become and be a beneficiary of the Resurrection of Jesus Christ means to live here and now in a way that upholds and honors the sovereignty of the Word of God in this life in this world.[44]

A liturgy of death is subverted by the liturgy of life.

In Luke's portrayal of the crucifixion the cry of Psalm 22 is less in the air. It is not, in any event, on the lips of Jesus. Rather, we find the famous words of forgiveness, which as public utterances serve much the same function. "Father, forgive them for they know not what they do" (Lk 23:34) is perhaps the gospel's single most notorious instance of the nonviolent love of enemies.

It is to this example that the early Christian martyrs looked, and we must recall Wink's description of its political meaning and function among them. By this prayer Pilate's administration and the Sanhedrin, their agents and minions, the Roman soldiers, and participant spectators are all brought before the sovereign judgment and mercy of God. This is to say that the loving intercession acts again as a liturgical subversion.

Parallel to this intercession is a second act of forgiveness, offered to the criminal who defends Jesus' innocence. Sovereignty is an issue here as well. "Jesus, remember me when you come into your kingdom" (which turns out, says Luke, to be this very day!). In the Lukan account those crucified on the left and the right are not armed revolutionary bandits (as in Mark and Matthew), but instead "evildoers." They "could comprise the classes of 'sinful' persons with whom Jesus had identified himself from the very beginning of his ministry: tax collectors, toll collectors, traders, merchants, usurers, gamblers, adulterers, and the like."[45] This conversation from cross to cross points to a liturgical practice of forgiveness rooted at the beginning of Jesus' ministry, a practice which ultimately finds its fulfillment in the cross.

And so to the beginning. As represented in the gospels, Jesus walks into his first experience of this liturgical practice in the baptism of John. There is general acceptance among scholars that the Baptist's enterprise was predicated on a Jewish ritual of proselyte baptism originating in the prior century. What is implicit, though little said, is that John had adapted a liturgy to his prophetic purpose. This riverside ministry revolved around a paraliturgical symbolic action, "a baptism of repentance for the forgiveness of sins" (Lk 3:3). The rite defined his movement, signifying both its ethic and expectation. If the gospels in their diversity are accurate, it called all of apostate Israel to repentance and offered forgiveness to a band which included Samaritans, tax collectors, and even soldiers. Herod, for his part, found the movement threatening if not outright seditious, and promptly executed its founder.[46]

In the wake of John's arrest, Jesus takes up not only the proclamation of the kingdom, but the tandem public ministry of forgiveness as well. In Capernaum (Mk 2:1-12 and par.)[47] he makes a flaunting public show of declaring the paralytic's sins forgiven. Whereupon the scribes looking on begin to question, "Why does this man speak thus? It is blasphemy! Who can forgive sins but God alone?" On the face of it the queries seem pious and sincere enough, even a defense of God's sovereignty. However, there *are* mechanisms of forgiveness, a ritual and liturgical apparatus controlled by the Temple hierarchy, including the scribal aristocracy. Jesus has not so much affronted God as transgressed their own turf of social sanction and control.

Hannah Arendt regarded this as Jesus' most threatening action, because she understood that the refusal to forgive sin (or the management of its ritual mechanisms) was a powerful instrument of social control.[48] Such means may even endorse class divisions or separate social groups.[49] To the individual, burdens like these are politically debilitating, a downward spiral of incapacitation. In circumventing and subverting these mechanisms, Jesus has claimed for himself, the Human One, the very prerogatives of the priests and scribes.

The Baptist, perhaps, had some legitimate claim to such authority by virtue of heredity. Luke 1:5-25 indicates that Zechariah, John's father, was from among the lower-class rural priesthood. This, however, merely names another point of tension with the Temple aristocracy in first-century Palestine. In that period the high priest was virtually an appointee of the Roman governor, and the aristocracy symbolized and served the Roman occupation; the rural priests operated with a looser rein. John's strongest language of castigation ("you brood of vipers") is aimed at those who presume to say to themselves, "We have Abraham for our father." The likeliest exponents of such theology of nearly idolatrous "trust" would be the Jerusalem priestly class.[50]

Jesus, however, did not even have the credentials of John for his liturgical improvisation. Eventually in Jerusalem it is reported that the chief priests and the scribes and the elders confront him pointblank: "By what authority are you doing these things, or who gave you the authority to do them?" (Mk 11:28). He answers with a question of his own, "Was the baptism of John from heaven or from human beings? Answer me." They know that any answer to that question is politically loaded. It is more than enough to put them off.

The issue of authority had been joined immediately, as the gospels are wont to say, first off in Galilee (Mk 1:21-28, par.). The setting is liturgical: the synagogue (sacred space) on the Sabbath (sacred time). His teaching authority is being publicly contrasted with that of the scribes, when a voice suddenly disrupts the scene, "What have you to do with us Jesus of Nazareth? Have you come to destroy us? I know you are the Holy One of God." Ched Myers suggests that in Mark's narrative the "demon" is heard to cry out in the voice of the scribes themselves.

> Upon whose behalf is the demon pleading? It can only be the group already identified in the conflict theme—the scribal aristocracy whose space (social role and power) Jesus is threatening. . . . [The] exorcism represents an act of confrontation in the war of myths in which Jesus asserts his alternative authority. Only this interpretation can explain why exorcism is at issue in the scribal counter attack upon Jesus later in 3:22f.[51]

There are a number of scholars who argue that Jesus' programmatic platform for the kingdom movement as Luke portrays it was liturgically shaped. The contention is that by his inaugural sermon (in Luke's account at the synagogue Sabbath day in Nazareth) Jesus was reviving the long-abandoned institution of the Jubilee or Sabbatical Year as described in Leviticus 25. [52]

> And he came to Nazareth, where he had been brought up; and he went to the synagogue, as his custom was, on the sabbath day. And he stood up to read; and there was given to him the book of the prophet Isaiah. He opened the book and found the place where it is written,
>   "The Spirit of the Lord is upon me,
>   because he has anointed me to preach good
>   news to the poor.
>   He has sent me to proclaim release to the
>   captives

and recovery of sight to the blind,
   to set at liberty those who are oppressed,
   to proclaim the acceptable year of the Lord."
And he closed the book and gave it back to the attendant,
and sat down; and the eyes of all in the synagogue were
fixed on him. And he began to say to them, "Today this
scripture has been fulfilled in your hearing" (Lk 4:16-21).

The premise is that the "acceptable year" is the year of Jubilee.
By Torah tradition provisions would include a general forgiveness of debts, liberation of slaves (including "indentured" debt
slaves), letting the land lie fallow, and preventing the consoli-
dation of capital by returning land to original owners. In a marginal, agriculturally-based economy such as Palestine, under the
burden of excessive taxation (both imperial and local), where
many farmers were driven into poverty, losing lands and becoming sharecroppers, day-laborers, or indentured servants, such
provisions would shake the roots of an entire system of domination. It is virtually a demand for land reform.

As to the Jubilee, I will belabor neither arguments nor prin-
ciples laid out lucidly elsewhere.[53] What ought to be underscored, however, is that the Jubilee, rooted theologically and
ethically in the exodus, was part of the liturgical cycle. It would
properly begin on the Day of Atonement, first day of the new
year, by announcement of the high priest. If the scholars have
this right, Jesus would be getting at economics liturgically — a
form we perhaps need to recover! And, once again, he is claiming or democratizing a priestly prerogative.

No survey of Jesus' liturgical practice would be complete
without mention of his relation to the Sabbath. There is no
scholarly consensus as to the origin of the Sabbath itself, but
Torah is clear in resting its meaning with God's work of creation
(Ex 20:8-11) and liberation (Dt 5:12-15). The former text stems
from the Babylonian exile, where the role of Sabbath in the
survival of Israel as a people is taken with deadly seriousness.
Another text from that period (Ex 31:15-17) proscribes the
death penalty for those who violate the day with work. No wonder the rabbis labored to define so precisely what was to be
forbidden and allowed! And no wonder the provocations of

Jesus rankle so. In every gospel account he is portrayed as violating the day, often quite deliberately and publicly, most often by the work of healing.

Jesus is regularly shown to enter into the debates of rabbinic logic (Mt 12:5-14; Lk 13:10-17; Jn 7:19-24), but his most telling argument is simple: "The sabbath was made for humanity not humanity for the sabbath; so the Son of Man [Human Being] is lord even of the sabbath" (Mk 2:27-28). It is to be a day of life, not a tyranny which hems in and binds up because it has been made an idol in the hands of Temple or synagogue bureaucrats. The Sabbath should serve life by way of creation and liberation. This is precisely the provocative work with which Jesus fills the day. The healings may undermine pharisaic authority, but they are right liturgy, true to the sacred day's meaning and purpose.

THE PASSOVER CONFRONTATION

In these few examples the genuinely prayerful liturgical action of Jesus is seen to subvert or transform the symbolic orders of either Roman imperialism or domesticated Judaism of first-century Palestine. However, in one act he confronted these dominant orders in combination. He goes up to Jerusalem for his final encounter with the powers at Passover time. He walks into an occupied city on the threshold of a liberation festival.

The earliest Christian writings, the letters of Paul, connect the death of Jesus with the feast: "Christ, our passover, has been sacrificed for us" (1 Cor 5:7); it is apparent that the passion of Jesus (his arrest, trial, and execution) has been told by the gospel writers with an eye to the festival and its meaning. They even quibble over the calendar in this respect: did Jesus eat the meal in underground fashion with his disciples (as in the synoptics), or was he killed on the Day of Preparation, at the precise moment that the paschal lambs were being slaughtered (as in John). In either portrayal the witness of his dramatic actions and the response of the authorities is shown played out in the context of the festival, its signs and rituals and texts.

Passover was a singularly tense and potentially explosive time in Jerusalem. An uprising at Passover time had been brutally crushed by Archelaus (Herod's son) in 4 B.C.E. He unleashed his entire army, including cavalry, against the crowds. The massacre sparked the notorious series of insurrections which erupted throughout Palestine that year.[54] A report of Josephus from the period a few years subsequent to Jesus' death gives a cryptic sense of the continuing tensions surrounding the celebration:

> When the festival called Passover was at hand ... a large multitude from all quarters assembled for it. [The Roman governor] Cumanus, fearing that their presence might afford occasion for an uprising, ordered a company of soldiers to take up arms and stand guard in the porticoes of the Temple so as to quell any uprising that might occur. This had been in fact the usual practice of previous procurators of Judea at the festivals (*Ant.* 20.106-107; cf. *War* 2.223-224).[55]

No wonder the eagerness of the chief priests to arrest and kill Jesus is mitigated by their uneasy concern: "Not during the feast, lest there be a tumult of the people" (Mk 14:2).

The public tension, of course, was the visible contradiction of celebrating freedom under foreign and domestic oppression. How are the ruling authorities to keep the explosive tension under control? Posting a guard of soldiers? Partly. But primarily in the domestication of the festival. The exodus could be made palatable and even serviceable to established political authority as in the enthronement festival under the Jerusalem monarchy. How about in an imperial situation? Make the sacrifice at the hands of an imperial appointee. Such was the effective position of Annas or Caiaphas or whoever was the high priest that year. Continuing a practice begun by Herod,[56] the Roman governors dismissed and appointed high priests at will, as political circumstance (or sometimes bribery) decreed. They controlled the office by taking possession of the splendidly elaborate vestments.

> Only thus can it be understood that neither Herod the Great, Archeleus, nor the Romans later could find a more effective safeguard against rebellion than to keep the high-

priestly robes in custody in the temple fortress of Antonia, handing them over to the high priest only on feast days.[57]

Indeed there was a tenacious continuing struggle to reclaim the vesture. Even after their release by decree of the emperor's own hand (45 C.E.), the appointment controversy continued. One of the first acts of the Zealot uprising in 67 C.E. was to depose the reigning high priest and reestablish the Zadokite line by casting lots for a successor.[58]

However, the most important aspect of domestication was surely the elaborate economic entrenchment of the feast in the life of Jerusalem. It is a simple fact that given geographic terrain, mineral and agricultural resources, the traffic patterns of international commerce, and geopolitical realities, Jerusalem as a city would hardly exist apart from the Temple.[59]. And among the three main pilgrim feasts, Passover was the centerpiece of the Temple's life. For Passover the city's population of thirty thousand could be inflated several times, perhaps even to Jeremias' calculated maximum of 180,000.[60] That's a lot of rooms at the inn. By Torah interpretation the "second tithe" was to be consumed in Jerusalem. Pilgrims from a distance would convert the tithe to money and spend it at festival time. Around that grew further commerce and an urban service industry. Moreover, the Temple was a massive stockyard and slaughterhouse; as many as eighteen thousand lambs might be sacrificed in the ceremonies. Think of the Temple workers involved, the money changers and sellers of animals (made famous by Jesus' action), but also the carpenters and construction workers in the building trades engaged in the luxurious rehabilitation of the Temple and its precincts.

Seen in this light, Passover as the central feast is the source of jobs, income, commerce. Vested interests abide at several levels of class and status. Passover generates capital. And what of its evangel of freedom? All but dead and buried.

It is almost as though, in confronting the powers, Jesus calls to the feast: "Come alive."

In the synoptic gospels Jesus is portrayed as going to Jerusalem only once, but it's a big trip. From Peter's Caesarea Philippi confession at the center of the story, Jesus has his eye on

the city. Indeed, everything in the story from that point forward
is on the road to Jerusalem. Along the way Jesus is making
preparations for the encounter. He repeatedly alerts the disciples to what they realistically may expect: the Human One will
be delivered up and crucified. When it comes time for the procession into town, preparations have been made (Mk 11:1-7,
par.). When it comes time for the Passover meal, preparations
are again found to have been made (Mk 14:12-16, par.). The
implication is that his going up to Jerusalem is well thought
through. And he arrives at Passover time. It would seem he
knows exactly what he's doing. The exodus history is aroused in
memory. The ancient texts and prayers are in the air and on the
lips. The people are astir in ways deeper than they know, the
authorities conspicuously nervous.

Jesus has chosen a liturgical context for his public confrontation. On entering the city, as Luke reports, he declares it a
kairos moment, a time of decision. By his design, calculated or
intuitive, all the events which transpire—from the Temple
action[61] and the public debate with the Pharisees, to the underground contemplative meal with his friends, to his own solitary
prayer ("Lord take this cup"), not to mention the trial and execution—are infused with the festival and against its backdrop.
The sovereignty of God and freedom from the powers are the
implicit topics at every turn. And the festival once again serves
to illuminate and expose the reign of God.

This is to say that Jesus embodies and enacts and transfigures
the Passover. It is not to suggest that he makes the feast "rel-
evant," but that he makes it present tense. An incarnational
feast. He gives it flesh.

All this is on the table in the attic "seder" (Mk 14:17-26, and
par.).[62] Here, in the course of the meal's homily, or perhaps in
the blessings at the beginning and the end of the ritual,[63] Jesus
interprets the events of the moment, his confession of faith, his
life and death in Jerusalem, all in the context of the Passover
meal. It is the reality of the festival. It is the living flesh and
blood of the ancient liturgy.

At the conclusion of *Binding the Strong Man* Ched Myers
offers a short reflection on Jesus as prophet, priest, and king.

The priestly section is compatible with the meaning I'm reaching for here and throughout:

> Jesus of Nazareth was also a "priest," in that he took it upon himself to mediate Yahweh's healing to the poor and outcast. He unilaterally declared a Jubilee for those doubly oppressed by the symbolic order; the unclean were pronounced whole, the debt-ridden forgiven. And he liberated Yahweh's presence from its controlled reclusion in the Holy of Holies, announcing that it dwelt among the people. The people could now eradicate debt by cooperating in a new community of sharing and forgiving: the people could welcome the impure and anoint the sick and cast out demons. Jesus' role as priest was to do away with priests, to radically democratize the body of Israel. The "blood of atonement" would no longer be a vicarious offering controlled by the temple stewards. The only acceptable sacrifice was of one's own lifeblood, shed in service to the people and in resistance to oppressors. So Jesus embraced this priestly vocation: not to rule over, but to be "reckoned with the sinners," and in the end to "pour out his soul to death" (Is 53:12).[64]

Here one thinks of the way this is discussed in certain other New Testament contexts. In Hebrews, for example, there is an extended comparison between Jesus' death and the Temple liturgies (chap 7). Jesus is said to be the true priest because he offers *himself*, not animals, as the sacrifice. His giving over of his life to the sovereignty of God manifested that sovereignty in the new covenant. According to the letter, Jesus' life and death thereby replaces the Temple ritual. "But as it is, Christ has obtained a ministry [*leitourgia*] which is as much more excellent than the old as the covenant he mediates is better" (Heb 8:6).

There is an obvious kinship here with the meaning of John's chronological claim that Jesus was executed at the very moment the Passover lambs were being sacrificed (Jn 19:14,31). This lends itself, of course, to all sorts of elaborate ritualized meaning, but the heart of it remains: Jesus fills up and transforms the

Passover by his death and life. Indeed this is the case with *all* of the major feasts in John.

Instead of the one big trip to town, John's gospel portrays Jesus making a series of forays into Jerusalem at various festival times. His trips may be regarded as punctuation marks for a running commentary on the meaning of the feasts and their transformation.[65] Not so remarkably, at each mention or visit a controversy occurs (see Jn 2:23, 5:11, 6:4, 7:2, 11:56). The threats against Jesus are almost invariably made explicit in these situations, and he is remarkably sentient about timing and risk.

On one occasion (Jn 7), when Jesus is lying low in Galilee because of death threats, his brothers (no less) encourage him to go public in Jerusalem at the Feast of Tabernacles. It was his obligation as a Jewish male to make the pilgrimage. He appears to decline because the timing isn't right and sends them on alone. Then he goes up after all, only quietly, observing the feast, presumably mingling with the crowd, overhearing the opinions of his work (mixed reviews to be sure), and staying clear of the authorities, who are in fact expecting him. Then abruptly in the middle of the feast (prompted by what? a prayerful rereading of the times? a contentious challenge? a burst of prophetic freedom?) Jesus emerges to teach in the Temple and openly discuss the plottings for his death. A spirited exchange follows. The people are divided, and the only reason he isn't arrested on the spot is because the Temple police are overcome by his eloquence and their own fear of the crowd, for both of which they are in due course reprimanded. All in all, the teaching is in keeping with Tabernacles, as Jesus offers living water (akin to the saving water from the wilderness rock). The people attend closely to his words because of the liturgical context and the risk he endures to utter them.

It has long been recognized that John's narrative is shaped by and addressed to the liturgical life of an early community.[66] Recent sociological work on the Johannine community suggests the sectarian strategy of a Jewish Christian community expelled from the synagogue, denied access to public liturgy, festivals and observances, even the scriptures held hostage in the sanctioned hands of their opponents.[67] In such a situation Jesus becomes the center of their world. No wonder the liturgist becomes the liturgy. None of this, however, mitigates the fact that such a strategy builds precisely on Jesus' own liturgical approach. As the synoptics testify, Jesus acts on the Passover festival and fills it up. As John portrays it, this is the case with respect to *every* feast.

THE CHURCH'S CONFESSION AS LITURGICAL ACTION

Luke extends this same logic, within his narrative and historical framework, to the praxis of the church. It is a further example of liturgical action notoriously underplayed by commentators. After the death of Jesus, when is it, according to Luke-Acts, that the disciples go suddenly bold and public? It is no less than the *very next festival after Passover* in Jerusalem, which is to say the Feast of Weeks, or Pentecost. Is this the shrewdness of the Holy Spirit or what? Because the Spirit so predominates the story in its rush of abruptness, the import of liturgical timing and context may readily be missed.

The church was "born" at a harvest festival, the feast of the ingathering. Pentecost (the Feast of Weeks) was the last of the Jewish agrarian festivals to be historicized. In fact, at this time it was in the very process of transformation. Its meaning and import were just being debated. At least since the Maccabean period, the Book of Jubilees[68] had been foremost in holding Pentecost in high esteem and connecting the feast with the covenant made at Mt. Sinai. According to Jubilees, it coincided with, recalled, and celebrated the founding of Israel as a covenant community.[69] At Qumran, the community held it in similar veneration, and likely made their own covenantal renewal on that day. However, it cannot be said unequivocally how widespread this interpretation of the festival, subsequently well established in Rabbinic Judaism, would then have been.[70]

In any event a pilgrim crowd is once again present (as we have it in Acts, from every nation under heaven). Are they particularly mindful of their historical roots? Are covenant and community in the air? People are surely ripe for preaching and repentance. The disciples appear to have taken an inspired clue from Jesus as to the liturgical politics of timely context. Made the occasion of their bold public confession, the festival reveals the "Day of the Lord," (the text of Joel in Acts). It marks a turning point in history, a world-shaking moment of *kairos*, both personal and political. In the streets they proclaim the sovereignty of God, exercise an untoward freedom, and forge a new community. *And* they introduce for the first time, says Acts, the paraliturgical Christian practice of baptism as sign of the new covenant. It's a lot of freight, but perhaps the feast may bear it, may interpret it, be filled and transformed by it.

"Let all the house of Israel therefore know assuredly that God has made him both Lord and Christ, this Jesus whom you crucified" (Acts 2:36). That is their new covenant and confession.

CHAPTER 2

A QUESTION of CONFESSIONAL Politics

"But who do you say that I am? . . . And he began to teach them that the Human One must suffer many things."
Mark 8:29,31

At the heart of the gospels is a confessional crisis. It is portrayed in the synoptics as the precise narrative center of the story, a watershed moment on which all other action turns. Who is Jesus Christ? (And what is his Way in the world?) The crisis provokes the question and the question the crisis. Close at hand is the disorienting voice of Satan, spreading its confusion. Indeed, the voice is heard within the discipleship community itself (Mk 8:33). And for the first time, openly and plainly, the cross is discussed and enjoined.

All readers of the gospel pass through that confessional moment, personally, and are compelled to declare themselves for one way or the other. In every age and place the community of faith must also make that declaration in answer to the Living Lord.

If recent scholarship has got it right, the community of the earliest gospel (St. Mark's), faced its confessional crisis in the midst of a civil war, after the first unsuccessful Roman siege of Jerusalem and before the last, which destroyed the Temple.[1] It was a heady, confusing time of revolutionary or messianic fever. Who, they were being asked in utterly concrete terms, is Jesus

Christ? And what is the form of discipleship for us here and now? The gospel of Mark is the document which addresses both question and crisis.

In church history, especially Protestant tradition, it is recognized that there are extraordinary times when the church's very identity is imperiled. If its confession is not made unequivocally clear, nothing less than the meaning of the gospel within the church and before the world is at risk. This special time, a *status confessionis*, is brought on by a historical crisis within the church or without. It is incumbent on the community of faith to discern and name the crisis and to distinguish, as clearly as it possibly can, between truth and error, even between life and death.

These reflections are made with certain questions in mind: Are we as North American Christians facing just such a juncture? A sea change is in the air. The eruption of serious non-violent movements in unexpected places (the Philippines, China, Eastern Europe, the Baltic states, Palestine, and South Africa, to name just a few) has shaken imperial power and set in motion major political and economic realignments. At the very same moment, first-strike nuclear weapons are being deployed, so-called low intensity warfare is being perfected and proving victorious in regions like Central America, the structural injustice of the global economy is verified daily as worse and worse, the planetary ecosystem is threatened with degradation and collapse. A historical crisis is upon us.

In many quarters the faith of the church has been awakened, vital as the day of resurrection. In others, specifically here in North America, the faith of the church remains confused and compromised by a cumulation of silence, seduction, and outright subversion. If believers continue in practical silence, the vitality of the gospel will be jeopardized within these United States. It is, in short, a time for confession. By the grace of God and the gifts of tradition, we do not grope about in a vacuum. There are some clues and precedents in our recent history. The famous one comes from Nazi Germany. So let us begin there.

THE NOTORIOUS PRECEDENT

Picture this: Swastikas ring the altar of Magdeburg Cathedral. It is 1933 and Adolph Hitler has just come to power. The dean explains from the pulpit: "In short, it has come to be the symbol of German hope. Whoever reviles this symbol of ours is reviling our Germany. The swastika flags around the altar radiate hope—hope that the day is at last about to dawn."[2] Paul Althaus, a notable German theologian, hails the rise: "Our Protestant churches have greeted the German turning point of 1933 as a gift and miracle of God."[3]

Following World War I Germany had suffered not only defeat, but a humiliating peace settlement, crippling reparation payments to the Allies, and then the effects of international depression. Hitler was elected in 1933, preaching an authoritarian society and traditional values based on family, religion, and German nationalism. When he came to power, he had a good bit of church support and he carefully curried more.

He threw the support of his own figure and voice behind the German Christians, a church unification movement, sympathetic to Nazi goals, including endorsement of the Aryan race and the building of a German Protestant church on this foundation. The German Christians prevailed in church elections and made sweeping changes, including provisions that ousted pastors and church officials of Jewish descent. Moreover, with the help of the German Christians, Hitler successfully installed his own "religious affairs" officer as bishop of the unified national church.

Meanwhile, under the guise of anti-communism, and in the wake of the Reichstag fire, he had arrogated dictatorial police-state powers to himself in the name of national security.

Dietrich Bonhoeffer wrote to Karl Barth, "There can be no doubt that the *status confessionis* has arrived; what we are by no means clear about is how the *confessio* is most appropriately expressed today."[4]

The form it subsequently took was the notorious theological declaration, drafted by Barth, and approved by a Confessional Synod at Barmen, May 31, 1934. The Barmen Declaration has been called a "fighting action"[5] of the church; it brought the crisis then brewing to a head.

It begins:

Jesus Christ, as he is attested for us in Holy Scripture, is the one Word of God which we have to hear and which we have to trust and obey in life and in death.

We reject the false doctrine, as though the Church could and would have to acknowledge as a source of its proclamation, apart from and besides this one Word of God, still other events and powers, figures and truths, as God's revelation.[6]

Hitler's name never comes up, but you don't have to be a political genius to read between the lines. On the face of it, the document reads as a mundane doctrinal statement (indeed one which functions today as a confessional standard for the Presbyterian church and appears liturgically in their hymnal). But the signers, it has been pointed out, were, every last one of them, pursued by the Nazis and subsequently exiled or imprisoned or executed!

Note also the yes/no format, affirmation followed by renunciation. This rhythm is sustained throughout the document, and it is a telling structure. Not only does it intimate resistance, but more precisely (and here the dreadful hazard of a confessional state) separation. The decision of the synod drew a line between itself and the German church's false doctrine and practice. Bonhoeffer went so far as to say: "Whoever knowingly separates themselves from the Confessing Church in Germany, separates themselves from salvation."[7] That is a theological mouthful. Yet the very substance of the gospel was at issue. That line marked off belief from unbelief. It unified and divided at once.

It is no surprise that there were heated responses and counter-confessions from the German Christians. One such statement was politically explicit:

As Christians we honor with thanks toward God ... every authority ... as a tool of divine preservation. ... In this knowledge we as believing Christians thank God that he has given to our people in its time of need the *fuhrer* as a "pious and faithful leader" and the National Socialist political system as "good government," a government with "decency and honor."[8]

The Barmen Declaration had dealt explicitly with the doctrine of the state — a thorny one for Lutherans prone to a "two-kingdoms" approach—and thereby paved the way for political resistance. It also addressed the servant character of church leadership (over against the heavy hand of Hitler's reichsbishop).

However, Barmen was deathly silent on the matter of the Jews. And while state intervention within the church is very much to the point, the confession betrays no rebuke of Nazi tactics: arrest without warrant, imprisonment without trial, intimidation and violence administered by the state. (I am aware that these will be recognized as commonplace in many client states supported and financed by the United States. But our consideration of that similarity to our own situation and silence must wait yet a moment.)

What Barmen effectively did was to declare the sovereignty of the Word of God in every aspect of life. In that sense it was like a breath of fresh air. An arena of freedom was created by the declaration, a space in which to think and move. The making and publication of the document was more like a liturgical event than a political manifesto, but the political implications and consequences were enormous. Members of the Confessing Church went in admittedly different directions, including ecclesiastical and overt political resistance, but all in the radical freedom of complete obedience to Christ.

Two postscripts are in order. Both report postwar convenings and declarations of the Confessing Church. The first took place in Stuttgart in October 1945. There the remnants of the church met to publicly acknowledge their guilt and responsibility. "Unending suffering has been brought by us to many peoples and countries," they confessed. "We accuse ourselves that we did not witness more courageously, pray more faithfully, believe more joyously, love more ardently."[9] Perhaps such a penitential spirit might have served well the original declaration. More to our own point, it may well be that any attempt to confess the sovereignty of God in a concrete situation of confusion or death is best served by an explicit acknowledgment of complicity in the sin which is being renounced.

The second document is a 1958 petition at least partially drafted by Karl Barth and spearheaded by Martin Niemoller and certain other leadership of the Confessing Church which sought to declare a *status confessionis* in Germany with respect to atomic weapons. The statement, submitted to the Synod of the Evangelical Church, invoked the Barmen, professed that modern weapons had created a situation in which the church could not remain neutral, and stressed that Christians must not participate in the design, testing, manufacture, stockpiling, or use of such weapons.[10] The petition garnered signatories and fostered a storm of debate, but never was adopted.

What happens, one may ask, when a confessional moment arrives, and the church passes it by, failing to speak or act? What is the toll exacted upon the body? What becomes of its capacity to discern or its ability to speak with clarity and be heard? These are questions that haunt us even today.

A BIBLICAL WORD FOR THE TIMES

Byers Naudé was the first person in South Africa to publicly suggest that a *status confessionis* had arrived for the churches with respect to apartheid. It was 1965. Naudé had spent some time in Germany during the 1950s studying the Confessing Church, and he became convinced that such a crisis, though uniquely its own, had arrived for the South African church.[11]

Certain parallels have been pointed out as obvious: racist ideology (though in this case targeting a black majority population rather than the Jewish minority); a false unity of church and nation; an emergence of Nazi tactics (there was in fact a historic affinity between Germany's National Socialists and the Afrikaner Nationalist Party, which was the architect of apartheid); government intrusion or pressure on church affairs; and the church's sin of silence before a massive, manifest injustice.

The twenty-five years since Naudé's original suggestion have been marked in South Africa by a continuing confessional struggle within the churches. There have been a series of statements, invoking or echoing in spirit and structure, the Barmen Declaration.[12] And Christians have also seen some watershed moments, decisive acts of truth risked.

One of the most remarkable of these moments came in 1982 at the World Alliance of Reformed Churches meeting in Ottawa, Canada. Dr. Allan Boesak asked that those gathered take special responsibility to recognize apartheid as irreconcilable with the gospel of Jesus Christ. "If this is true," he said, "and if apartheid is also a denial of the Reformed tradition, then it should be declared a heresy."[13] In a moment of courage and clarity the world body agreed, suspending from its membership the two white Afrikaner Reformed Churches until such time as they should renounce the doctrine.

Historically the church has understood a heresy to be a fundamental distortion of the gospel that leads to division within the body of Christ and a false witness before the world. Apartheid clearly qualifies. As a political policy it has been sanctioned with an array of theological justifications ("Calvinist" predestinarian social arrangements, promised-land white destiny of chosenness, Blacks as the cursed offspring of Ham, and the like). As an anthropological heresy which impugns and denigrates the very humanity of black people, apartheid functions to divide the church at the altar, separating the body of Christ at the precise point of its visible public union: the table of the Lord.[14]

God knows there are frightening dangers in pronouncing against a heresy. It smacks of a witch-hunt—and we know in retrospect how violent and mistaken they turned out to be. Self-righteousness is a patent temptation, and dialogue would seem to be foreclosed instead of invited. All that notwithstanding, if the gospel itself is jeopardized by confusion, if the integrity of the church's commonlife is at risk, and if silence permits the most horrifying crimes, then it is not a rash step. Indeed it remains an invitation to reunion and reconciliation based on the gospel of Jesus Christ. And the evidence is that the black churches in the Dutch Reformed family have continued to call their sisters and brothers to account in the most loving and passionate face-to-face terms.[15]

An edifying complication of the theological issues in South Africa is that the so-called English-speaking churches made, over this same twenty-five-year period, repeated public statements of one strength or another condemning apartheid, but effectively did nothing to implement them in their own life or in the life of South African society. These churches have continued to indulge what has been called "a heresy of practice."[16] They generally failed to translate their theology into concrete action in solidarity with South Africa's poor.

Events, however, and the emergence of a new document generated from the grassroots of the church struggle effectively
forced the issue. The theological statement is the Kairos Document. Written collectively by more than fifty black pastors min-
istering in the townships around Johannesburg, it has for several
years been getting broad circulation and study. Many more have
signed it. The document names a decisive moment in South
African church history and demands a choice by Christians of
every sort. Hence, its title.

Kairos, as many will recognize, is one of the New Testament
words for "time." In contrast to *chronos*, which means "the
chronological flow of time," "clock time," *kairos* tends to mean
the fullness of time as a ripeness, or a moment of crisis. It has
come to signify the decisive, critical moment, the time of opportunity, a crisis hour dense with the possibilities of grace.

It is clear, for example, that Jesus recognized such a moment.
His first words in the earliest gospel are: "The *kairos* is fulfilled,
and the kingdom of God is at hand; repent, and believe the
gospel" (Mk 1:15). In Matthew's portrayal he criticizes the Pharisees for knowing how to read the skies but not the *kairos* (Mt
16:3). And in Luke, on his march to the Temple action in Jerusalem, he weeps for the city because it does not know its *kairos*
and the things that make for peace (Lk 19:44).

Beyond that it may truly be said that the gospels themselves
are *"kairos* documents." The work of Ched Myers cited earlier
suggests that the gospel of Mark was also a call for decision in
a concrete moment of historical circumstance (Galilee just prior
to the final Roman siege and destruction of Jerusalem). Each
of the gospels, in fact, is written for and to a particular moment.
They are confessional statements defining a community, inviting
decision for its struggle and practice. They are each a *"kairos*
document" in narrative form.

The South African Kairos Document names a moment and
demands a decision of faith and conscience. It is a theological
broadside aimed at the continuing political situation in that
country. Like its confessional predecessors, it does not hesitate
to use the strongest terms in describing things theologically.
Apartheid is a "heresy" and the god of the South African State

is not merely an idol or false god, but "the devil disguised as Almighty God—the antichrist."[17]

In the document both "state theology," which abuses chapter 13 of Romans to justify unquestioned obedience to the government, and "church theology," which distorts the meaning of nonviolence, justice, and reconciliation into passivity and gradualism, are critiqued biblically. Then the challenge of the moment is thrown down to the church: to "take sides" with the poor, to join actively in the struggle, to begin by transforming its own life, and to engage as required in open acts of noncooperation and civil disobedience. It has a biblically discerning eye.

The challenge to the churches was inescapable in part because it was so clearly articulated in the light of scripture, but even more so because it was incarnational. *Kairos* became the symbol of an actual movement, signifying the emergence of a "church within the church."[18]

As the Kairos appeared, the government thrust this church into the spotlight of the frontlines politically by banning virtually all other alternative organizations and by subjecting its leadership (one thinks of Boesak or Desmond Tutu or Frank Chikane) to public attack. It is as though the powers had acknowledged that the fundamental issues are, in truth, theological and consequently marked off the appropriate grounds for combat.

If the outcome is shifting, it still hangs in the balance.

COMING CLOSER TO HOME

Meanwhile other *kairos* documents have appeared. On Easter day 1988 upwards of eighty people gathered in Managua to draft and sign a Central American Kairos.[19] In keeping with the familiar Latin American method, which insists that theology is not the point of departure, but the "second act" of reflection, it begins with a painfully sober account of this current political moment in the five-hundred-year struggle of the Central American peoples.[20] Only then does it apply the eyes of faith to identify signs of the kingdom which may be seen. Among those are the growing number of Central American martyrs, the new forms of pastoral work emerging, the resources of hope which are being nourished, the ways in which the cross and persecution are being embraced. If there are specific points where other Christian sisters and brothers might disagree, that is specifically encouraged and invited. Please circulate and criticize, they say. Write us, they urge. Let's be in conversation.

The document casts a pointed sidelong glance toward the imperial center. It does not mince words about our complicity, lamenting Christians here and there who "remain buried in their comfort, excusing themselves because of distance, the lack of clear information, their pretended neutrality, the complexity of the problems . . . while the poor die."[21] Nevertheless, they invite the churches of the United States, even as they commit themselves, to acts of penitence and self-criticism, solidarity, and political intercession.

It is in this last regard that *The Road to Damascus,*[22] a kairos document even more recent, is the most pointed. No sidelong glance. It is addressed to us.

> What was revealed to Saul was that God was not on the side of the religious and political authorities who killed Jesus. On the contrary, God was on the side of the One who had been crucified as a blasphemer, who had been handed over as a traitor, an agitator, a pretender to the throne of David and a critic of the Temple (Mt 26:62,65-66; Lk 23:1-2,5,13). On the road to Damascus Saul was faced with this conflict between these two images or beliefs about God. He was struck blind by it. It was his kairos. Saul became Paul when he accepted faith that the true God was in Jesus and that the risen Lord was in the very people whom he had been persecuting. This kairos on the Road to Damascus must be taken very seriously by all who in the name of God support the persecution of Christians who side with the poor. The call to conversion is loud and clear. We must be converted again and again from the idol of mammon to the worship of the true God. We cannot serve two masters, we cannot serve both God and mammon.[23]

Here is a document that has our theological and political number. Its appearance is among the signs of the current historical crisis, naming in judgment and grace a God-given moment of decision for North American Christians. By it we are called upon to endure the transformation of our lives, our church, our nation—probably in that order.

The *Road to Damascus* document makes clear that in the struggle between the poor of the world and the dominating Northern powers, biblical issues are at the heart of the matter. The Damascus theologians recognize that virtually since the time of Constantine, Christianity has been made to legitimate and serve the imperial project of colonization. However, since the awakening of the faith of the poor to see that "Jesus was one of us," a scandal and a crisis has arisen, a conflict has been set in motion; "The Church itself has become the *site of struggle*."[24]

The document is thoroughly biblical and utterly lucid in naming and exposing the imperial "faith." As a prophetic act it calls *idolatry* the bondage to Mammon in consumerist materialism which places money and property above people.[25] It names *heresy* the other-worldly, dualistic, individual and spiritual reductionism of what they term "right-wing" Christianity.[26] They call it *blasphemy* to misuse God's name, invoking it to justify death and destruction.[27] The authors see *hypocrisy* in the silent neutrality which effectively supports the status quo while attacking as divisive those who speak out, and in the proclamation of "nonviolence" which rebukes armed struggle but silently endorses military action.

In setting the historical context of this kairos, the document begins, virtually with the fall, in the first act of human violence: Cain's murder of his brother (p. 3). This seems thoroughly right to me. However, the only place nonviolence comes up is in the discussion of hypocrisy (p. 22). This saddens me, for I believe the document puts its finger on the biblical story for North American Christians: the conversion of Paul. There we ought to linger and return, to look and look again. Conversions do not (any more than correct theological ideas) fall from heaven. The conversion of Paul is literally inseparable from the witness and martyrdom of Stephen. If Paul encounters the Risen One on the road, it is because he has seen the Crucified One face to face in the death of Stephen. In that death we are mindful not only of his diaconal commitment to the least, or his fearless and scathing critique of Temple-State idolatry, but also Stephen's love for his enemies, this intercession of forgiveness on their behalf. With Jesus' doings in Jerusalem it is among the preeminent acts of nonviolence in the New Testament. It is a weakness that our friends do not invoke it as well.[28]

A NORTH AMERICAN KAIROS?

The overall effect of these documents is to raise the question of whether a decisive American moment is upon us. Is it time for North American confession?

This is not the first time this has been asked in America. The crisis times of the civil rights movement or the Vietnam war have put it within the minds of Christians struggling with church and state. And the periodic anniversaries of the Barmen Declaration have raised it inevitably as the subversive memory against which to measure our own times, our own theology, our own action.[29]

Barmen and its story function for us not as a prescription but as a parable. We must not be reduced to scrutinizing our times for the technical parameters of a *status confessionis* or looking for precise analogies (even if there are a few to be found) with the Nazi era.

Perhaps we would do well to identify these previous "confessional times" in America, especially as they are rarely so articulated. The civil rights movement, in fact, did serve as a kind of "church within the church." Christ was confessed in the music and the preaching and the prayer which preceded and accompanied those actions and campaigns. The movement's leaders, most notably Martin Luther King, Jr., were among the greatest American theologians of this century, and they didn't hesitate to cast political issues in fundamental theological terms.

A story is told of William Stringfellow which exemplifies the misunderstood confessional character of the movement. At a National Conference on Religion and Race convened in Chicago 1963, Stringfellow mounted the podium for an address. "The issue, the only *issue*, at this conference is baptism," he began.[30] The session never got beyond that opening one-liner. Jewish participants sat in stunned silence. The other delegates rose to their feet and the place was reduced to uproar.

What was the issue? Precisely this: the solidarity with all human beings — indeed all of creation — that Christians affirm in their act of baptism. The undivided unity of humanity as celebrated and verified (ostensibly) within the commonlife of the body of Christ. Simple as that. It was for the church what might be termed a confessional issue, close to the heart of the gospel.

Throughout those years of struggle Stringfellow never ceased the work of naming racism as a demon and an idol which had invaded the church. To my knowledge he never specifically invoked Barmen in this connection, but he consistently pressed, heard or not, the confessional issue.

So are we in the midst of a crisis today or are these ruminations an undue hankering after Barmen nostalgia? We are indeed suffering a crisis. Is it recognized within the churches? Barely.

In line with the thinking of others who have been writing and speaking about these same things, I will name four specific elements of our historical crisis, though more might well be added.

FIRST-STRIKE NUCLEAR WEAPONRY

As the nineties begin, political geography is everywhere changing; the Cold War is thawing; Europe unites; and at least prior to events in the Middle East, armaments reductions and "peace dividends" were much discussed. But at this self-same moment, the elements of a first-strike nuclear system, long in preparation, are finally being deployed. The USS *Tennessee* finds its new homeport in Kings Bay, Georgia. The *Tennessee* is a floating historical watershed. It is the first Trident submarine to be outfitted with Trident II missiles and D5 warheads. Along with the MX, Midgetman, and stealth-type cruise missiles (now in the pipeline), it signifies the deployment of pinpoint accurate first-strike nuclear technology.

There is plenty of reason to be wary of the incipient despair implicit in certain technological timelines which would mark off a historical point of no return. They are doomsday calendars.

However, when their red-letter date is upon us and goes all but unnoticed, I shudder.

Since Hiroshima, first-strike has been structured into military policy, end to beginning, top to bottom, from Pentagon nuclear scenarios down to the terrors of covert warfare. It will not go easily away. First-strike weapons are now being loosed upon the earth, and that betokens a crisis.

Moreover, this has for years been parallelled by a theological crisis. The passivity of the church in the face of this military policy would itself be sufficient to name it so. However, "nuclearism," the ideology which has accompanied these weapons, also has the character of a secular religion. Robert Jay Lifton summarized it a decade ago as,

> the passionate embrace of nuclear weapons as a solution to death anxiety and a way of restoring a lost sense of immortality. Nuclearism is a secular religion, a total ideology in which "grace" and even "salvation"—the mastery of death and evil—are achieved through the power of a new technological deity. The deity is seen as capable not only of apocalyptic destruction but also of unlimited creation. And the nuclear believer ... may come to depend on the weapons to keep the world going.[31]

In the next chapter we will look more closely at this aspect of American culture. But for now it is sufficient to note that the intrusion of that "religion" into the church under the guise of political pluralism constitutes a heresy to be named and renounced. More than that, as Jürgen Moltmann among others contends, the elevation of the bomb to divine status is not merely a heresy, it is "apocalyptic blasphemy," the blasphemy of the antichrist.[32]

THE THREAT OF ECOLOGICAL COLLAPSE

Present patterns of production and consumption within the international economy are assaulting the ecological support base of all life. We are reaching the limits of what earth, water, and air may bear of toxic poisons. The rain forests are being razed and the atmosphere depleted. The ozone layer is suffering a tear. Have we damaged it to the point of fundamental climatic change?

The coincidence of this crisis with the implementation of first-strike nuclear weaponry is ironic in the very least. Its causes are rooted in industrialization, but accelerated in the same postwar period by recent consumer technology, the fossil energy required to drive the military-industrial complex, and the advent even of missile engines.

There is, moreover, a kind of spiritual connection between this crisis and the arms race. Once you have declared as a matter of national policy that you are prepared to incinerate half the planet for the sake of national security objectives, then a practical indifference to the long-term consequences of this or that economic practice seems small potatoes indeed. Or said differently, once you have radically called into question the assumption of the future (nuclear weapons do this at a depth of our psychic and cultural assumptions), then there is pressure and license to use resources to the point of exhaustion—which is happening.

There are theological issues aplenty in this—some even blame a human-centered Christian theology for the crisis—but the main one will be the place of genuine repentance in concern for creation. A technological fix, the perennial American temptation, apart from a fundamental act of repentance, will only yield new forms of the same crisis.

THE STRUCTURED INJUSTICE OF THE GLOBAL ECONOMY

The poor of the world, as many as forty million a year, are being killed by hunger and hunger-related causes. The view from North America is that they go quietly. No one notices. As with the weapons deployment, it goes unnoticed because it has become so normal. Is it really a crisis? Ask the forty million.

The widening of the North-South gap is parallelled by a similar gap within our own country, the development of a permanent underclass of homeless and unemployed who live in a separate, and again mostly invisible, socio-economic world.

The financing of our churches, from lifestyles in the pews to the offering plate passed, from the pension fund to the property-laden tax exemption, is deeply implicated in this structural economic injustice. In Europe theologians are giving serious study to whether the global economic system itself, and the church's place within it, don't constitute in and of themselves a *status confessionis*.[33] This must be considered by North American Christians.

WAR ON THE POOR

A kind of warfare dubbed "low-intensity conflict" has become more and more perfected as the imperial strategy of preference in the Third World. The deftly combined economic, diplomatic, psychological, and covert or proxy military warfare employed against Nicaragua for nearly a decade is one prime example. The 1990 elections were declared a vindication of the method. The financing and manipulation of dictatorial regimes, as in El Salvador, where death squads hover in the streets, popular leadership is assassinated or disappears, administrative torture is practiced, and popular organizations destroyed — all in the name of democracy — is another adaptation of the same thing. It is systematic. And it is well thought through and coordinated.

It is totalitarianism, and we are party to it. We are also victimized by its largely covert character, carried out as it is by enterprises, secret teams, special forces, client states, the CIA, and other extra-constitutional authorities of hidden government. These subvert the remnants of democracy at home, effectively numbing and deceiving people.[34]

OF DOCUMENTS AND DEEDS

Nevertheless, signs of a North American response are in the wind. An annual gathering of Christian peacemakers wrestles with whether this is indeed a *kairos* moment. They commit themselves to a year of focused reflection in their local communities and form a committee of correspondence to keep in touch.

Elsewhere, a small informal meeting of theologians takes up a discussion of whether the time is right for a North American document. What would be the process? How would discussion be stimulated? Who would do the writing? They send out a circular letter inviting grassroots reflection.

Or again, a coalition of activist Christians first convened at the margins of a World Council of Churches meeting in Seoul, South Korea, begins to organize around the five-hundredth anniversary of Columbus's "discovery." They ask: Could this anniversary and its attendant imperial celebration be the occasion to discern the *kairos*? Might *kairos* communities be organized specifically to seize the moment?

Such conversations are happening all over. Communities and congregations, some independently, some by way of studying *The Road to Damascus*, are putting these questions straightforwardly among themselves: Is it time for some explicit form of confessing community? Is it time for a kairos-type document for Christians living in the United States? Could we incarnate confessional words into creative actions that would breathe new life into our communities and nation?

"Another document?" some will say. Even among those encouraging it there is necessarily a reticence that comes of knowing the poverty and humiliation of words in this culture, and in the church in particular. American Christians crank out statements in convention and conference by the volume. Condemnations of injustice, pastoral letters on the arms race (even good ones), resolutions, and covenants gather dust without action. The American idols of religious and political pluralism grant them a wide dismissive tolerance. They neither bind the church nor truly guide it. In the end they seem to signify so little.

John DeGruchy makes much of Bonhoeffer's ecclesiological reflection that "the first confession of the Christian community before the world is the *deed*."[35] In point of fact, we may rejoice to recognize that there are communities of the deed in North America. There is, among the church of the poor, among nonviolent resistance communities, the sanctuary congregations and refugee workers, the communities (rural and urban) of simplicity and service, a de facto confessional movement nourished by prayer and sacrament and scripture study. It is happening after a fashion; it simply is.

It is within this loose movement, no coincidence, that experiments with liturgical direct action have begun. These may be counted, interpreted, offered as confessional deeds. They are among the ways in which the *kairos* is concretely announced. Here, they say, is an aspect of the crisis. Now, they declare in lives and action, is the sovereignty of God. At the very least they may be said to pose the confessional question in a powerfully public and personal way.

How they do that is a matter to which we will come; first, we will examine a specific instance of why.

CHAPTER 3

THE ENGINE of HISTORY: A RELIGION of NUCLEAR IMPERIALISM

We state with clear conscience that our action at Griffiss Air Force Base was an act of obedience to the law of God, indeed an act of religion and worship of God.

It is our conviction, which we will seek to prove, that such action is protected by the First Amendment to the U.S. Constitution, which states that "Congress shall make no law respecting and establishment of religion, or prohibiting the free exercise thereof."

We find our religious faith and practice . . . in conflict with the conduct of our government, especially as regards its sanctions of nuclear war preparations, and the monies, the resources, the trust it puts in them. In short, we are compelled by this government into a stance of false worship unless we act against them as we have sought to do. . . .

McGeorge Bundy called the United States "the locomotive at the head of mankind [sic] pulling the caboose of humanity along behind." Any engine-of-history outlook requires the displacement of the one who is the Lord of History. . . . We live in a situation where we must exercise our consciences and choose the sovereignty of God or the sovereignty of nation.

From a defense brief proffered at the trial of seven men and women who hammered and

*poured blood on a B-52 converted to carry
cruise missiles, Thanksgiving Day, 1983.*[1]

This astonishing trial brief of the Griffiss Plowshares did not carry the day legally. The jury was permitted neither the benefit of their argument nor the expert testimony which supported it. The seven were convicted for their action of symbolic disarmament and served sentences ranging from two to three years. Still, as with the action itself, it raised in a most explicit way the fundamental conflict, at once religious and political, between biblical faith and the system of nuclearism.

This was a genuine legal argument eloquently pressed.[2] Other, more common attempts to raise viable legal issues such as those stemming from the body of international law violated by weapons of massive, indiscriminate destruction, and explicitly honored by civil resistance, have also never been permitted to carry the day in a U.S. court.[3]

Still the brief, as with the trial and the action itself, is also a confessional word in the sense already raised. Yes, the Constitution is rightly invoked. Recourse to its authority is made against those powers which, abusing its name, have subverted the founding document in more ways than one. The argument is employed to expose the subtle establishment of nuclear religion, but also as an opening to make a confessional statement within the legal forum. In the Griffiss trial brief it is the Bible and the biblical view of history which is held to be normative and binding on Christians, namely those who acted.

Their argument is organized around three of the Ten Commandments and the prophetic mandate of Micah 4. This latter injunction, which envisions the beating of swords into plowshares, has been the guiding image, the very form, of all the plowshares actions. However, it is the first commandments and their explication which are most decisive: "You shall have no other gods to set against me," and "You shall not make carved images for yourself or worship gods of metal."[4] Our lives in nuclear America, the Griffiss Seven aver, "have been twisted into disregard of these laws and the God of the Bible"[5] because a cult of national sovereignty has been established as the major religion. Americans are required to worship the imperial god and the idols of its weaponry.

"NUCLEAR FUNDAMENTALISM": WHO IS LIKE THE BEAST?

One of the expert witnesses denied a hearing at the trial was Robert Jay Lifton, the teacher and writer in psychiatry who came to prominence through his work with Hiroshima survivors. Their experiences, overpowering traumas, coping mechanisms, and patterns of reaction had never been examined prior to his thorough 1969 study. The neglect itself may be something of a cultural defense mechanism, an avoidance and denial of the ground-level human reality of these weapons.

It was his subsequent discovery, however, which was of import to the trial and so for us here. North Americans, living with the bomb and beneath its shadow, have suffered some of the same patterns, syndromes, and incapacitations as the first victims. Lifton, for example, popularized the term "psychic numbing," which applies to both the survivors who, immersed in a sudden sea of death so massive and grotesque, simply shut down and closed off completely their feelings, and also to Americans, who respond in a similar deadened fashion to the image of extinction implicit in these weapons. Hiroshima, he says, is our own text.[6]

In *Indefensible Weapons,* Lifton mapped the individual and collective terrain, counting and naming the uncanny ways in which the bomb penetrates the American psyche. There he lists the illusions and delusions which proliferate with the warheads. He demonstrates the evidence of radical insecurity residing just beneath the surface of consciousness which, on the one hand, oddly helps drive the race for more and more weapons, and on the other, fosters the pervasive doubt that anything will last, from committed relationships, to works, to the elements of culture itself. All in all this engenders in its turn a consuming passion for the present. On the unconscious symbolic level the biological connection to future generations is broken and abandoned, hope in the endurance of creative works diminished, the human relationship to nature itself perverted and severed, and even religious recourse to images of immortality (though sought the more fervently) rendered inadequate.[7]

Lifton argues that this radical insecurity, these broken connections, the assault on immortalities, evoke the desperate attempt to preserve some fundamentals. Witness, he says, the resurgence of fundamentalisms, not simply the cults and new religions, and the Christian versions which have been so subject to political manipulation, but a veritable worldwide outbreak of fundamentalisms, religious and political, in the '70s and '80s.

Here we arrive at key coordinates in the symbolic terrain:

> In an age of potential nuclear genocide, we may expect these waves of fundamentalism to become relatively permanent manifestations of our collective experience. But we are in grave difficulty if that is also true of the most corrupt and dangerous of all fundamentalisms, that focused on the nuclear devices themselves. I have in mind here the condition of *nuclearism*: the embrace of the bomb as a new "fundamental," as a source of "salvation" and a way of restoring our lost sense of immortality.[8]

Is he saying that nuclearism is a religion? Lifton is still talking about the appeal of an ideological totalism to a psychological state, but he is surely brinking on such a claim. Moreover, he compiles a striking collection of descriptions and responses from eyewitnesses to the first atomic test explosion in the New Mexico desert.

Brigadier General Thomas Farrell invoked the "awesome roar of doomsday" and imagined it "blasphemous to dare tamper with forces heretofore reserved to The Almighty." (Not that he ever opposed its development or its use against human targets.) "The effects," he said,

> could well be called unprecedented, magnificent, beautiful, stupendous and terrifying. The lighting effects beggared description. The whole country was lighted by a searing light with the intensity many times that of the midday sun. ... It was the beauty the great poets dream about but describe most poorly and inadequately.[9]

Here is the language of the numinous, the holy. Here is the experience of overpowering awe. In an association now become notorious, Robert Oppenheimer, the bomb project's director and something of a metaphysical poet himself, thought of lines from the Bhagavad Gita, "If the radiance of a thousand suns/ Were to burst at once into the sky/ That would be like the splendor of the Mighty One. . . . /I am become Death/ The shatterer of worlds."

Andrew Lawrence, the professional science writer cum official spokesman on matters of the bomb, beheld images of creation, "the first cry of a newborn world." He wrote, "If the first man [sic] could have been present at the moment of Creation when God said, 'Let there be Light,' he might have seen something very similar to what we have seen."[10]

This sense of the divine infusing the first bomb is reflected already in the code name for the secret test operation: Trinity. Since that time, and certainly under the same impulse, the weapons themselves have been granted mythic and religious names: Atlas, Nike-Zeus, Orion, Titan, Poseidon, Trident, and such.

Long before the nightmare images of hell now connected with Hiroshima, the earliest and longstanding mythology of that first bombing was a story of salvation. Hiroshima saves. Americans were spared, so the account goes, the beachhead deaths, the loss of life certain in the protracted struggle to take the Japanese mainland. No matter that this version of events has long been disproven.[11] Hiroshima was no military necessity. Indeed, with the collapse of Japan's war effort imminent, the bomb project was rushed forward for geopolitical reasons and a technological impetus all its own. But in the mind of an entire generation, Hiroshima was a saving event. It is hard to quarrel with the jubilation that accompanies the end of a world war.[12] Hiroshima occasioned, understandably for many at first sight, celebration. A divine gift. A messianic power. A source of life.

Even thirty years later (though admittedly impossible in the present political climate) a club of retired military officers called the Confederate Air Force, which owned and operated the last flying B-29 (the kind that dropped the first bomb) could be engaged by local air shows to simulate or reenact the Hiroshima event. The bomber would make a pass before the crowd of fer-

vent watchers as a small, ground-based explosion created a min-
iature mushroom cloud. Cheers and applause would go up. Such
reenactments may be understood liturgically, and we will return
to this aspect of nuclear symbolics.

At its birth the bomb was hailed as the harbinger of peace.
And though it was shortly employed in secret threats of massive
retaliation to achieve political objectives[13] and was made the
keystone of an imperial military policy, the public language surrounding it foresaw the beginning of an era in which war would
become impossible, a time of unprecedented peace enforced by
the bomb. Pax Atomica.

Its beneficence was to include an unlimited source of clean
efficient energy, a source of power too cheap to meter. No matter that nuclear energy research was in large part a masterful
cover for continued weapons development (in the same labs and
facilities), the postwar "Atoms for Peace" program held the
vision of a bountiful world of unlimited resources, a time flowing
with all good things. In short, a paradise of sorts.

True, these promises were delusions or fabrications or outright lies. They have been surpassed and refuted in experience.
Yet, in tracing the symbolics in the system of nuclearism, these
powerful roots in the collective American consciousness must
be named. The mythologies have shifted over the years, as have
the doctrines and policies and delivery systems, but the stark
early images hold a certain sway. They figure in the religious
symbolism of the bomb. Hiroshima, to a certain extent and in a
variety of ways, remains our text.

A MYTHOLOGY LIKE UNTO BABYLON

Hiroshima is the creation story of nuclearism's imperial
world. It is historical act perceived as primordial, primeval event.

In *The Symbolism of Evil* Paul Ricoeur lays out four mythical
"types" of representation concerning the origin of evil. Pertinent
here is the "drama of creation" in which,

> the origin of evil is coextensive with the origin of things;
> it is the *"chaos" with which the creative act of the god strug-*
> *gles.* The counterpart of this view is that *salvation is iden-*

tical with creation itself; the act that founds the world is at the same time the liberating act.[14]

It is notoriously the ancient Babylonian creation drama which epitomizes this type. In that story, reenacted at the New Year's festival, the young god Marduk engages in fierce cosmic combat with Tiamat, the goddess of chaos. Victorious, Marduk divides Tiamat's monstrous fishlike body, thereby imposing order upon the world and paving the way for his enthronement among the gods as the very god of Order.

Note that it is by violence that chaos is overcome and the orderliness of the cosmos established. It is by disorder—murder and war—that the original enemy, disorder, is vanquished. This is imperial state mythology par excellence, and it functions politically, needless to say.

The story sanctions the Babylonian state as the very world of order. (Indeed, the cosmos itself may be conceived as a state.) And a theology of war emerges which identifies every enemy with the original Enemy, chaos. The king as divine representative embodies the sovereignty of imperial order, a role authorized and ritualized in public festival.

> The magnitude of the New Year's festival at Babylon is well known. A whole people, in the presence of the gods assembled in effigy, relives the fundamental emotions of the poem—the cosmic anguish, the exaltation of battle, the jubilation in triumph. By the celebration of the festival, the people place their whole existence under the sign of the drama of creation.[15]

In nuclear mythology, and Hiroshima as creation drama, Babylon finds a typological kin. The war fought to make the world safe for democracy, to preserve Western civilization, was won by the purveyor of unimaginable destruction. By that bombing the postwar world was created. Salvation and creation were one and the same.

It is more and more understood that the atomic bomb was used against the Japanese in order to use it against the Soviets, to prevent their entrance into the Asian theater, and so subse-

quently into Asian markets. Moreover, its use was hastened—
lest the war end before it could be employed—to demonstrate
dramatically both the bomb's existence and the requisite will to
use it against cities and human targets. It ordered and guaranteed the dividing of the world, East and West, on terms dictated
by the bomb users. "Order" of a certain sort was wrought and
the bomb enthroned.

The chaos contained and kept at bay, so goes the narrative
of the mythic drama, was both the Soviet Union, openly deemed
the "evil empire" not many years back by a United States head
of state, and the nameless terror of nuclear war itself. Deterrence is better understood as a religious doctrine than any sort
of rational policy. And it is with this element of American religious symbolics that we are concerned.

To challenge in a serious way the imperial system of nuclearism, or even one of its doctrines, is to be seen as invoking chaos.
The civilly resistant are often subjected to judicial tirades on the
threat they engender against the fundamental blessings of order.
A district judge once remonstrated my friends and me: "Now,
the holocaust that comes about by people who take the law into
their own hands is as horrendous as any type of holocaust that
may come about down the line." He enlarged upon the theme.[16]

In similar fashion any agent of "domestic disorder" during
the Cold War years, anyone advocating a reality alternative to
that prevailing, was named with the primary political epithet of
the demonic—*communist*—a purveyor of chaos as if from the
very far side of the wall itself. New labels forever emerge. *Ter-
rorist*, for example, is coming into some currency. Such labeling
and tirades were rendered in the same way as scribal accusations
against Jesus that he was "possessed by Beelzebul, and by the
prince of demons casts out demons" (Mk 3:22).

SHRINES, RITUALS, AND NUCLEAR LITURGIES

One of the few academic attempts to articulate the religious
function of nuclearism was undertaken by Ira Chernus, a historian of religions. Published in a series on comparative religions, his book, *Dr. Strangegod*, concludes, much as I have here,
that

When a form of behavior is repeated largely for the sake
of repetition—to provide a sense of fixed regularity and
unchangeable pattern in life—and when that behavior provides a recurring relationship with limitless power, it can
be called a religious ritual. . . .

In acting, in preparing for nuclear war and building up
our nuclear arsenals, we are engaging in sacred behavior
or ritual.[17]

From this perspective, and particularly in the light of the
Babylonian analogy, the arms race itself may be seen as a form
of massive ritualized combat. In earlier periods the irrational
accumulation of megatonnage or numerical advantage, and
more recently the perpetual development and deployment of
newer, more advanced weapons systems, function to signify the
symbolic victory over nuclear chaos.

Such deployments themselves are occasion for explicit ceremony. Dignitaries and the press are in attendance. Prayers are
uttered, the glories of American technology invariably intoned.
Perhaps the cruise missile has herewith come to a Strategic Air
Command Base, or a new bomber (the B-1 or the Stealth) is
being rolled out for the first public glimpse. These rites of technological passage are episodes or rehearsals of the larger nuclear
drama of mock creation.

I vividly recall driving cross-country to be at the christening,
so-called, of the second Trident submarine, which was named
The Michigan after my home state. (A christening, the formal
naming ceremony in which the boat is launched, by the way, is
distinct from the commissioning, a military ritual in which the
sub passes from the builder's ownership into Pentagon authority.)

Outside, I joined with many others engaged in offering a
counter-liturgy, as it were. Workers and townspeople streamed
in, if a little slowed by our presence. The air of the event was
solemnly festive. The Trident itself, two football fields long and
four stories high, is such a massive and compelling thing, horrid
and fascinating. Bearing twenty-four missiles loaded with mul-
tiple independently targetable warheads, it is the most deadly
powerful single weapon system of any arsenal in the world. It

begs to be worshiped. Such rituals grant form and moment to the impulse.

On another occasion, personally my first face-to-face recognition years ago of the religious impulse, I witnessed a military air show. It was, in fact one where the Confederate Air Force proposed to reenact the Hiroshima bombing. One hundred thousand people, families with children in tow, poured onto the airfield. There, arrayed before them, accessible to touch for the day, were the objects of their interest and desire—a diverse range of aircraft, some of Vietnam fame, many nuclear-capable. A palpable spirit of awe prevailed. It seemed a pantheon of idols had come down and assembled to be reverenced.

It could be argued that technology itself is the concrete realm of the sacred in America, indeed in first-world cultures as such. Jacques Ellul, for example, claims technology is one of the tangible poles around which the modern sacral world is organized.[18] It has its own mystique and thrall and saving power. It is the subject of a deep and unrelenting faith. Even granting this, in military technology, and nuclear weapons in particular, that techno-religious impulse is then compounded by its merger with the power of unimaginable destruction and with the myths of manifest destiny, the omnipotence of the imperial nation-state. It is a compelling convergence.

As it happened, this air show coincided with the United States bicentennial celebration, conspicuously hyped and manipulated and extended by the then-current political administration, so all the elements of civil religion were prominently in the wind. I had come with friends in the Great Lakes Life Community, a collection of nonviolent communities then lively in southern Michigan. The focus of our interest was the B-29 Hiroshima-type plane. Some of our group fasted that day and held a vigil in front of it, effectively preventing its use in any flyover ceremonies. Later in the day, however, another group of us crossed the rope barricade which guarded the plane and spray-painted the word *DEATH* on both sides of the fuselage. The point here is in the reaction of the crowd. They went berserk. They swarmed over us to protect and vindicate the plane. We were dragged and assaulted and screamed at. Had it not been for the intervention of the military police arresting us, we would certainly have been beaten. Whatever else may have been at work, I take the fury of that passion as a measure of the religious investment such weapons invoke.

As Ellul writes:

> The absolute value is one of the sure signs of what a given person or group holds sacred. There is the untouchable, or again, that which cannot be called into question. This defines the boundary of the sacred. ... Criticism is not acceptable. The very being of the person seems under attack. The nerve of a tooth has been exposed. The reaction is vital. Even if they have no clear knowledge of what the sacred is for them, even if they can't explain it, they are laid bare at that point.[19]

Gods of Metal, whose title is drawn from the images of Psalm 115, is a film which makes the religious impulse visible and explicit. It begins with footage shot from the perspective of a B-1 bomber in test flight, harrowing the earth. The sense of speed and omnipotence is seductive, contagious, frightening. But the scene suddenly shifts to the Smithsonian Air and Space Museum in Washington, D.C. We are along on a guided tour. The pilgrims smile and lift their eyes up to the heights of towering missiles. It takes little imagination to see here this same reverence for the technology, this ogling of the devices and, yes, the weapons, which are prominently included. The museum may be thought of as a shrine of sorts. Here again the pantheon is gathered: a model of "Little Boy" (the Hiroshima bomb) and mockups of the Poseidon, MX, and cruise missiles. Nearby a TV monitor plays video footage of successful test flights. The worshipers stare transfixed.

Tests must be counted, themselves, among the rituals of religious nuclearism. One thinks of the H-bomb demonstration in the Marshall Islands, the careful documentation of destructive power rising from the sea, lifting battleships straight up in its plume. The eyes of the world were called to watch. Or there are those surreal photos of military men in sunglasses and deckchairs, lined up for front-row seats at an above-ground test in the Nevada desert.

No sampling of nuclear liturgies, even a brief one such as this, would be complete without mention of the civil defense drills of the 1950s. They imprinted the psyches of an entire generation of school children with the shadow of the bomb. Lifton reports the findings of a study on the pervasive impact of such "duck and cover" drills and concludes that the findings "have relevance for all of us. The air-raid drills are a metaphor for the nuclear age."[20]

I remember from school the preparatory pep talk, the repeated bursts of the bell droning its warning, the somber single-file walk down into the otherwise hidden depths of the school basement, the nightmarish free-play of imagination to be quartered there for ... how long? Later as a Boy Scout I worked toward a merit badge in preparedness: how to build a family fallout shelter in your own home. In New York City during that same period there were annual drills of compulsory shelter-taking mandated by the Civil Defense Act.

All these examples are suggestive of nuclearism's ritual aspect. That they are diverse in time or form is not an issue. They point to its fundamental religious character. And the functional effect of such nuclear liturgies may be thought cumulative. That active civil defense drills have ceased, or that gross reenactments of Hiroshima are no longer politically viable, does not mitigate their liturgical function and effect. The forms have changed over these forty-some years, but the grip (in dread and awe) upon the American psyche remains.

Chernus puts it thus:

> When some particular symbolic meanings come to the forefront of our consciousness, others recede. But all retain their hold over our unconscious thoughts and feelings, in the depths of the psyche where religious symbols have their true home. New images embrace rather than displace old ones; nothing is ever lost. Perhaps the clearest proof of this is the Strategic Defense Initiative, or "Star Wars" proposal, in which all the symbolic motifs of the nuclear age are tied together in one comprehensive package (which may explain the plan's widespread popularity.)[21]

HIGH PRIESTS AND THE CULT OF SECRECY

It will come as no surprise to suggest that nuclearism comes equipped with its own "priests" and "theologians." The latter, called precisely that in Pentagon circles,[22] are the grand theorists, the thinkers of the unthinkable, the Herman Kahns and Henry Kissingers and Edward Tellers (the physicist actually dubbed by his colleagues the apostle of the H-bomb), who argue targeting doctrines and envision integrated long-term strategies. It is their function to think and *speak* at such levels of abstraction as to impose the appearance of rational discourse and control upon these endemically irrational weapons. These are men (invariably) steeped in the mythology and history of nuclearism. They are its exemplars.

The "priests" are the experts, the hired brains, the engineers, and military technocrats, whose access to the information, the codes, and the weapons themselves make them intermediaries to the bomb's sacred realm.

Both "priests" and "theologians" operate at an expertise supposedly beyond the ken of the ordinary layperson. Both employ language which is esoteric, arcane, and euphemistic. The language of "nukespeak" (after Orwell's term) has long been recognized. The narcotizing abstraction yields such terminology as *nuclear umbrella, counterforce, escalation dominance, collateral damage, window of vulnerability, megadeaths,* and *strategic exchange,* all of which mask murderous realities with sophisticated obfuscation. The priestly experts similarly utter a jargon of coded phrases, acronyms, and technical language that serves to mystify and limit access to the ordained and initiated.

Moreover, both operate with security clearance.

The technocrats and theorists alike serve within the cult of secrecy which envelops the bomb and all its systems. That secrecy has a military function, and moreso a political one, but at root the impulse is religious.

From most ancient times the secret and the sacred have been linked, most prominently in the mysteries of the centralized Temple-State. Together they elicit feelings of what Rudolph Otto called "numinous consciousness" which simultaneously combines dread and allure. Both are set apart, demarked as needing protection from violation or despoilment.

Of course as an exercise in grand physics the bomb project was from the outset designed to unlock "the secret powers of the atom" (this way of putting it was constantly recurrent). The alchemists, cloistered in their hidden laboratory, delved into the mysteries of nature. "This implies that the atom itself, like God, held this secret mystery, this deepest of all wisdom, from the very beginning. But only in the twentieth century have human beings become privy to it."[23]

Around the bomb project grew an entire secret city, and perhaps eventually, one could say, an entire national security state. Los Alamos, New Mexico—its site chosen by Robert Oppenheimer from the secret places of his childhood camping experiences[24]—had all the mystery of a hidden city. Young physicists and their families would suddenly disappear, no questions asked, from university campuses to be collected in the desert. To be so elected was a heady honor, and all were drawn thus into the necessity of secrecy. Many of them were not even told the scope or aim of their research, by virtue of General Leslie Groves's military management policy of compartmentalization of knowledge. Each one should know everything needed for his or her own job and *nothing else*.[25]

Pseudonyms and code names (like "Trinity") proliferated. Personal letters to friends disguised the work and location or degenerated into empty generalities. Oppenheimer himself wrote to a friend, "For the last four years I have had only classified thoughts."[26] For the moment we set aside the extent to which that burden of secrecy was morally debilitating and dehumanizing. Suffice it to say that the extent of the secrecy was astonishing. They blew off an A-bomb in North America unbeknownst to anyone. Truman, though he grew bossy at Potsdam (July 1945) under knowledge of the successful test, kept the news from Stalin, then a United States ally with whom he was celebrating defeat of the Germans. And the Hiroshima bombing was carried off with such secrecy that even for days after the Japanese did not know what hit them.

Our enemies, the Soviets above all, or the dreaded terrorists, became the "stealers of the secret." An entire American era was preoccupied with the infiltration of such spies into our scientific culture. The execution of Julius and Ethel Rosenberg, non-scientists whose espionage role was dubious, testifies to the passion which attended this sacred violation.[27]

In another revealing incident a few years back, Howard Moreland was prosecuted for publication of simple instructions in the construction of a small atomic weapon. It was a symbolic and political act which raised a huge storm, prompting the government to attempt prior censorship of the article, court injunctions, and more. Yet all the information was, in point of fact, presently available in public journals. The secret was the secret.

I believe the bomb may be considered the seed of the present national security state with its contemporary *arcana imperii*. The bomb was born in wartime secrecy, but notice that every nuclear power (Soviet Union, Great Britain, and France, not to mention Israel or South Africa) subsequently pursued it without public knowledge or debate. Secrecy is part of the meaning of the bomb.

Encodements, loyalty tests, rituals of initiation or access, systems of classification, the hierarchical emanations ascending in ranks of security purification, all betoken the cultic character of the security apparatus. Nuclear weapons were the sanction and justification for its growth.

That secret has issued in a fundamental assault on democracy. Basic discussion of nuclear policy decisions—from the very first to the present moment—are circumvented, and basic decisions are made apart from public view. In addition, as hinted by political revelations such as the Pentagon Papers, the Watergate matter, and the Iran-Contra affair, there is a full-blown shadow government which usurps the Constitution and even the pretense of democratic control.

The real secret kept from the American people is that there is to be no restraint on the nuclear deity. It has always been the policy of these United States to be willing to use nuclear weapons in a first strike. And we have *used them*.

Daniel Ellsberg, the former Rand analyst whose act of civil disobedience made the Pentagon Papers available, was among the first to collect a long series of instances in which the United States has actively threatened to use nuclear weapons against

an adversary—not always the Soviet Union by any means—for
the purposes of achieving a military or political objective.[28]

> The notion common to nearly all Americans that "no
> nuclear weapons have been used since Nagasaki" is mis-
> taken. It is not the case that U.S. nuclear weapons have
> simply piled up over the years ... unused and unusable,
> save for the single function of deterring their use against
> us by the Soviets. Again and again, generally in secret from
> the American public, U.S. nuclear weapons *have* been
> used, for quite different purposes: in the precise way that
> a gun is used when you point it at someone's head in a
> direct confrontation, whether or not the trigger is pulled.[29]

Now, using Freedom of Information Act access to recently
declassified materials and other documents which appear from
time to time mailed in brown paper envelopes out from behind
the shroud of secrecy, Michio Kaku and Daniel Axelrod have
assembled a detailed history of those events and the specifics of
the Pentagon's assorted war plans.[30] The history they recount
demonstrates how nuclear weapons have, since World War II,
been the capstone of all military policy structure.

By quick degrees we have passed from consideration of the
bomb's religious phenomenology to its pragmatic imperial function. Yet it is the one which has enabled the other. The aura of
sanctity has facilitated, nay encouraged and driven, the criminal
machinations of nuclearism. There is no getting at the latter
until we comprehend the former.

This is precisely the complaint Chernus makes of the nuclear
disarmament movement.

> The movement has tried to move us from the level of
> numbing to the level of awareness by urging us to imagine
> the literal horrors of nuclear war. Yet its alarms have fallen
> on deaf ears. ... In its commitment to literal thinking it
> has ignored the third level of symbolic meaning. ... It is
> clear that the nuclear issue goes beyond ethical consider-
> ations, and it is equally clear that the antinuclear campaign
> cannot succeed merely by stressing the irrationality of

nuclear armament, for the Bomb's nonrational symbolic meanings lie at the heart of its appeal.[31]

In *Facing the Nuclear Heresy* Clark Chapman levels the identical criticism against the church. It is *moral* issues which have predominated in the churches' efforts at arms race opposition. He is on target when he stresses that this is not enough. His primary illustration is the United States Roman Catholic bishops' pastoral letter which, when it comes to cases, focuses substantively on the morality of deterrence. "The distinctive religious challenge of the Bomb, however, is not examined."[32]

The same could be said of the United Methodist bishops' letter "In Defense of Creation." A wonderful document in many respects, it goes so far as to name deterrence an idol and a "position which can not receive the church's blessing."[33] So it brinks on the right questions, but apart from that reference, barely gets beyond ethics or psychology.

One of the few documents to treat nuclearism as a religious, indeed an explicitly confessional issue, was a study document of the Presbyterian church, *Presbyterians and Peacemaking: Are We Now Called to Resistance?*[34] It enjoyed a brief controversy but is now out of print.

So Chapman and Chernus are right as far as they go. Indeed in the foregoing analysis, I acknowledge a debt to them and hereby part company.

My thoughts turn to the faith-based resistance community which has in word and deed been forthrightly exposing the religious worship of the bomb for a decade or more. I think on liturgical symbolics in which they struggle to pray and act. Chernus knows not a whit of them, Chapman barely (he does quote two imprisoned resisters in his Postscript testimonials). It is toward those symbols, and those prisoners, that we are steadily making our way.

However, there is more, from an unapologetically biblical point of view, to be said about the power of imperial nuclear religion. It is a spiritual power. The idolatry inherent makes it so. Nuclearism is thus more than a false doctrine, though when found within the church or claimed to be compatible with the gospel, it is just that, indeed a heretical false doctrine as we have already suggested. Nuclearism and its institutions are still not fully understood; nor will they have been fully named until they are counted among the principalities and powers of this world. Then may they be rebuked with right worship.

CHAPTER 4

PRINCIPALITIES AND THE POWERS THAT BE

What is most crucial about this situation, biblically speaking, is the failure of moral theology, in the American context, to confront the principalities—the institutions, systems, ideologies, and other political and social powers—as militant, aggressive, and immensely influential creatures in this world as it is.

William Stringfellow[1]

A REVIVAL OF INTEREST

When William Stringfellow, who must be credited with the theological and political discernment that has awakened so much of the recent practical interest in the powers, first began to speak and write on the topic, he met a strange mix of acceptance and rebuff. He loved to tell the story of an early presentation, in fact two of them, given in Boston. Scheduled to give similar talks the same day at Harvard Business School and a seminary there, he debated with himself about excising from the business school version any explicit biblical reference or language, but decided in the end to let it stand intact. The business school students, it turned out, engaged him thoroughly, bending his ear long past the hour appointed, with numerous examples from their own experience of corporate dominance and possession by the commercial powers. Their experiences verified his own observations.

Later at the seminary, with the identical speech, he was ridiculed and written off. Ruling authorities, principalities, world rulers of the present darkness? Come now! These were but the incidental vestige of a quaint and archaic language, an esoteric parlance now obsolete, with no real meaning in history or human life.

Needless to say the New Testament view of the powers, its cosmology and insight, has not always been available to the church. Virtually since the church, its scriptures in tow, was seduced and taken captive by empire under Constantine the Great in the fourth century, the powers have been conveniently misread as insubstantial demons floating about in the cosmos.[2] There could be speculation, within certain limits, on the hierarchies of their being. They could be envisioned as a plague of disembodied spirits hovering to prey upon the individual, but it was not politically expedient that they be read in relation to social institutions preying on the body of humanity. The biblical reference, rest assured, My Lord, is not to empires and their minions, but to some other order of beings altogether.

Any social critique was thereby effectively eviscerated and rendered harmless. It evaporated, so to speak, into thin air. Any restraint on political idolatry was minimized, if not completely foregone.

Moreover, the history of biblical criticism has by and large aided and abetted this reading. From the very beginning of critical New Testament studies, it had been assumed that when St. Paul and his followers spoke of authorities or angels or powers, they were suffering the superstitious remains of an archaic worldview. On that score their observations might be passed over, dispensed with, or even justly attacked.

For example, S.G.F. Brandon, otherwise notorious for his maverick political reading of the gospels, castigates Paul for obscuring the real political facts of Jesus' arrest and trial with an overlay of this esoteric theology. He cites 1 Corinthians 2:7-8, "But we impart a secret and hidden mystery of God, which God decreed before the ages for our glorification. None of the rulers of this age understood this; for if they had they would not have crucified the Lord of Glory." He comments on the "rulers":

> They denote the demonic powers that were believed to govern this present world-order, and their use in this passage reveals that Paul was thinking in terms of current Graeco-Roman astralism. This was a very esoteric system, based upon an ancient tradition of belief that the stars, particularly the planets, ruled the destinies of men [sic]. . . .
>
> In this truly amazing statement Paul is obviously referring to the crucifixion of the historical Jesus of Nazareth. But he has, in effect, lifted the event completely out of its historical setting and assigned to it a transcendental significance.[3]

Such a reading has been typical of biblical commentary. Fortunately, however, there has been a revival of interest in the principalities and their pointed political meaning. It has come generally in two waves. The first coincided with a historical crisis, namely, the events that shook the world in the '30s and '40s.[4] When Protestant theology was sent groping for a biblical handle on demonic historical forces raging out of control, the significance of the powers more readily commended itself. Not surprisingly, the Confessing movement in Germany was a primary forum of exegetical debate.[5]

As a matter of parallel interest, this was the same period in which Carl Jung's depth psychology was opening on the field of the collective unconscious and naming the Germanic god, Wotan, as a cultural archetype formerly suppressed, but then rising with a vengeance in the Third Reich. In 1936 Jung had ventured the suggestion that economic, political, and psychological factors were insufficient to explain the pending fury. Beneath and within them he beheld that "an ancient god of storm and frenzy, the long quiescent Wotan, should awake, like an extinct volcano, to new activity, in a civilized country that had long been supposed to have outgrown the Middle Ages."[6]. He flatly regarded the phenomenon as a state of being seized or possessed. The year following he commented on the individual normalcy which accompanies the grip of such a collective hysteria:

> Look at all the incredible savagery going on in our so-called civilized world: it all comes from human beings and their mental condition! Look at the devilish engines of destruction! They are invented by completely innocuous gentlemen, reasonable, respectable citizens who are everything we would wish. And when the whole thing blows up and an indescribable hell of devastation is let loose, nobody seems to be responsible. It simply happens, and yet it is all man-made. But since everyone is blindly convinced that he is nothing more that his own extremely unassuming and insignificant conscious self, which performs its duties decently and earns a moderate living, nobody is aware that this whole rationalistically organized conglomeration we call a state or a nation is driven on by a seemingly impersonal but terrifying power which nobody and nothing can check.[7]

His observations have figured in some of the biblical and theological explorations of more recent powers study.

If there was an urgent historical context for the earlier awakening of attention to the principalities, the same may be said for this recent work. In North America it coincided roughly with another period of crisis, a comparable rage of demonic powers requiring comprehension. The utter resilience of racism, the brutal prosecution of war in the Third World (especially in Southeast Asia), the growth of predatory multi-national corporations, and yes finally, the nuclear arms race, all figure in the background.[8]

Stringfellow's work has been mentioned. Nobody on the theological scene has been his match for incisive, intuitive grasp of the powers' deadly reality, their strategies and tactics, their pervasive claims and pretensions. It is as if he looked them unflinching in the eye, sized them up, and rebuked them from within the Word of God itself.

However, the most wide-ranging, thorough study of the powers is being undertaken by Walter Wink in a trilogy, of which the first two volumes are complete. With exhaustive New Testament research Wink confirms in the main what Stringfellow intuited over the years through his own Bible study and writing. Indeed, Wink recognizes Bill Stringfellow throughout and specifically acknowledges first conceiving the entire project in 1964 under the impetus of reading his *Free in Obedience.*[9]

Wink's first volume, *Naming the Powers*, is the exegetical foundation, undertaking the word studies and closely reading the disputed or neglected passages for their first-century meaning. The second, *Unmasking the Powers,*[10] is a set of interlocking cultural essays on aspects of power addressed as the phenomenal categories developed in the first book. They are thoughtful reflections on topics long banished from our own rationalist and materialist vocabularies — Satan, the demons, the gods, the angels of the nations, the angels of the churches, and the like. The essays are polemical insofar as they make frontal attacks on the ideology of materialism, but they are Christian apologetic insofar as they use sociological analysis and Jungian depth psychology to make these biblical persona more readily comprehensible. Between the two is the attempt toward helping construct a postmaterialist cosmology, as he terms it, by drawing on the biblical resources.

Because our assumptions run so deep, any approach to the intentions of the New Testament writers must proceed carefully, mapping out the mythic worldview within which they conceived of power and examining their special vocabulary. Wink discovers that terms such as "rulers," "powers," "thrones," "realm," "authorities," (and a host of others by no means limited to Paul), are fluid and ambiguous depending on the context. But it is this very ambiguity, this *studied* ambiguity, now earthly and temporal, now cosmic and spiritual, that apparently served the New Testament communities so well in comprehending the versatilities of power which they confronted. Such terms are often paired ("rulers and elder," "principalities and powers") or may be strung together in a series "as if power were so diffuse and impalpable a phenomenon that words must be heaped in clusters in order to catch a sense of its complexity."[11] (Readers of Stringfellow will recognize his own unconscious and exaggerated mimicry of this New Testament style.)

Wink admits to beginning the study with the naive precon-
ception that the powers could be facilely "demythologized," that
is, rendered without remainder into modern categories. By
materialist assumptions he expected to find nothing more than
institutions, social systems, and political structures, but he was
in for an exegetical surprise: their mythic spiritual dimension
wouldn't go away.

In the end he has come to argue that they are *simultaneously*,

> the inner and outer aspects of any given manifestation of
> power. As the inner aspect they are the spirituality of insti-
> tutions, the "within" of corporate structures and system.
> As the outer aspect they are political systems, appointed
> officials, the "chair" of an organization, laws — in short, all
> the tangible manifestations which power takes. Every
> Power tends to have a visible pole, an outer form — be it a
> church, a nation, or an economy — and an invisible pole,
> an inner spirit or driving force that animates, legitimates,
> and regulates its physical manifestation in the world. Nei-
> ther pole is the cause of the other. Both come into exis-
> tence together and cease to exist together. When a
> particular power becomes idolatrous, placing itself above
> God's purposes for the good of the whole, then that Power
> becomes demonic. The church's task is to unmask this idol-
> atry and recall the Powers to their created purposes in the
> world — "so that the Sovereignties and Powers should learn
> only now, through the Church, how comprehensive God's
> wisdom really is"[12] (Eph. 3:10, JB).

So, to take as an example the central case of Jesus' trial and
execution, the powers may be in one rendition "the rulers and
elders" or Pilate, and in another, "the rulers of this age" who
crucified the Lord of Glory. The latter, Brandon notwithstanding, is no abstract theologizing or political misdirection; both
speak of the realities of political power in different aspects.

Or, to draw a striking instance from a different class of powers, the "prince of the power of the air" (Eph 2:2) is not to be
cast off as some spooky and ephemeral first-century superstition.
The power of the air may be recognized as a kind of world

atmosphere, the general spiritual climate that influences human interaction, what Paul in another reference calls "the spirit of the cosmos" (1 Cor 2:12). It is, says Wink, the "invisible dominion or realm created by the sum total of choices for evil. It is the spiritual matrix of inauthentic living."[13] This pseudo-environment is the constellation of forces which he sees touched on by such contemporary terms as *zeitgeist* or ideology, cultural expectations, climate of public opinion, mob psychology, even negative vibes. Essential to its functioning is that we are not even aware that it exists. To seem not to appear is part and parcel of its power. Somewhere I have heard that at the Pentagon, the in-house term for its own military propaganda is "atmospherics."

FROM THE EXPERIENCE OF ISRAEL

Both because they figure so prominently in the development of the Hebrew background to Paul's usage, indeed the New Testament cosmology in general, and because they get at our current concern for the religious dimension of the nuclear-armed state, attention must be given to the *archai*, the princes or angels of the nation.[14]

After the liberation from Egypt, when the Hebrews gathered in Canaan they were confronted, as again and again in their history, with the reality of political authority and its religious expression. Hence was posed a perennial question: If Yahweh is sovereign, then what in heaven's name are the gods of the nations? (And how do they do so well?)

In answer, there were three basic choices. These may be thought of as three ideological strategies in a budding conflict of class and myth, or simply as options in the process of struggle and communal discernment which shaped Israel's identity. The first was plainly to identify Yahweh with the supreme god El, or with the up and coming young rival, Baal, who subsequently usurped El. Such syncretism was safe and accommodationist, and there is plenty of evidence within the canon that the tactic was tried.

The second path was to categorically deny there was any substantive spiritual reality behind the gods. Here is Elijah (emblematic of the whole prophetic tradition) ridiculing the empty powerlessness of Baal on Mt. Carmel: "Cry aloud, for he is a god; either he is musing, or he has gone aside [to relieve himself], or he is on a journey, or perhaps he is asleep and must be wakened" (1 Kgs 18:27). Here the mythic conflict is literalized, a public contest. Or again, subjected to mockery the Psalmist strikes back:

> Their idols are silver and gold,
>> the work of human hands.
> They have mouths, but do not speak;
>> eyes, but do not see.
> They have ears, but do not hear;
>> noses, but do not smell.
> They have hands, but do not feel;
>> feet, but do not walk;
>> and they do not make a sound in their throat.
> Those who make them are like them,
>> and so are all who trust in them.
>> (Ps 115:4-8)

Those empty piles of sticks and stones.

Still, they were sometimes victorious, often had the upper hand (as in the Canaanite feudal-states), were certainly seductive, and perhaps after all not to be taken too lightly. Hence the third option, which ultimately prevailed: the gods are subordinates to Yahweh. Hereafter they came to be known as *elohim* (the gods) or *bene Elohim* (the sons of God[15]). They were envisioned as forming something of a heavenly council about the throne of Yahweh. This, too, is commonly celebrated in the psalms:

> Let the heavens praise thy wonders, O Lord,
>> thy faithfulness in the assembly of the holy
>> ones!
> For who in the skies can be compared to the
>> Lord?
> Who among the heavenly beings is like the
>> Lord,

> a God feared in the council of the holy ones,
>   great and terrible above all that are round
>   about God? (Ps 89:5-7)

Not to be missed is the element of wry political humor, seeing them grouped in obeisance round about the throne as advisors, messengers, choir members, subordinate gofers, and lackeys. Sing, ye gods.

If, as suspected, this view emerged at the time of the Judges, then it would coincide, according to Caird, with the title "Yahweh of hosts."[16] In the Hebrew Bible "host of heaven" most often refers to the stars, the sun, the moon, but it may also, by a *studied ambiguity*, such a useful literary device, portray the courtly council. The two are rendered in parallel by God's creation song, the answer to Job:

> Where were you when I laid the foundation of
>   the earth?
> . . . On what were its bases sunk,
>   or who laid its cornerstone,
> when the morning stars sang together,
>   and all the sons of God shouted for joy?
>   (Job 38:4,6-7)

In point of fact, the nations and their gods are *creatures*. By the period of the exile this element of the cosmology and primordial history is becoming well formed. Deuteronomy 32:8-9 reads, "When the Most High gave to the nations their inheritance, when God separated the sons of men, God fixed the bounds of the peoples according to the number of the sons of God. For the Lord's portion is Israel, Jacob is God's allotted heritage." Here things are being spelled out further: the nations themselves are not human creations (see Genesis 10); over each one God has appointed its own angelic ruler, devoted to guarding its identity and responsible for its fate. They have a place and function, a proper vocation even, in the created order. From Israel's perspective they are to be granted a respect, but *not* worship.

Elsewhere in Deuteronomy the warning is explicit and

stern. "Beware lest you lift up your eyes to heaven, when you see the sun and the moon and the stars, the whole host of heaven, you are drawn away to worship and serve them, which Yahweh your God has allotted to all the nations under the whole heaven" (Dt 4:19).

Perhaps in exile, under the overpowering sway of Babylon, this line was the most difficult to tread. The success of massive, imperial power seemed to validate Marduk and his kin, the Babylonian pantheon. A grave and seductive temptation was the issue. Whom to follow? Whom to worship? Whom to remember or forget? It was a temptation which recurred in the victory of Cyrus over Babylonia. Thanks to whom for liberation? A whole new pantheon?

These are the questions proper to a reading of the Genesis 1 creation story which originated in that period. They are questions which the story has every intention of addressing. The account is properly read, in all its renowned beauty and poetry, as a parody of the Babylonian creation liturgy. It's been called in that regard a "theogonic satire."[17] In one fell swoop gods of chaos and their subduers, Persian dualistic gods of light, sun gods (both Egyptian and Babylonian), moon gods, and the multitude of astral deities associated with the nations, even fertility (and the Baal cults attending it), are all located within the created order of the one God. The worship of all else is rendered patently ridiculous. It is a sweeping and politically subversive account.

By envisioning the Genesis creation poem in action, which is to say employed liturgically in a political situation of exile, we come upon a substantial hint in what remains our central concern: the power of liturgy in a "war of myths" to break and undo the pervasive claims of a spiritual and symbolic order. At the very least it evinces, as we have seen, the capacity to preserve the freedom and identity of a community.

In the first two volumes of his powers trilogy, Walter Wink makes much, and rightly so, of a wonderful and provoking story in the tenth chapter of Daniel, a later work of Jewish apocalyptic. In the remarkable events narrated there, Daniel, a Babylonian Jew who has risen to prominence in the court of the conquering Persians by virtue of his gifted political discernment, begins to fast and pray on behalf of his captive community. Three weeks later a messenger angel arrives in a burst of splendor to explain that he'd been dispatched from God on the first day of the fast bearing a prophecy of Persian destruction and defeat, but had been waylaid all this time by the angel-prince of Persia, who apparently was eager that such news be suppressed. The messenger was able to escape only with the aid of the chief angel Michael, who was even then holding the Persian to a heavenly standoff. Pardon him if he rushes off quickly to rejoin Michael in that fight.

What does all this portend?

Either it is a large and mythic way of speaking about Daniel's struggle against the internalization of the imperial program, foreign interests occupying his heart. Or, as Wink concludes, the angel of Persia is the actual spirituality of the nation which, in pursuit of its "self-interest," effectively for a time resists the will and Word of God. Of import here, and also for later liturgical reflections, is that his prayer and fasting initiate war in heaven. "If we conceive of heaven not as some super-terrestrial realm in the sky, but think of it instead as the interiority of earthly existence in all its potentialities, the image of war in heaven can be understood as the struggle between two contending spiritualities or national spirits for supremacy."[18]

All the foregoing, as one variety of power, comports well with the New Testament view of the authorities, at once earthly and heavenly. It is after all the very history which has nourished and formed it. Paul writes to the Colossians that in Christ "all things were created, in heaven and on earth, visible and invisible, whether thrones or dominions or principalities or authorities— all things were created through him and for him. He is before all things and in him all things hold together" (Col 1:16-17). In so saying, he puts the powers in their place. They are creatures under the sovereignty of the Lord. They are grouped around, held together in Christ. Created in him, they are by implication, originally "good," having a vocation in the right order of things.

FALLEN: THE LAW AND THE STATE

And yet it is the powers, the rulers of this age, who crucified Christ. That is perhaps the single most edifying point in comprehending them. They are at best confused and blind to their vocations. And if all the New Testament references are amassed, from the lowliest human agent to the powers in high places, from the Pharisaic party to the Beast rising out of the sea, the preponderance of them report demonic agencies, a host in rebellion against God. They are among the forces which separate human beings from the love of God (Rom 8:39); they blind the minds of unbelievers (2 Cor 4:4); they enslave human beings (Gal 4: 1-11); they are in league with death (1 Cor 15:24-27); and they are the true forces against which believers, in faith, contend in mortal combat (Eph 6:10-20).

The powers are fallen by virtue of idolatry. In the biblical saga human beings neglect the stern warning, lifting up their eyes and worshiping that which is not God. In consequence they come into bondage, and the powers are twisted and inflated, mushrooming out of control.

We might easily take the nations as the ready example of this. Israel's history is surely a litany of suffering one imperial occupation after another. The social order of creation has been experienced as corrupted and in disarray. From one prophet to the next the cause of this is laid to idolatry.

Let us, however, try an example closer to home, at least firstly to Paul's home: the law. The law is no mean principality. It must be so counted and numbered. Moreover, it is the one with which he is most intimately acquainted. He knows it as agent and insider. With legal credentials he's been jealous on its behalf even to the point of official violence. No wonder, this side of his conversion, the question which exercises his mind so much in correspondence is how could the law, a good gift of God, become an instrument of blindness, a vehicle of ignorance, a tempter to sin, an ally and accomplice of death itself?

The law is the good creation of God (Rom 7:13). It has a given vocation in the social order. It probably is imprecise to speak of an angel of the law, though there is a tradition mentioned in Acts (8:53) and cited by Paul in Galatians (3:19) that it was delivered by angels. As we have come to expect of the powers, there is certainly a visible aspect to the law—the written code, the public symbols, and rituals of interpretation—and there is most assuredly an invisible, interior aspect (even today a lawyer will argue a case on the "spirit of the law"). But how does it come to be in a trio of powers, in alliance with sin and death?

We may draw again on G. B. Caird who recounts a brief literary history of Satan.[19] His survey doubles as something of a parable which illuminates the mystery with which Paul struggled. "Satan" means adversary, and early on that came to have a legal meaning in relation to divine judgments. In the prologue to Job Satan is one of the angels with rightful access to the heavenly court of Yahweh, there to serve as public prosecutor, defender of the law. In that pursuit Satan goes to and fro upon the earth garnering evidence. (Notice that even in the New Testament period certain juridical duties remain. Satan is the legal adversary in 1 Peter 5:8, and in 1 Timothy 3:6 those who are conceited come under his legal condemnation.)

Later, in rabbinic literature Satan has a tendency to be executioner as well, dishing out punishments in accord with the sentence. Paul himself reflects this when he mentions a person being handed over to Satan "for the destruction of the flesh, that his spirit may be saved in the day of the Lord Jesus" (1 Cor 4:5). In the extreme, Satan becomes Destroyer, holder of the power of death.

Meanwhile, Satan expands his responsibilities with the zealousness of an agent provocateur, canvassing business for the lawcourts, tempting and inciting people to disobedience. By degrees the servant of God has become the enemy of God, with whom Jesus contends in the gospels. Caird concludes:

> We cannot say that in the process he loses anything of his original character. Throughout his tragic history his zeal for justice remains unimpaired. He is a martinet, who demands that men shall be dealt with according to the rigor of the law, and will go to any length to secure a verdict.[20]

Satan has made an idol of the law and so becomes himself the raging power of death. The fall of Satan appears here to be one with the idolatry of law. Not that we should let the parable confuse us on this point: idolatry is a *human act*. Think about

the zeal of Paul himself. All of the principalities become inflated
in their power; they are all implicated in the fall; they are confused in their vocations; they usurp the very place of God —
because human beings grant them worship.

In the case of law, that comes of mistaking something deriv-
ative, secondary, and conditional for the absolute will of God.
It comes of seeking self-justification, meaning, and identity in
law. (To seek justification by the law is the form of idolatry that
most concerns Paul.) In consequence the law itself becomes
accuser, tempter, and executioner. Human beings are then "in
bondage to beings that by nature are no gods" (Gal 4:8). To put
it another way, the law was made for humanity, not humanity
for the law. Paul never quite speaks of it so, but I believe he
experienced his relation to the law as a kind of possession. The
sudden violence of his conversion, as portrayed in Acts, may
suggest its powerful grip upon him.

We have already touched on the nations as prototypical powers. And while there is little difference in the ancient world
between nation and state, they do name distinct principalities
in our own. Much is written on the state in New Testament
literature, a preponderance focused upon Romans 13, because
that chapter has been so abused as an isolated text sanctioning
an unqualified obedience of Christians to any established
regime. I forbear to dwell on it, but the passage does speak of
the vocation of political authority to order society. The word
Paul uses for authorities is the same one he employs in other
places referring to the angelic powers, which is to say their heavenly, interior aspect, and most often with respect to their
demonic rebellion against God. In the thirteenth chapter of
Romans the reference is clearly to the most mundane human
agents who wield the sword and issue taxes. Their authority,
says Paul, comes from God. They are servants of God, not that
different in conception from the subordination of the nations to
Yahweh's divine sovereignty. And not that different from what
Jesus is reported in John 19 to have pluckily said to Pilate on
the occasion of his sentencing to death.

This admonition of Paul to obey the state authorities is often
rightly juxtaposed with the version of the Roman state portrayed
in Revelation 13: the Beast rising from the chaos of the sea.

There the angelic being "behind" the Beast is the Dragon, an "interiority" from hell itself. In this vision the state has lost any vestige of legitimate vocation in a frenzy of idolatry and blasphemous pretension. It is experienced as virtually out of human control, transfixing and enslaving human beings, demanding their worship. This is an image which has provided grist for thoughtful meditation in our own time.

Second Thessalonians, a Pauline letter, seems to combine the views:

> Let no one deceive you in any way; for that day will not come, unless the rebellion comes first, and the man of lawlessness is revealed, the son of perdition, who opposes and exalts himself against every so-called god or object of worship, so that he takes his seat in the temple of God, proclaiming himself to be God. Do you not remember that when I was still with you I told you this? And you know what is restraining him now so that he may be revealed in his time. For the mystery of lawlessness is already at work; only he who now restrains it will do so until he is out of the way (2 Thess 2:3-7).

To say the least, this is a more ambiguous view of the state. In a narrow historical sense it may reflect the impact of Caligula's decree, never accomplished, that his image be erected in the Temple of Jerusalem, but more broadly it evinces an understanding of the general idolatrous tendencies of political authority. That a restraint is seen (perhaps in Caligula's removal) implies the continuing vocation of the state, not as yet altogether lost. However, the fact of deep corruption remains, a fallenness which seen full-blown could be adequately described only with recourse to the beastly images of apocalypse.

HUMANITY BE DAMNED: A PRESUMPTION OF SURVIVAL

It is suggested that the Roman Imperial cult, made notorious in history by the Christian refusal to worship the emperor, was not at the outset a conscious political manipulation, a religious apparatus contrived and constructed to hold disparate pieces of empire together. Instead, it appears to have begun spontaneously in the far-flung provinces, and only subsequently been adopted as an ideological strategy of Rome.[21]

The same may be said of the religious character of nuclearism examined in the previous chapter. If it was periodically enhanced or consciously manipulated for the sake of political interests, it was nonetheless neither conspired nor invented in some closed room of the national-security state. The idolatry which inheres to nuclearism arose gradually and spontaneously, as the utterances of those who beheld the first bomb test bear witness.

That is the example, again only the most explicit of truly innumerable instances on the current scene, which has never been far from mind as the New Testament view of the powers has been unfolded here. The idolatry of the bomb has exactly the effects the biblical view describes and anticipates: its grip on society and culture is deepened and its power over human life has become more entrenched. Its institutions take on a life of their own and rise up chaotically out of human control. People who imagine that they direct its movements—the planners, theorists, politicians, and technocrats—are instead its victims, consumed and possessed by its ethos, the driving spirit of power. It becomes insufficient merely to say, "This is a religion," however true that may be. It has become a power whose first concern is its own life and survival.

Stringfellow spoke of this trait: "The principalities have great resilience; the death game which they play continues, adapting its means of dominating human beings to the sole morality which governs all demonic powers so long as they exist—survival."[22] With respect to the nuclear powers this is astonishingly explicit. Their commitment is to surviving even a nuclear war. The fantasy is almost comically portrayed in those revelations which appear from time to time in the media about the Postal Service's contingencies for reestablishing mail routes after the cataclysm, or the Internal Revenue's plan (it even enhances their fearsome reputation for tenacity) to go on collecting taxes come what may.

Survival is now applied not so much to human beings (humanity be damned!) as to systems and technology. Thirty or fifty or one hundred and fifty megadeaths (that is millions of deaths) may be anticipated in this or that scenario, yet the war-fighting capacity, the second-, third-, and fourth-strike responses are deemed survivable. Hardened command centers will abide; communication systems will be trucked out and redeployed as more weapons beneath the earth or in the depths of the sea await their orders.

Another example of this ethic is the presumption of technological survival implicit in the creation and storage of nuclear waste. What other theological meaning can be made of the willingness to concentrate and store a material which will require sophisticated technological monitoring and oversight for the next five thousand years (or some other unfathomable half-life). In just a few short decades management of nuclear waste storage facilities has reached a state of breakdown and disarray, but it is deemed that megabucks and technology and political coverup can handle the crisis. The presumption and testimony remain: deadly by-products continue pouring out of the weapons and power plants.

In a changing political climate, which is so much touted these days, the intransigence of such powers should not be underestimated. Are alliances shifting? They regroup. Is the Cold War at an end? They simply declare a victory and roll on. New enemies are readily found. Perhaps it serves their purposes to further arms control talks at this point or some other; perhaps cuts in number of certain weapons will be encouraged, but the fundamental structures, the institutions, the powers themselves will tenaciously refuse any talk of dismantling. Their ethic, their sense of survival dictates it. These powers have a life of their own, in effect beyond human direction.

OUT OF HUMAN HANDS: THE COVER OF DARKNESS

By the lights of a biblical view it should come as no surprise that the powers enjoy an autonomy which refuses submission or slips human control, but what remains so astonishing is the variety of ways this may be spoken of or verified in experience.

In the plainest of political terms there is the aforementioned subversion of democracy, which has accompanied nuclear weapons from their conception. The decisions to build and to use them, each of monumental historical moment, were undertaken in the shroud of wartime secrecy, necessarily (so the argument goes) without the slightest recourse to public discussion. In the aftermath of the war, however, the entire apparatus of that secrecy was expanded, institutionalized, and made a permanent feature of American military power.

The Pentagon, then rapidly nuclearizing and overseeing the largest military machine in history, moved to consolidate its power against the intrusive restraints of any democratic control. (The actual Pentagon building was designed for conversion to a hospital after the war, when the massive administrative complex would no longer be needed; now in the ethics of survival, there is no talk of dismantling or peacetime conversion.) The National Security Act of 1947 formalized and structured a configuration of agencies, the first of which was the National Security Council (NSC), composed of the president's highest military and political advisors. These consultants set policy, both foreign and domestic, related to broadly conceived United States national security interests. The Act also established the twin partners of the CIA and the Department of Defense. All three were cloaked in official secrecy.

Moreover, the Act granted the presidency emergency powers beyond those conferred in the Constitution, including the authority to suspend civil liberties and undertake otherwise illegal covert operations such as widespread surveillance of citizens. Over the years these emergency powers have been so interpreted as to sanction covert military operations whose aim is to destabilize and overthrow legitimate foreign governments. The operations against Iran, Guatemala, Vietnam, Chile, and Nicaragua are only the most notorious.

At the same time the Act gave the presidency exclusive and unlimited power to use nuclear weapons. It is precisely this expansion of authority which has made possible the long list of nuclear first-strike threats determined and exercised within NSC secrecy. In the National Security Act the veil came down and the restraints were simultaneously lifted. That may be thought one symbolic moment in the powers' unleashing. It remains the primary element in their functioning autonomously, out of sight, above accountability, and beyond reasonable control.

TECHNOLOGY: THE AUTONOMY OF MEANS

Now and then it is said that Hitler won the Second World War. Jacques Ellul, himself a participant in the French resistance, wrote to that effect in 1948 with the publication of *The Presence of the Kingdom*.[23] That remains perhaps the soundest and sanest and most accurate sense to be made of the some four decades since. Hitler won. His spirit rules.

That may also be said to be the meaning of nuclearism and the national security state. Hitler's enemies imitated him and mastered his means, which is to say, perfected them. If he could sponsor *blitzkrieg*, they could manage first the firebombing of Dresden and Tokyo, and then Hiroshima and Nagasaki. The bomb itself was conceived in the mind of the Nazi regime. No matter that Hitler abandoned the project. A kind of technological momentum pulled the United States version forward, not merely to production but to its use against a civilian population, and then finally to become the cornerstone of military policy. Here was sign and seal of Nazi victory.

It was in *The Presence of the Kingdom*, a genuinely prophetic book, that Ellul first articulated the radical separation of means and ends taking place in modern society. Indeed, he beheld that everything was becoming "means," that "ends" as such had been reduced to abstractions or disappeared altogether. Thus life was being rendered absurd.

> All that science can do will be used to save one life, and then millions of men will be massacred by bombs, or in concentration camps: both are products of the enormity of means. . . . In this terrible dance of means which have been unleashed, no one knows where we are going, the aim of life has been forgotten, the end has been left behind. Humanity has set out at tremendous speed—to go *nowhere*.[24]

The time has passed, writes Ellul, when "the end justifies the means." Instead the means, by sole virtue of their efficiency, justify themselves. This may frankly be understood as a form or variety of idolatry. The means, in society, were thus passing beyond judgment or limitation; they were freed of any moral hindrance. Humanity was losing control and mastery, even choice, of the means. The efficiency of technics itself chooses with a precision and exactitude humanity cannot attain. Personal responsibility for the use of means is eliminated. Simply put, *there is no choice.*[25]

These postwar social reflections were offered in a theological context, but they have been elaborated and verified with a lifetime of sociological examination. They presaged the monumental work Ellul has undertaken analyzing the full-blown emergence of technological society. Several of his characterizations of the technological system are directly pertinent to the discussion here.

Ellul effectively demonstrates the "automatism" of technical choice. "The one best way," rationally measured and calculated, effectively precludes human choice, and by this process the technical movement becomes self-directing.

> The system's automatism is the application of technologies according to choices that are induced by previous technologies and that can be shunted and diverted only with great difficulty. Hence, this automatism has a large measure of indetermination. In each new situation, for each new area, the technologies combine in a certain way that *as a result*, and independent of human decision, a certain technology (new or old) is applied, a certain solution is contributed.[26]

The cumulation of such results issues in a process of technological progress which is "self-augmenting." By this Ellul means that things occur as if the system were growing by an intrinsic, internal power, without decisive human intervention. It seems to operate by a kind of automatic, self-generating logic, which may be formulated in two "laws":

1. In a given civilization, technical progress is irreversible.
2. Technical progress tends to act, not according to an arithmetic, but according to a geometric progression.[27]

This progression is a matter of *necessity*. The preceding technical situation alone, which is to say even apart from an economic or social condition, determines the next. Techniques and technologies recombine in incessant new discoveries and innovations. An apparent barrier to any particular technique is overcome by these combinations and new ensembles. One implication is that the role of individuals, or in a general way of human beings themselves, is rendered increasingly unimportant.

> The more factors there are, the more readily they combine and the more evident is the urgent need for each technical advance. Advance for its own sake becomes proportionately greater and the expression of human autonomy proportionately feebler. ... In this decisive evolution, the human being does not play a part. Technical elements combine among themselves, and they do so more and more spontaneously. In this sense it is possible to speak of the "reality" of technique — with its own substance, its own particular mode of being, and a life independent of power and decision.[28]

It is indeed characteristic of technology that *it* becomes autonomous. This is simply to say again that technology depends upon itself, "mapping its own route." Two aspects of that autonomy concern us here. The first is the measure of autonomy from the state and political direction which technology enjoys. This will appear at first a fantastic claim. Ellul is not about to renounce the existence of the famous "military-industrial complex." The technocratic state, as our experience attests, is deeply entangled in, nearly merged with the technological milieu. But there is more to be said of the accepted aphorism sponsored by theorists and politicians and philosophers that the state decides and technology obeys, or the simplistic notion that the state will serve as recourse against the abuses of technology.

How in fact does the state intervene? How is a decision reached, and specifically, by whom? A closer look reveals that it is the state technicians who are the origin of political decisions. And in what direction might their decidings go?

We perceive very quickly that a remarkable conjunction occurs. The state is furnished with greater power devices by technology, and, being itself an organism of power, the state can only move in the direction of growth, it is strictly conditioned by the technologies not to make any decisions but those to increase power, its own and that of the body social.[29]

A certain drift is by necessity implied.

The other aspect of technological autonomy which especially concerns us is that autonomy from value and ethic. Like the much touted value-free environment of its predecessor and companion, pure scientific research, technology does not endure any moral judgment. It simply is. Whatever has been found is to be applied. The corollary is similar: "Since technology does not support any ethical judgment ... it does not tolerate being halted for a moral reason."[30] Happily we have entered a period where moral limits are being vocally raised. However, there abides a powerful presumption, in society and system, that anything scientific and technological is legitimate, practically by definition. Technology is a self-justifying system.

> Here we have the same reversal that I studied in detail with respect to the sacred: The desacralizing factor becomes in its turn the sacred. Likewise, the fact of having become autonomous gives technology a supreme *situation*. There is nothing above it that can judge it. Hence, it transforms itself into a supreme *authority*: Everything has to be judged in technology's terms.[31]

This analytical observation has profound theological implications. The situation itself brinks on the blasphemous.

Ellul has sometimes been criticized for indulging a "mythic exaggeration" with respect to technology. In fact, his prolific lifetime of writing has proceeded along two distinct, if actually parallel, tracks: sociological criticism and biblical reflection. (It is always striking to encounter people who know the one but not the other. The discovery leaves them mystified or nonplussed.)

He tends to be scrupulous, especially from the sociological side, about keeping the two distinct.[32]

> It is obvious — and this comment holds for all the rest of this discussion — that when I say technology "does not admit," "wants," etc., I am not personifying in any way. I am simply using an accepted rhetorical shortcut. In reality, it is the technicians on all levels who make these judgments and have this attitude; but they are so imbued, so impregnated with the technological ideology, so integrated into the system, that their vital judgments and attitudes are its direct expression. One can refer them to the system itself.[33]

Even here one might recall Wink's reading of the "spirit of the power of the air." Moreover, the self-generating autonomy of technology comports well with Ellul's own view of the principalities as expounded in his theological work. That view lies somewhere between seeing in them powers which have an existence and reality of their own, independent of human decision, and seeing in them human dispositions constituted as powers because they are exalted that way by human beings. He is indeed close to Wink and the view I have been generally setting forth:

> No one has ever yet been able to find the basis of political power or the reason why people always irresistibly and irremediably obey it. . . . Political power has many dimensions, e.g., social, economic, psychological, ethical, psychoanalytical, and legal. But when we have scrutinized them all, we have still not apprehended its reality. We cannot say with Marx that power is an ideological superstructure, for it is always there. The disproportion noted above leads me to the unavoidable conclusion that another power intervenes and indwells and uses political power, thus giving it a range and force that it does not have in itself. . . . One might ask whether technology is not also one of these powers. The answer seems simple enough.[34]

In drawing on Ellul's technology writing, I have dwelt upon those characteristics and mechanisms which show how one variety of powers operates beyond human control. In so doing I have been mindful that nuclearism and the arms race would furnish abundant examples at every point.

They begin, as one might imagine, with the very first bombs. From the formation of the Los Alamos research city, to the testing of the bomb, to the destruction of Hiroshima and Nagasaki, a scientific and technological process was at work driving the project forward, even apart from the emerging power struggles of the postwar world, and certainly apart from the military exigencies of the war. The bombing was completely unnecessary from a military standpoint. As early as 1945 the U.S. Strategic Bombing Survey reached the conclusion "that certainly prior to 31 December 1945 and in all probability prior to 1 November 1945, Japan would have surrendered even if the atomic bombs had not been dropped, even if Russia had not entered the war, and even if no invasion had been planned or contemplated."[35] Truman's circle of prominent military advisors was of much the same mind.[36]

There were powerful *political* reasons to destroy Hiroshima, namely, to end the war quickly before the Russians could enter the Asian theater, staking a claim to the division of geopolitical spoils, but more especially to put the Soviets on notice that the United States possessed the bomb and the will to use it against human populations.[37] However, it was the technological *fact* of the bomb which set the policy in motion. In that sense technology led and policy followed almost necessarily. It was because the weapon was in the secret pipeline that the politicians and diplomats began to foresee and plan for its usefulness. No matter whatsoever that the military need had disappeared.

Ellul quotes a remark which goes to the heart of things: "Since it was possible, it was necessary." (In this respect atomic weapons are emblematic of technological evolution in its entirety.) Or as Truman put it with a certain naive aplomb, "We found the bomb and we used it."[38]

One testimony to technological predomination may be recognized in the choice of targets. They were cities otherwise largely undamaged by previous aerial bombardment; effects would be more readily measurable. Why two cities? There were two bombs; one plutonium, the other uranium. For further scientific comparison, the landscapes varied. Hiroshima was inland, surrounded by mountains; Nagasaki was a coastal city. And finally, under the guise of the barest of treatment, the victims were medically studied for years to come by the United States Atom Bomb Casualty Commission.

The same logic of technical necessity has dominated the research and development think-tanks to the present moment. "If it can be made, it must be made." Put with an ideological slant: "If we can make it, they can make it, and since we know they are just wicked enough to do it, we better make it first." In the arms race the pace of self-generated necessity is accelerated by the logic of competition. While a given system is still in development, the counter-system is already being worked on.

> At bottom, it is the old argument between "the breastplate and the projectile." And in this indefinite competition, we see the process of self-augmentation, for every obstacle presented by the breastplate is an obvious and indispensible provocation to find a more powerful projectile, and vice versa. There is no human "participation" here; deliberation is wiped out by the crushing presence of technology. We would have to reach a peak of *collective spiritual* independence to challenge this process, and this gets all the more improbable and difficult as technology *creates* inevitable situations in which there is no other solution than to keep advancing.[39]

Technology does determine policy. This is by no means an exclusive or entirely one-way process, but the extent of it needs to be grasped. A few examples may suffice.

Cruise missiles—small, pilotless jet planes capable of delivering nuclear warheads with extreme accuracy—have a history which may be said to originate in Hitler's World War II buzz bombs, which were part rocket and part airplane. Early Pentagon attempts to develop the weapon further were essentially abandoned with the successful deployment of ICBMs. However, in the early 1970s several simultaneous technological breakthroughs—miniaturization of fanjet and turbo jet engines, nuclear warheads, and electronic mapping and computer guidance elements, along with the concentration of jet fuel, combined to make feasible an accurate and effective cruise. Henry Kissinger used the threat of its development as a "bargaining chip" in arms-control talks. Once developed, however, it was deployed in a variety of land, air, and sea-based systems. (All branches of the armed services had fallen in love with it. Each wanted it among their own arsenal of available weapons.) Moreover, its deployment in the early '80s coincided with the development of the doctrine called "protracted nuclear war," wherein a limited nuclear exchange in a particular theater of war— Europe, for example—is envisioned to result not in a full-blown nuclear war, but in a long, slow, "protracted" series of nuclear shots escalating horizontally, as they put it, into other theaters. A global test of wills is thereby envisioned, one which may last for a period of weeks or even months. This policy was formalized in the Single Integrated Operational Plan, specifically SIOP-6, the master targeting plan set in place under the Reagan administration.[40]

To reiterate more simply: An ensemble of technologies makes a weapon possible. It is developed as a bargaining chip, but once developed is withdrawn from the table and deployed. Its deployment results in a new rung on the ladder of escalation dominance;[41] a new element of policy is formalized. Furthermore, it's a policy not of deterrence but implying first-use and nuclear warfighting scenarios.

It is certainly true that the Pentagon pours research and development money into areas which constitute "missing links," for example, in an overall first-strike strategy. Hence the furious research proceeding in areas related to anti-submarine warfare, the remaining arena of Soviet invulnerability. But it is also certain that weapons and systems do emerge from the darkness of military think-tanks, which by their very nature alter strategy and policy.

Twenty years ago Robert Aldridge, then an engineer for Lockheed in California, discerned the necessary policy implications of his work on greater missile accuracy for the Trident missile, then under development. Greater accuracy seems like a simple improvement, natural enough in the progress of perpetual modernization. However, greater accuracy, specifically an accuracy sufficient to hit and destroy a missile silo, has profound implications. Aldridge foresaw them and resigned from the project.[42] He saw, in short, that the only reason to hit missile silos is if the missiles are still in them. Trident signified the capability of launching an unanswerable first-strike nuclear blow.

Perhaps more to the point, the capability signifies the policy. Since it is possible, it is necessary. If it can be done it must be done. If we can do it, someone else can do it, so we best do it first. The deployment of pinpoint accurate weaponry, like MX and Trident, represents the piecing together of a gigantic technological ensemble, a first-strike machine. That, of course, is an element of the historical crisis which has already been mentioned.

As this is written, there is a much touted reduction of Cold War tensions. The Eastern European bloc is breaking up and breaking free from Soviet domination. Politically, there is a great global flux. Historical surprises seem to be in the air. Yet in the midst of that, there is the technological autonomy of the system, proceeding apace.

One thinks of Ellul's two "laws," that technological progress is irreversible and that it proceeds geometrically. The former (thus far) is verified in the experience of the arms race. (Edward Teller is reported to have compared the "silly" attempts to reverse the arms race to a futile theological effort to "unbite the apple." Indeed.) And the latter geometric axiom could practically be plotted on a curve of warhead and weapon production.

Kaku and Axelrod, whose work was cited and commended in the previous chapter, are not the least bit naive about the intent of Pentagon military strategists. They recount frightening meetings and memos of the Joint Chiefs and the National Security Council. They demonstrate that the willingness to use nuclear weapons to achieve political objectives is a simple fact, and they reveal the history of threats and plans. By this they show the deception which the American people have suffered since the use of the first atomic bomb. However, they betray little comprehension of the extent to which technology has a hand in shaping policy. Perhaps this is a peculiar naivete endemic to scientists and technicians, which they are. A blindness which goes with the territory.

Conscientious scientists and technicians have on occasion voiced political opposition to the military use of their works. Leo Szilard, who first broached the possibility of the atomic bomb with Roosevelt and who oversaw the first controlled atomic chain reaction at the University of Chicago during the war, circulated a petition signed by sixty-seven other atomic scientists urging Truman to restrain the dropping of the bomb until other steps to induce a Japanese surrender had been undertaken.[43] This was truly a conscientious action—effectively suppressed by the Pentagon. Even so, it was not a refusal to work on the weapon, but rather an attempt to control its use. The naivete regarding technological determinism remains.

The more recent instance several years ago of the "Pledge of Non-Participation" with Strategic Defense Initiative research needs to be mentioned here. Eventually more than twelve thousand signatures were garnered in a significant refusal of lucrative contracts and effective refusal of cooperation. The situation was unique in certain respects. Rather than a technological possibility emerging from the laboratories and think-tanks, Star Wars had more to do with a shrewd political strategy of the Reagan adminstration. Under pressure from a then-burgeoning peace movement worldwide, and a new wave of nuclear anxiety within the culture, SDI purported to offer the vision of a world in which nuclear weapons would be rendered "impotent and obsolete" by virtue of a nearly blind faith in a technological fix. The combination was politically effective to an enormous degree. The real possibility of it, however, remains thoroughly dubious. While the objections of the Pledge foresaw that such a system could in fact trigger a nuclear war (it would, as a matter of further fact, be quite useful in a first-strike system), it also objected that the project was not "technically feasible." Reagan may have counselled briefly with the Joint Chiefs, but when he made his Grand Vision speech in March of 1983, his own science advisor was stunned and shocked. The Office of Technology Assessment, against heavy political pressure, repeatedly found the scheme to have only a remote chance of working, which is to say that the needs of domestic politics created a rare situation in which the president initiated public debate on a weapons system before it was a practical reality.[44]

A CASE OF POSSESSION

There is a very good film called *Day After Trinity*. It's about Robert Oppenheimer, the scientific city of Alamogordo, and the making of the first atomic bomb. The story is told in stills and footage and interviews with the participants.

On the one hand, it is the story of Oppenheimer and his driven, singleminded preoccupation with the breakthroughs and necessities of building the bomb. It is a biographical account which begins with his poetry and politics, passes through the scientific and technological enthusiasm of the Alamogordo days, and ends in his tragic brokenness—even his security clearance revoked—on the trashheap of the McCarthy attacks. It is, as the filmmakers have it, a tragedy of classic proportion.

In the light of our foregoing discussion, we might be more precise. It seems more a classic case of *possession* in a very concrete and demystified sense. This is not to suggest something spooky. There was no disembodied spirit lurking in the desert to hover and swoop down upon Oppenheimer. The bomb project, however, did have a spirit to it, an interiority which may be said to have enveloped and gripped and blinded the participants. It was surely a constellation of forces: the moral isolation generated by extreme secrecy, the bondage of necessity implicit in the logic and ideology of technology, the spirit of power rooted in the very conception of the bomb, even the spirit of violence which rises to meet the Nazi spirit—all of these and more were thoroughly embodied in the situation. Oppenheimer was one prominent victim.

At one point in the film a young scientist even reflects that Oppenheimer had made a "Faustian bargain" with the Pentagon's General Groves, who was able to offer him all the resources in half the world to do history-making physics on a grand scale in simple exchange for certain successful products. He delivers, it seems heart and soul. Oppenheimer, with both political fervor and scientific fascination, is captivated and captured. Under the pressures and influences of the project, his personality even changes. The metaphysical poet becomes the great administrator. Ego inflates. He is virtually consumed.

In parallel fashion the film is also concerned with the scientific city, the technological boomtown of Alamogordo, New Mexico. As though conjured by the Pentagon, it grows *ex nihilo*, out of nothing in the middle of nowhere. People tell lightheartedly of being carried off to be involved in the military's historic endeavor. No questions asked.

One citizen of Alamogordo remembers that an invitational sign was posted late in the project to gather a modest, informal, living-room conversation about "the impact of the gadget on civilization." It's not clear if Oppenheimer pulled down the notice himself, but he effectively squelched the discussion with force of argument as unnecessary, inappropriate, premature. For the time being, such questions were better left unasked.[45]

In this sense Alamogordo becomes a parable of sorts, a compact instance of collective possession, a technological realm where moral questions were effectively banished, a city of blindness, rife with victims.

Robert Jay Lifton has noticed a phenomenon pertinent here. He was struck by "the way men, at or near retirement, renounce precisely the nuclearistic structure so central to their entire professional lives."[46] He terms it "nuclear backsliding" but it may better be understood as akin to exorcism or escape. Oppenheimer, in fact, is one of the examples he catalogues. His turnabout from insistence that the atomic bomb be used to a position against the next generation of development, H-bombs, once he was out of active military employ, is typical.

The most famous example in recent memory is Admiral Hyman Rickover, who oversaw the development of the nuclear navy, including the basic decisions about the Trident submarine system. Upon forced retirement in 1982 he averred that nuclear weapons and nuclear power both ought to be outlawed! He said he was not proud of the part he had played in the making of these weapons, warning that they would likely be used in a future war because history demonstrates that nations employ whatever weapons are at hand.

The conversion of Robert Aldridge has already been mentioned. Former scientists and technicians have been the driving force behind the *Bulletin of Atomic Scientists*, an important source of critical information on the weapons establishment, or such groups as the Federation of American Scientists and the Union of Concerned Scientists.

There have been dramatic defections from the Central Intelligence Agency, where courageous individuals have broken ranks and then worked to expose deception and covert terrorism. Philip Agee, Victor Marchetti, and John Stockwell come to mind. More recent examples include David McMichael and Ralph McGehee.[47]

Presidents themselves may be similarly disabused. One thinks immediately of President Eisenhower, who administered a huge military build-up, expanded nuclearism under the first-strike doctrine of "massive retaliation," and made the nuclear weapons the centerpiece of American military policy. His celebrated and much quoted Farewell Address of 1961 warned against "the acquisition of unwarranted influence . . . by the military-industrial complex."[48]

Then there is Jimmy Carter, who may be the most striking example of all. He ran for the presidency with decidedly do-something-about-the-arms-race campaign rhetoric. Early in his administration he shocked the Joint Chiefs of Staff by solemnly proposing reduction of the nation's nuclear stockpile from thirty thousand down to a barebones two hundred warheads, sufficient for a deterrent force. Yet in office he initiated the cruise and MX missile programs, sponsored the neutron bomb, continued Trident development full steam ahead, and signed the infamous Presidential Directive 59, which made counterforce targeting and nuclear warfighting strategies official and even to a degree public. So what was his message upon leaving office? A dire warning against the dangers of nuclear war.

This is not to question Carter's dovish sincerity. As much as anything it illustrates the fundamental impotence, even incapacitation, of the president. To sit in that office is to live at the vortex of incredibly powerful forces, material and spiritual, including the ideologies and structures of nuclearism. It is not so much that a person takes possession of the presidency as that the presidency takes possession of a person. Carter was simply overwhelmed and victimized.

Stringfellow writes of this more broadly:

The American problem is not so simple that it can be attributed to a few—or even many—evil men in high places. . . . Besides, our men in high places are not exceptionally immoral; they are, on the contrary, quite ordinarily moral. In truth, the conspicuous moral fact about our generals, our industrialists, our scientists, our commercial and political leaders is that they are the most obvious and pathetic prisoners in American society. There is unleashed among the principalities in this society a ruthless, self-proliferating, all-consuming institutional process which assaults, dispirits, defeats, and destroys human life even among, and *primarily* among, those persons in positions of institutional leadership. They are left with titles but without effectual authority; with the trappings of power, but without command over the institutions they head; in nominal command, but bereft of dominion. These same principalities, as has been mentioned, threaten and defy and enslave human beings of other status in diverse ways, but the most poignant victim of the demonic in America today is the so-called leader.[49]

It is more than simple analogy to suggest that what happens to individuals happens as well to whole societies. Americans suffer this possession widespread. That has virtually been the topic, all but unnamed, of this entire chapter. We stand in need of what the gospels call exorcism, liturgies which engage the powers at the level of their mythic and psychic and spiritual claims on human beings and human cultures. We need liturgies that meet them toe-to-toe in a war, albeit nonviolent, of myths. We need liturgies that declare freedom, indeed enact it, that break the logic of necessity, the imperial spirit of triumphant fatalism with its claims upon us. We need confessional liturgies which, by the grace of God, undo the power of death. Come, Lord.

Chapter 5

Liturgical Direct Action

Politically informed exorcisms which I believe to be as exemplary as that involving the pharaoh do still occur, if occasionally. This, indeed, was the witness of the Catonsville Nine, when they burned draft records in May of 1968. As those attentive to their trial . . . can apprehend, the action at Catonsville was a sacramental protest against the Vietnamese war — a liturgy of exorcism, exactly. It exposed the death idolatry of a nation which napalms children.

William Stringfellow[1]

POLITICALLY INFORMED EXORCISM

It is timely to invoke again the recent examples of such public liturgy as Catonsville. They ought not have been too far out of sight and mind all along. These actions comprise something of a liturgical renewal movement that has flourished at the margins of the church. Indeed, they take place in the streets, where the element of polemic and nonviolent combat — virtually a "war of myths" — may be most explicit. In seasons and on feast days hymns are sung at the gates of military bases, corporate headquarters, the front steps of power. Standard lections and prayers (so tamed and domesticated, like psalms in the royal sponsorship) are being heard in new ways and their power set loose. Then *simultaneously* a self-conscious act of delegitimation accompanies; some deed of civil disobedience — a trespass or fence-cutting or blockade or such — occurs. There, in that moment, the grip of militarism is in fact and in reality broken, the deconstruction of its world begun. A certain spirit is rebuked and renounced, a mythic claim slipped, an entire world unmade.

Any catalogue of these recent public liturgies would acknowledge a seminal inspiration from the late fifties: the Catholic Worker's six-year resistance campaign against New York City's annual air raid drill, required by the Civil Defense Act. The drill, compulsory for New Yorkers, was itself precisely a nuclear liturgy of the variety described in Chapter 3. It socially constructed and maintained the reality of the bomb's world and signified the submission of citizens to its sovereignty. The young Catholic Workers declined to partake in this rite. At the sound of the siren, they gathered in the streets, each year with more and more support from other pacifist organizations, refusing to take shelter and suffering arrest. Dorothy Day drafted the religious leaflet which declared that one could not have faith in God and depend on the atom bomb at the same time. In 1961 two thousand people joined in public refusal, and the compulsory drills simply ceased. So went an early skirmish in the war of myths.[2]

One thinks in a new way of the Plowshares actions, so often maligned for their property destruction. Seen in this light, as liturgical direct actions, this ritualized unmaking of a weapons system, this naming and neutralizing of the technology, a literal deconstruction of nuclearism's world, might simply be called a forthright form of confession and praise. Or an exorcism.

The precursor to these, another in the stream of tradition deemed the Catholic left, is the action of the Catonsville Nine in 1968. It is pivotal and formative. As the war in Vietnam was being escalated yet again and official mythology justified further conscription of American young men, this circle of friends entered a draft board in Catonsville, Maryland, removed 1-A files to the street, and burned them with homemade napalm. This endeavor galvanized a movement and set in motion a series of similar actions. In an address to the Liturgical Conference, Dorothy Day named it "an act of prayer."[3]

William Stringfellow, however, was the first to pronounce it a politically informed exorcism. And his assessment of how the Catonsville witness came to be shaped is especially edifying:

The Berrigan brothers and others of the defendants had
been involved over a long time, particularly since the
extraordinary papacy of John XXIII, in the renewal of the
sacramental witness in the liturgical life of Christians. They
had become alert to the social and political implications
of the mass. . . . [It was] a liturgy transposed from altar or
kitchen table to a sidewalk outside a Selective Service
Board office, a fusion of the sacramental and the ethical
standing within the characteristic biblical witness.[4]

It is no coincidence that Daniel Berrigan was able to edit the
transcript of their trial into a poetic and liturgical form which
has been published and repeatedly performed, mostly in
churches, as a drama, *The Trial of the Catonsville Nine*.[5]

These public actions are liturgies insofar as they declare the
sovereignty of God. The reign of God is celebrated and enacted
in the lives of people and communities. And they are exorcisms
insofar as the powers, and the power of death behind them all,
are named and exposed and rebuked on behalf of human life.

Occasionally the element of exorcism is fully explicit. I have
participated in exorcisms at the headquarters and plants of
weapons manufacturers. These liturgies were modeled specifically on the Roman rite, which begins by invoking a litany of
the saints. (We included a host of our own naming, not traditionally mentioned.) The ritual prays fervently in the name of
the incarnate Lord, makes the sign of the cross (we marked it
on sidewalks and drives), and circles the place dispersing holy
water.

On another occasion I was part of a Witness for Peace delegation to Nicaragua, which accompanied a woman back to her
home in the hills, a site filled with terror because her husband
and several children had been dragged from the house and brutally murdered by the Contras. We granted her space for wailing
and tears, standing around awkwardly like so many gringos. But
we also came prepared with a small service of confession. Readings of scripture and the Lord's Prayer in both languages were
followed by a dispersion of blessed water. The young Argenti-
nean priest who served the parish and its wide circle of base
communities was wary at first, eschewing any pretense of magical

power or superstition. However, he consented to preside, blessing the water with a simple prayer on behalf of life, and grace-
fully scattering it with leaves upon us and the house to reclaim
the space from death. The woman, Juana Franchesca, and her
family and friends were most grateful for the act. By it they
seemed to claim a measure of freedom and peace.

These are only suggestive. I know of a pastor in Missouri who
was sentenced to several months in jail for transgressing the
sanctity of a missile silo with holy water and ritual in hand. Or
again: the Methodist Federation for Social Action undertook a
public exorcism of the church's Board of Pensions, renouncing
the power of death in South African apartheid and the invest-
ments sustaining it—in this case accompanied by remarkable
changes![6]

By and large, however, exorcism is the implicit meaning of
liturgical actions. They confront and rebuke in part by their very
geography, declaring as counterclaim the sovereignty of God and
interceding concretely for a renewal of humanity.

EXAMPLES ABOUNDING

All the foregoing actions, as well as those found in the Intro-
duction, are drawn from the faith-based, nonviolent, anti-
nuclear, and non-interventionist movement. (There's a hyphen-
ated mouthful.) We should be aware that other examples
abound, though only a few are named here.

With respect to the assault on the biosphere by industrialism
and technology, there exists a vital history of nonviolent direct
action. It's strong and creative. The Greenpeace network and
the various regional alliances typify this activist strand. However,
for various reasons, less of an explicitly liturgical dimension has
emerged in this arena. A prominent exception is the ritual which
convenes a "Council of All Beings." A contemplative exercise
originating in the "deep ecology" movement, the council encour-
ages, by listening and imagination, an inner identification with
another creature, perhaps a species endangered or even an
entity like a river or mountain. Convened as a "council," the
creatures "speak" for themselves and on behalf of all creation.[7]
Embodied and enacted is a world of ecological integrity which

subverts the human-centered, objectified world of domination. A further step in the ritual has occasionally involved a process of mask-making to represent the creatures and then walking them publicly in procession to a site of industrial assault, a toxic incinerator or the like, where they too may speak in delegitimating action.

Although biblical warrant might be found for such a rite,[8] these gatherings tend in the main to be non-Christian, even expressly neo-pagan.[9] Many who participate would view the Bible as at the root of the problem. Here the mythic conflict engages that particular variety of so-called biblical worldview, truly a perversion, which has been appropriated and endorsed by Western industrialism and materialism.

In my hometown of Detroit, as in a number of cities around the country, a form of paraliturgical action has arisen and spread in the last year: neighborhood anti-drug marches. They emerged in Detroit first when a wave of crack houses invaded a certain neighborhood on the northwest side. The story is worth telling in some detail. With such invasions comes a palpable spirit of fear and intimidation. The acrid smell can almost be tasted; a shadow of death settles in. Against the houses and their spirit, residents made repeated police calls without response. Finally one day the cops made a bust, a buyer coming out. Across the street an older black woman who had made the call raised her arms and rejoiced, "Thank you, Jesus! Thank you!" It was perhaps too public a display; some would say she was unduly and indiscreetly bold.

The following morning an ambulance arrived at her home summoned by an emergency call. A shooting had been reported. She was dumbfounded; they had been misinformed. She couldn't imagine who had called. The following morning the "dead wagon" arrived from the nearby funeral home. They had been called to pick up a body.

These, of course, are death threats, and sophisticated ones at that, but the older woman was having none of it. She went to her friends and pastor and subsequently convened a meeting in her church to plan a response. The following week they gathered as planned in a storefront, were led in prayer by their Baptist pastor, and began a slow procession through the community pausing before the known drug houses to sing "We Shall Overcome." This, too, is an exorcism, intuitive and politically informed. It is less combat with a mythic formation—though I suppose the drug culture does have its own street level symbolic structure—as it was a discernment of the spirit of death and despair, and a public rebuke. The procession refuses death's claim and grip. It is a public liturgy of freedom, for person and community. At this writing, these things are happening all over the country.

Fundamental to the *kairos* moment, as many have named it, is the overpowering mythology of the global economy. Consumption and exploitation are richly justified. New economic forms and commitments are emerging, but I am not aware of many creative liturgical confrontations with their underlying assumptions—the myths of mammonry. Here is a need, a call. We have already mentioned the confessional character of the civil rights movement. One also thinks of the Poor People's campaign and the frustrated attempt to build a "Resurrection City" in the heart of Washington.

One resource perhaps pointing a direction and offering a clue is Jacques Ellul's wonderful and under-read little book *Money and Power*.[10] The book is lucid in identifying money as one of the powers, indeed the one expressly named mammon by Jesus himself. He recognizes the power of the sacred which accrues to money in this, and nearly every, culture. Breaking the bondage to money means making it *profane*:

> Now this profanation is first of all the result of a spiritual battle, but this must be translated into behavior. There is one act par excellence which profanes money by going directly against the law of money, an act for which money is not made. This act is *giving*. Individuals as well as authorities know very well that giving attacks something sacred. They know full well that it is an act of profanation, of destruction of a value they worship.[11]

Where this happens liturgically, albeit unbeknownst and unrecognized, is in the Sunday morning offering. We are accustomed to imagining, often as a thin guise for utilitarianism, that money

brought to the altar is thereby "sanctified" to God's work. Let
the profane be made sacred. So go our prayers. To the contrary,
says Ellul, exactly the opposite transpires. "The offering, the
moment of giving, *should be* for us the moment when we desa-
cralize the world."[12] In order for further forms of liturgical economic action to emerge, the first task, it would seem, is to get
this commonly understood. However, we should note that the
offering plate has already been invaded and claimed by mammonry in and through the enormously seductive and effectively
confusing power of tax exemption in U.S. churches.

This raises the question, and properly, of Christian tax resistance. Here is a phenomenon, indeed a movement, more widespread than publicly acknowledged. *And* it is very interesting
that the perennially invoked key scripture text in this regard
puts tax paying and tax resistance in a liturgical context! When
under questioning Jesus calls for the Roman coin (Mk 12:13-
17), he holds up to view the image of Caesar. The coin was itself
a text of imperial liturgics. Stamped on the denarius was the
profile of Tiberius and the telling inscription, "Tiberius Caesar,
son of the divine Augustus."[13] Jesus practically rubs the coin in
their noses: "Whose image?" As with current Christian war tax
resistance, the question of idolatry, of sovereignty and allegiance
is clearly in the air.[14]

There is one further arena of politically alert liturgical
reflection and action which must be mentioned: the Christian
feminist movement. There, as perhaps nowhere else, comprehension has arisen that language and ritual utterance reflect
and shape social relations. Within the churches pronouns
rightly become a topic of heated debate. The translation of
the scriptures and the modification of prayer book rites have
been passionately pressed, and passionately resisted. A marginalized community, in some cases virtually underground with
respect to official church structures, has flourished with its
own creative liturgical life, one which takes on the myths of
patriarchy, clericalism, and even the historical legitimacy of
apostolic succession. Rosemary Ruether, one of the most
articulate theologians of the movement, writes:

> The feminist religious revolution thus promises to be more
> radical and far-reaching than liberation theologies. It goes

behind the symbolic universe that has been constructed by
patriarchal civilization, both in its religious and modern
secular forms. . . . One needs not only to engage in rational
theoretical discourse about this journey; one also needs
deep symbols and symbolic actions to guide and interpret
the actual experience of the journey from sexism to liberated humanity.[15]

She recounts the history of this counter-cultural movement,
which declines both sectarian departure and accommodation-
ism. She describes the means by which women "delegitimize the
theological myths that justify the *ecclesia* of patriarchy and begin
to form liturgies to midwife their liberation from it."[16] Half the
book is a collection of such liturgies, drawn from a variety of
women's base communities, and covering traditional sacraments,
rites of healing, plus life-cycle and seasonal rituals. While I have
no doubt that this critical culture would criticize my remarks
here, I have their "public works" and commonlife concretely in
mind, along with the others mentioned, as I pursue these reflections on the politics of liturgy.

A SUBVERSIVE CALENDAR OF THE HEART

Because the Detroit Peace Community of which I have been
part is typical of many who have experimented with this kind of
confessional and liturgical action, I will tell its history of awakening to the church year as a rubric for discernment and liturgical action, a subversive calendar of the heart. Like others, we
moved piecemeal into this discovery. We began with the passionate days, those in which the suffering and fate of victims
may be made visible. We began with public "stations of the
cross," walking through the streets of the city on Good Friday
and pausing to pray at sites of oppression, before the signs of
manifest suffering, or at places of compassionate ministration.
We exposed a local geography of Christ's suffering.

In like manner we remembered the blood of the children on
the Feast of the Holy Innocents, seeing Herod's slaughter of the
Bethlehem infants in the military violence of this moment. On
behalf of the children of Salvador or South Africa, the feast

subverted the numb reality of normalcy. And we have regularly scattered the ashes of Hiroshima on that anniversary, which weighs in our hearts like another passion, a day of remembrance that actually coincides with the Feast of the Transfiguration.[17]

Gradually the whole calendar commended itself to us, beginning with the penitential seasons of preparation—Advent and Lent—which lend themselves so readily to vigils or calls of repentance and conversion. Most remarkable of all, however, was the discovery of power in the high feasts themselves—Christmas, Easter, Pentecost—the seasons of intervention and liberation, freedom and victory.[18]

In several instances the cycle was linked with an ongoing campaign of presence and action at a particular site. For several years it ordered for us times of liturgical incursion with some form of civil disobedience into the world headquarters of Bendix Corporation, then overseeing manufacture of hydrogen bomb parts. We would walk in, taking them unawares, though it always surprised us that they were surprised. After all, it was Ash Wednesday, or the first Monday in Advent, and we were there to repent, calling one another to conversion. But they were typically stunned and unprepared. It just never dawned fully on them. They were like a certain Circuit Court judge we met in the course of trials over the years who was utterly mystified by our timing. He expressed publicly the conviction that behind our actions lurked a "world-wide conspiracy." The evidence spoke for itself. After all, these things happen in so many places on the same day!

Another campaign was different. Williams International, the cruise missile engine manufacturer, became more alert. They remain generally tighter in their security measures and aggressive in their surveillance. They quickly comprehended the rhythm and would beef up security according to the season.

In the course of things we have struggled with the fundamental questions this book has tried to take up: Does the liturgical form and context further the power or the truth of such actions? Does it engage the corporate principalities and their own mythic forms in a substantive way? Are the nuclear or imperial or economic myths in any way confronted or subverted? Does liturgical action, when coupled with lives and communities of service, reveal the reality of God's reign here and now? Does it acknowledge and declare the sovereignty of God? Does such action serve social transformation as well as preserve an identity in faithful endurance?

We pray yes. And wager these public acts upon it.

Political culture would certainly regard the festivals and liturgies of the Christian year as an irrelevant distraction at best. The church has perhaps aided and abetted the presumption. However, we are being convinced that those liturgies and symbols have deep and hidden power, not in any magical sense,[19] but because they draw on ancient memories to envision and embody an alternative reality. Even in our technocratic culture, the mythic symbols of these rites may touch otherwise inaccessible places of the individual and collective psyche.

THE TURNING WORLD: A BIBLICAL REPRISE

The rhythm of the church year is a deep one, ancient with history and meaning. Any thoughtful comprehension of the Christian cycle needs to recognize the Hebrew pattern beneath, a pattern whose origin is firstly pastoral and agrarian. This common memory has roots deep in the earth and its turning. The earliest versions of the Jewish feasts celebrated natural events of life: the new grain, first-born lambs, the wheat harvest, and the new wine. Respectively these came to be Passover (*Pesach*), the Feast of Weeks or Pentecost (*Shavuot*), and Tabernacles or the Feast of Booths (*Sukkot*).

Behind Passover, on which we shall concentrate because of its relationship to the single most central feast of Easter, there were two distinct festivals, one a shepherds' festival, the other a farmers', both springtime rites offered in connection with fertility and the blessings of new life.[20] (It is a fitting irony that Easter itself should be named after an Anglo-Saxon fertility goddess, who also enjoyed spring rites at the vernal equinox.) The lambing festival celebrated the fecundity of the flock by sacrificing a lamb and smearing its blood on the doorposts of the tents, most likely as a prayer of blessing and protection as the tribe broke camp for a migration under the spring full moon.[21]

The agricultural rite of unleavened bread, essentially a

Canaanite festival, marked the spring barley harvest by throwing out the old leaven, the fermented sourdough "starter" which raised their bread. The old and the new grain were not to be mixed. A new beginning was made in the year's first batch of bread, a simple flat hearthcake, before the new fermentation.

It is perhaps tempting to pass easily over this literally pre-historic level of festal origin. These roots are regularly denigrated or even suppressed, but they bear attention. Understanding that a seder meal or an Easter morning eucharist are connected in history's longest running continuous feast, one begun and anchored in the earth's irrepressible seasonal regeneration, adds a potent dimension of meaning and power. In the industrial or post-industrial societies which supplant and assault the natural world, social orders ruled more and more by technological rhythms, this recourse to the earthly cycle is itself an act of exposure and confrontation.[22]

Over the course of a millennium this ancient earthly cycle was historicized or politicized. It was made the vehicle for remembrance, celebration, and reenactment of the Hebrew historical saga, the story of Yahweh's transforming action in their life. On foreign or familiar soil, the lambing festival recalled the exodus movement out of political tyranny; the Pentecost wheat harvest eventually remembered the convening of the assembly and the giving of the Law in covenant at Mt. Sinai; and the new wine feast with its leafy harvest-time huts (Booths or Tabernacles) came to signify the wilderness sojourn.

Although this historical transformation touched all three of the major feasts, it began first with Passover and Unleavened Bread. All the literary source traditions which make up the Pentateuch connect one or the other or both of these feasts to the exodus event.[23] Indeed, in the current form the narratives portray the two feasts as first celebrated simultaneous to the turning of historical events; they are "prescribed" and performed in the very moment of liberation. Hence their origins are reformed and resituated as liturgical actions that enable and enjoin the freeing work of Yahweh. They serve to mark the community's identity and its readiness to walk out, to follow at the decisive moment.

Parenthetically, there is an intriguing strategic element of the exodus narrative wherein Moses is charged to approach the king of Egypt with an urgent proposal: "The Lord, the God of the Hebrews, has met with us; and now, we pray you, let us go three days' journey into the wilderness, that we may sacrifice to the Lord our God" (Ex 3:18). Here an additional dimension of liturgical action is stressed. Liturgy figures into the struggle with oppressive political authority. The story as it stands clearly enjoys the humor of seeing Moses negotiate terms with Pharaoh, who makes concessions as the plagues mount. You may sacrifice, but stay in the country (Ex 8:20-25); all right, the men may go but not the women and children (Ex 10:7-11); well, the women and children may go, but leave your belongings and all your flocks and herds (Ex 10:24). Moses hardlines him in offering the final terms: "You must also let us have sacrifices and burnt offerings, that we may sacrifice to the Lord our God. Our cattle also must go with us; not a hoof shall be left behind, for we must serve the Lord our God, and we do not know with what we must serve until we arrive there" (Ex 10:25-29). This is not a mere ruse. Ritually acknowledging Yahweh's sovereign claim upon them and exercising their freedom go hand in hand.[24]

For a remarkably long period of Israel's history the feasts of Passover and Unleavened Bread apparently coexisted, separately remembering the liberation, the former as a family feast and the latter as a pilgrim festival of the central sanctuary, subsequently Jerusalem. (Two ancient liturgical calendars from the pre-monarchial period of tribal confederation list the three pilgrim feasts including Unleavened Bread, but either omit Passover or mention it only separately and incidentally: Ex 23:14-17; 34:18-25.) So when were these two first united? It is possible that they came together when Passover was made a pilgrimage festival under the centralizing reforms of King Josiah (622 B.C.E.).[25] But most likely this fusion happened in exile under Babylon.

A key text in this regard is from the Priestly version of the exodus account (Ex 12:1-20) as produced in the exilic period. Here they are first linked by *reason* of haste: eat the Passover lamb with your sandals on and staff in hand ready for departure, and eat bread unleavened because you won't have time for it to rise. Truly a "movement" ritual. And also, in the Babylonian context, one of resistance. The text begins by specifying that to remember the liberation the feast will be celebrated in this month which "shall be the first month of the year for you" (12:2). This is one of the indications of Priestly/exilic authorship. Prior to exile, the new year began in the autumn, as recounted in ancient liturgical calendars already mentioned. A spring new year reflects the Babylonian imperial calendar! There is, of course, political import here. The liturgical cycle of Babylon began with the ritual victory of Marduk over chaos and the enthronement of the king in a lavish New Year's festival. At precisely the same time, in private family units (Ex 12:1-6) without so much as a role for priests, dressed for departure, the exiles held a counterfeast: Passover/Unleavened Bread.[26]

Throughout its history, which has been grossly oversimplified here, there was an abiding tension in Passover between its family-centered, "liturgically democratic," priesthood of all Israel character, and its centralization in the service of nation and state. We have already touched on Passover's elaborate domestication in the golden age of the Temple into which Jesus walked and acted. We have seen how he reclaimed and celebrated, filled and transformed it by his life and death.

In the early church that transformation yielded two liturgical forms which shaped life and social reality in the Christian community. One was the weekly common meal partaken on the Lord's Day, and the other was the annual festival of the resurrection, the Christian *Pascha*, the new feast of freedom. As to the former, suffice it to say here that the common meal signified the oneness of the community under the sovereign Lordship of Christ — an allegiance subversive with respect to imperial rule — and made visible in the sharing of their commonlife, with an implicit economic dimension (Acts 2:44-45; 4:32-35; 1 Cor 11:20-34).[27] It quite simply proclaimed and revealed the reality of a new creation, a new social world.

As to the latter, the feast of the resurrection was the central, and at first sole, festival of the church year. It was a "unitive feast," extending for fifty days from Easter to Pentecost. Here the Passover theme of liberation from political oppression was deepened to celebrate liberation from death in all its guises and forms. This does not mean, as is often said, that in Easter the Passover was somehow spiritualized. It had simply become for

Christians what Jürgen Moltmann has called the "festal protest against Death," anticipating the day when along with death, "*every* rule and authority and power" are neutralized or abolished (1 Cor 15:24).[28]

The confessional character of Easter is underscored by its function in the reception of new members into the community by baptism. The personal confession of the sovereign Lordship of Christ in their lives was made one with the proclamation of the whole community. In the pre-Constantinian period, when the church was outlawed and with some regularity systematically persecuted, the reception of members was a rigorous and often risky proposition. Those wishing to become "hearers" (*catechumens*), were brought to the community by sponsors who could vouch for them. Thereupon they entered into a three-year period of prayerful instruction and preparation, which concluded with an intensive time of examination and exorcism and fasting.[29] In an act of solidarity, others would join this fast anticipating the Easter Vigil. Indeed, from these fasts, accounted variously in different places, the Lenten fast of forty days, echoing Jesus' struggle with the powers of death in the wilderness, subsequently developed. Hence, the greatest influence upon the Christian liturgical year in this period was the confessional rigors of baptismal preparation.[30]

It was in this same period, beginning in the mid-second century, that the Christian year began to be punctuated by the annual celebrations of the martyrs on the anniversary of their deaths, often at the place of their burial. The purpose of these commemorations, as recounted in the *Martyrdom of Polycarp*, was "both in memory of those who have already contested, and for the practice and training of those whose fate it shall be."[31]

It was, however, following the so-called conversion of the Roman Emperor Constantine and after the legalization and expansive domestication of the church, that the Christian year developed more fully. The emperor, for example, enabled the construction of churches in Jerusalem at sites traditionally revered for the notorious deeds of Jesus in the city. Pilgrimages to these, and from one to another, in the week prior to Easter eventually gave place to the days of Holy Week. There is a conspicuous irony here. It is akin, at this same juncture, to the ironic emergence of Christmas coinciding (be it by sublimation, Christianization, or convenient political syncretism) with the established annual feast of the Roman sun god, Sol Invictus.[32]

Here the world-making power of liturgy was once again bridled in the service of empire, now coterminous with the church. The liturgical calendar flourished freely and functioned increasingly as the civil calendar, the framework of business and social life.[33] However, the elaboration of the liturgical year in the imperial church never fully domesticated it because the roots went so deep, because the gospel story it enacted was so irrepressibly subversive, and because it retained the world-breaking and world-making tension of eschatological expectation. This latter, of course, is nearly a synonym for liturgy's world-making social energy.

If anything, the historical roots in Judaism came clearer and clearer in this period. The feast of Tabernacles and the Hebrew autumn New Year festival that anticipated the reign of God[34] informed Advent as it evolved from Christmas.[35] And the Feast of Weeks (Pentecost), marking the first gathering of the assembly (*ecclesia*-LXX) of Israel at Sinai, could be understood as now celebrating the "founding" of the Christian church (*ecclesia*) by the power of the Holy Spirit.

And all of it looked forward in the end to historical transformation. Rosemary Ruether comments on this dimension of the year:

> The core of the Christian calendar is eschatological or messianic. It builds upon the future dimension of Hebrew hope. But it also sees itself as already empowered by the advent of the final deliverance of the world from sin and death, even while still looking forward to its future completion. This element of a foretaste of things to come is the key dynamic of Christian ritual. One cannot understand the yearly reenactment of advent expectation, leading to the messianic birth, the Lenten preparation for the final passion and resurrection of Christ, and the feasts of Christ's ascension into heaven and the outpouring of the Holy Spirit "in the last days," unless one understands that these are not simply remembrances of events completed

in the past. Rather, they look back to experiences which themselves point forward to that final time when the bondage of evil and mortality is lifted from humanity and from all creation and the fullness of God's reign of peace is established.[36]

She argues for the Christian feminist community in particular not to abandon the liturgical year as patriarchal or exclusive, but to claim it consciously (as a rubric for social transformation) on all the levels of tradition we have discussed: the natural earth cycle of the seasons, the Hebrew story of historical liberation, and the messianic drama of Christian hope.

At such a depth of tradition and community, the year may become once more a kind of counter rhythm for the Christian life, a subversive calendar of the heart. We are now again far removed from the time when the church year was the civil calendar, when courts recessed, battles abated, shops closed, and labor ceased in accord with the holy days. There are "liturgical calendars" which vie for attention and set the rhythm of life in society. We are subjected to an array of state and commercial holidays, to shopping seasons of consumption, to a cycle of professional sports which captivate large portions of the population in the manner of "bread and circuses," and the more general seasons and cycles prescribed by the commercial media, especially television. We are regularly assaulted by the political noise of the pretentiously messianic electoral cycle. Beside all these, the church year, in both its contemplative aspect and its public enactment, may become a counter-cultural rhythm, the different drummer, the recaller and invoker of a world not yet seen, a subversive agenda for our collective hearts. By it we may see our own history through gospel eyes. And by it we may intercede and intervene, praying to act with the Word of God.

LITURGY AND ACTION: *KAIROS* AND THE CONFESSIONAL MOMENT

Now. There is something in the character of Christian liturgy which is powerfully present tense, be it the anticipation of final release from bondage or the lively remembrance of God's past liberating actions, say in Jesus Christ. All come to bear on this present moment, perhaps this decisive moment. Thomas Merton once put it in a way now rendered quaint by liturgical reform: "Whenever the Gospel is sung in the Liturgy it begins with the formula 'at that time' (*in illo tempore*) and the formula, in effect destroys the passage of time, annuls all the time that has passed since 'then,' for in the liturgy the 'then' of Christ's actions is 'now' in the redemptive mystery of the Church's prayer."[37]

Inasmuch as Jesus named and defined a *kairos* moment and called for a decision of allegiance to the reign of God, that choice is presented in liturgy as current. All his deeds and teachings, which provoke that choice, come to bear on this moment now. Indeed, this is virtually another and perhaps more conventional way of defining *kairos* as time which has as its content the work of Jesus Christ and the decision of human beings to accept or reject this liberating event.[38] Perhaps we begin to imagine how a *kairos* moment in history, a moment full of God's judgment and mercy, ripe for personal and collective choice, may be pointed to and embodied liturgically. The seasons of the liturgical year, which in part dramatize the work of Jesus, may likewise serve in pointing to this decisive moment.

Here and now we arrive at the heart of this book, the page to which all others repair by preparation or reference. Here arguments and trajectories meet, impressions coalesce or not, examples come to bear, inferences are ready to be tested. Do these disparate pieces fit? Is there a center in all of this?

Let us take an example from the range of current liturgical direct actions, and examine it for function and effective meaning: an Easter morning eucharist and trespass at the manufacturer of cruise missile engines, an action close to my home and heart. This is a simple, modest, and prayerful action. Yet, if all the foregoing rings true, it portends much. By its simple public character a measure of light is directed upon an otherwise hidden and inconspicuous evil. By it an aspect of the historical crisis is expressly identified, in this case the deployment of an array of first-strike nuclear weapons. Within that crisis is recognized God's grace. A *kairos* moment of decision for the community of faith is named and commended and acted upon. The Word of God in common history is discerned and joined.

By it a community is gathered in solidarity of spirit with all of humanity, indeed standing for and interceding on behalf of all human life. That community offers a confessional act which honors the sovereignty of God, the Lordship of Christ in lives and history, expressly rebuking the nuclear heresy. By word and deed it engages in a war of myths with imperial religion, subverting and unmaking nuclearism's world.

It takes seriously the church year and says to it, "Be alive with Christ!" Be lived and walked. By means of the year a community through time is remembered and invoked: from the slave camps of Egypt to the shepherds of Canaan, exiles and outcasts and underground communicants. In a sense not utterly mystical these too are gathered at the gates.

The layers of tradition are all, more or less, in the air. They nourish the community but also carry and convey public meaning. The cycle of creation itself, so relentlessly attacked and targeted by the weapons, is marshalled in the irrepressible energy of spring renewal. The Passover of historic liberation from oppressive political authority is enjoined. And the resurrection, which breaks the power of death and thereby undoes *every* power and rule and authority, is claimed.

The authority of the resurrection is experienced first of all in the freedom the participants evince. They have "died to" the logic of imperialism and nuclearism, and they demonstrate that here. They declare a measure of freedom from fear of the sanctions which the powers wield. Indeed, they come prepared to suffer those sanctions, relatively modest in this instance, if so required.

However, the action also rebukes the principality which is the corporation, even the entire configuration of powers which is nuclearism. Yes, the employees are addressed personally and straightforwardly, but they are also understood and addressed as victims of the principalities. If truly done so, they are pastorally addressed.

Before the table of the Lord the corporation is reminded of its mortality. It is subject not only to international law, which a trial may give opportunity to recall, but to the judgment of God, even if that judgment is not finally or fully known. In effect, the frailty of all political authority is underscored.

By anticipating the transformation of all things in the end, the liturgy unveils the reality of a new world. A new society being constructed in the shell of the old. Gathered at table, in the streets, the community sits down to a new social order.

In this action liturgy is filled with lives and vice versa. It thereby implies a fuller life. The participants insinuate an integrity; this direct action is offered in continuity with their prayer discipline and service and ethics. The campaign is more than a campaign. It is an expression of a deeper and wider commonlife rooted in the gospel.

All this and more is expressed by simple sharing of bread and wine as the sun comes up on a certain day in a certain forbidden place. The truth may swirl furiously about so bare a still point.

WITH EYES OPEN: WARNINGS AND HESITATIONS

Needless to say, the church is implicated and addressed in this sort of action from beginning to end. In such liturgies, even the most ecumenical and informal, the church is gathered and to a degree bound. It is to be expected that these actions will provoke discussion, complaint, official suppression in some cases, and even counter-liturgies within the church.

In the 1930s, when the Confessing Church was taking so much heat from its detractors for pronouncing Nazism an outright idolatry and blasphemy, Karl Barth replied on behalf of the movement:

No one has the right to complain when he must listen to such a witness and confession, even though it is not at first his own! And he has no right to complain when he must hear and take notice that the other is not bringing forward what he has to say as only a personal—where possible "only" political—expression of opinion; but that he is bringing it forward in the proper form, i.e. in unity with the confession of Jesus Christ, as he sees this, and hence in all seriousness as true and binding. . . . But what have these others to do? They have to *set over against* this witness, in the same bindingness, a firmly grounded opposing witness. They have to *rely* on the strength of their own good cause and that of their opposing witness. And then they have to leave it to the witness of the Holy Spirit in the congregation, i.e. to the further common enlightenment through the Holy Scriptures.[39]

This is strong encouragement for confessional and in our related sense liturgical politics. However, it ought also give us pause. It demands a faith which loves and trusts the church. In liturgical direct action we address the church and also name it as a site of struggle. The caution is that this could be entered into with a calculated cynicism as if the "religious sector" were merely another arena for ideological combat, or as though religious symbols were nothing more than instruments for social manipulation. The integrity of their use is basic.

I would be saddened if this book, by beginning with a functional analysis of worship, were to be taken as sanction for an essentially instrumental view of liturgy, reducing faith to functionalism. Liturgy has transforming social power because human beings give their lives and live their lives within the community and Reality to which it testifies. We are following a God who acts and trusting in God's grace.

The prophets regularly railed against the liturgy of Israel's cult whenever it was reduced to magical manipulation. In yearning for a "circumcision of the heart" (Jer 4:4 or Dt 10:16) they insisted on the commitment of the person, an integrity of liturgy and life. In this sense they denounced reductionism and pressed a demagicalization of the cult.[40] We do well to attend their voices in taking up liturgy as direct action.

To this, Rafael Avila adds two further prophetic critiques of Israel's worship by which any liturgical reflections (even ones intended as our own) might be continually chastened. One is that ritual was so often disconnected from context and celebrated abstractly without reflecting or questioning history. This we have explicitly renounced. And the second is like unto it: that ritual worship can passively coexist with injustice.[41]

> Is such the fast that I choose,
>   a day to humble oneself?
> Is it to bow down the head like a bulrush,

> and to lie in sackcloth and ashes?
> Will you call this a fast,
>   a day acceptable to the LORD?
> Is this not the fast that I choose:
>   to loose the bonds of injustice,
>   to undo the thongs of the yoke,
> to let the oppressed go free, and to break
>   every yoke? (Is 58:5-6; NRSV)

Could a liturgical renewal which is grounded in history and justice and community integrity still fall prey to the confusion Isaiah discerns? Let the liturgists take care.

Prophetic voices who rightly utter the same today include the theologians of liberation. In general, liturgy is regarded warily by them. They labor in situations where ritual is most commonly in the service of status quo social arrangements, bitterly unjust. Among their number, "materialist readers" of the Bible detect the culmination of scripture in the hands of a priestly elite domesticating and inverting the popular subversive or revolutionary energy in which its narratives began. Amos is their patron prophet on this score:

> I hate, I despise your feasts,
>   and I take no delight in your solemn
>   assemblies. . . .
> Take away from me the noise of your songs;
>   to the melody of your harps I will not listen.
> But let justice roll down like waters,
>   and righteousness like an everflowing stream.
>   (Am 5:21, 23-24)

Biblically, let us recall, the first act of violence was conceived during the first liturgy. Cain's design against Abel came as he lifted his hands to the Lord at their common altar. The Bible is clear that liturgy can hide sin; it can mask unjust human social relations. In the early church catechism of the Sermon on the Mount Jesus discusses the interconnection of the forms of violence and then advises: "So if you are offering your gift at the altar, and there remember that your brother or sister has something against you, leave your gift there before the altar and go; first be reconciled to them, and then come and offer your gift" (Mt 5:23-4). Do not make liturgy a lie, using it to cover broken-ness and injustice. Let it, instead, bring such violations into the light of day. This very admonition is given tangible and symbolic form in the eucharistic liturgy by the passing of the peace prior to communion.

Let us not omit St. Paul from this litany of the dubious. It must be admitted that his skepticism included the feasts, the very liturgical cycle we have lifted up. "You observe days, and months, and seasons, and years! I am afraid I have labored over you in vain" (Gal 4:10-11). Specifically, and no doubt out of his own zealous experience as a Pharisee, he was concerned that the festival rubrics, like the whole of the law, could become an idol and thereby in the service of the powers, the "elemental spirits whose slaves you want to be once more" (Gal 4:9). In this instance the liturgy could divide the community whose unity was in their common freedom. With respect to legalistic ritual-ism, Paul was capable of counselling tolerance (Rom 14:5), but more often he preached passionately against it.

Any reclaiming of liturgy in action must attend to these voices. There are manifest dangers and temptations in the exer-cise of liturgical direct action.

The year or its forms could be treated as a slavish rubric. Instead of stimulating prayer and discernment, instead of free-ing imaginations, it might in certain instances limit responses. Events and moments which demand public outcry might be neglected because they don't conform to the cycle. Or liturgical actions could be repeated year after year irrespective of events in our own history. We might lock ourselves in or out with legal-isms that forgo or preempt creative new symbols which present themselves.

A movement acting liturgically could generate its own "priestly elite" with jailhouse credentials who alone know the "proper" forms of action.

Liturgical action could divide a community or cut it off from allies in a common struggle. When Christians act publicly, it is in solidarity with and on behalf of all humanity. A certain litur-gical piety, even a politically conscious piety, could obscure and deny that. There is a true dilemma here. Over the years I have suffered both sides of it. On one extreme is a lowest-common-spiritual-denominator approach to symbolic action. Symbols and liturgies may be reduced to applesauce. On the other is a Christian sectarianism, hopelessly alienated from our true friends. What is required of us here specifically is a certain freedom, which I suspect is a gift and a grace. On the one hand it is the freedom to act openly as Christians, not hesitating to employ and declare our symbols, enjoining them in the public arena. At such events we welcome our friends for whom these symbols and liturgies may seem foreign and strange. Such friends and allies will, more readily than we generally imagine, recognize the integrity of our lives and symbols. In any event the welcoming, invitational posture may be thought evangelical in the truest sense. Conversely, and on the other hand, we need the freedom to stand as well, even in risk, with friends and allies in the use of other symbols, both religious and political.

Another temptation, and our experience verifies this, is to cloak a political position in liturgical garb and thereby secure a smug self-righteousness. Liturgical direct actors will be accused of this in any event, but that shouldn't prevent an honest, confessional, self-examination to make certain it isn't true.

It is possible to engage in liturgical action as some sort of political expedient without a commitment of the heart to its language and symbol, a commitment which necessarily has integrity in the full life of a Christian. Several years ago there was a conscious shift within the Pledge of Resistance, a national campaign in which thousands of people committed themselves to civil resistance in the event of a United States invasion of Nicaragua. The move, rightly and thoughtfully done, was intended to revive the original religious character of the Pledge. In many communities the religious community had been edged out or supplanted by secular organizations of the Central America solidarity movement. In some quarters the revival was resisted and fought, but in a few it was embraced ingenuously; demonstrations wielded Christian symbols simply to put a religious face on the protests. I do not suggest this is common, but the temptation is real.

Liturgical and symbolic actions may mask in some people an

incipient lack of hope. Despairing of the possibility of real and substantial change, they throw themselves into "absurd" acts of desperation parading as liturgy. This element of the movement's dark side is simply a reality which cannot be denied. It is a pastoral question to which our communities must be alert.

Hidden despair may be accompanied by a zealous indifference to the action's comprehension by the wider public audience. There is a certain sense in which a liturgical action stands complete in and of itself. The visible sign speaks for itself. Still, there remains a necessity to interpret these things to the fuller church and the wider culture. An irony and an obligation: confessional apologetics.

It must finally be admitted that liturgy can be a convenient cover for actual shallowness, for failing to do the real homework, the hard research, or clear political thinking. Its form may excuse all manner of fuzziness about the processes of social change and transformation.

Where any of these seductions or distortions prevail in the movements of faith and resistance, they signify a true bondage to the elemental spirits. Eyes must be open and hearts alert.

IN SPIRIT AND TRUTH: LITURGY AND NONVIOLENCE

What has gone largely unsaid for pages may now be made explicit: liturgical direct action is a unique variety of nonviolence. There are no guarantees, as the foregoing temptations attest, but public action offered in the context of worship can express and discipline and nourish a nonviolent spirit.

An image and icon of sorts comes to mind. It is from *The Mission*, a film which appeared several years ago. In general, the movie itself operates mainly on the level of images; the story is carried forward on a series of moral decisions. There is the decision of the sixteenth-century Jesuits to persevere in their missionary work among the indigenous people of Paraguay after the first attempt ended in martyrdom. There is the decision of the papal emissary, arriving poshly arrayed and equipped, to consider the fate of the missions, now established, in the light of shifting new world geopolitical arrangements between Spain and Portugal. The lives and deaths of the Indians hang in the

balance. Will the missions, which have become both model economic cooperatives (competing successfully with their imperial
counterparts) and sanctuary cities of refuge against the Portu-
guese slave trade be supported and sanctioned by the church?
Or will the Jesuits be ordered home and the Indians abandoned,
left to a bloody fate?

Beyond that, will the Jesuits comply, bending to a hierarchy
for whom authority and control — the issues sound vaguely familiar — outweigh the primacy of gospel demands and options for
the poor? They do resist and rightly so, but this only raises the
further moral question: by what means? Paths diverge as one
priest, a former slave trader and fratricide whose conversion is
poignantly told takes up the sword he once laid down in becoming a Jesuit. Is he, as his mentor and counterpart contends,
betraying not only the order but the gospel?

And finally, the compelling image. The mentor also chooses
resistance and takes his place with the Indian community gathered in the mission chapel. As the military troops approach,
having brutally defeated the armed resistance, the community
emerges from the church in liturgical procession. In front, most
vulnerable, is the priest bearing the ornate sanctuary of the con-
secrated eucharist. Together they carry it toward the soldiers,
offering it as the very truth of the moment, and yet another
choice. The soldiers pause and nearly balk under orders. But
orders prevail and they fire massively and indiscriminately upon
the crowd.

The image betokens much. For one thing, to my way of seeing,
all of those choices from the pope to the soldiers, all of the
choices which participated in that decisive *kairos* moment for
the church and Latin America, are summed up and named and
clearly put in that moment of eucharistic direct action. For
another, the Jesuit and the community cling to the host as to a
nonviolent discipline. It shapes and defines the spirit of their
resistance.[42]

I think again in this same regard of Jesus' entrance into Jerusalem. Through the gospel accounts one may imagine it to be a
day of turbulent temptation for Jesus. He, too, is setting before
the city a *kairos* of visitation (Lk 19:45). Such events may have
their own momentum: a cheering crowd building as it goes, a

confrontational target at the Temple with strong and dramatic action planned. Certain of his friends and disciples want to see it spark an uprising, a violent insurrection. I wager Jesus struggles to keep his spiritual and political balance. And the colt helps. Entering the city on the back of a donkey has loaded messianic meaning. It signifies in the symbolics of the tradition (Zec 9:9). But it may be as much for his own sake as for the crowd or the authorities. He rides the donkey as a self-conscious act of humility. It defines a preeminently nonviolent posture. It disciplines the strong action to come. Liturgy, its forms and symbols, may do the same for us.

There is another, relentlessly perennial question, which is raised by these sorts of direct action. It is put by the bloody denouement of the eucharistic image: faithfulness versus effectiveness. Ought our first concern be deeds which generate immediate and visible results? Or should it rather be unerring fidelity to conscience and the gospel? In liturgical actions there is a certain resolution of this dilemma. On the face of it they press the latter point. However, I have tried to argue that symbolic struggle is real struggle, that liturgy can effectively subvert or resist or even transform a political situation, that the world-making power of liturgy is a real force of social construction. On the other hand, liturgical actions exhibit what Gandhi called "non-attachment to results." Since their intention is not firstly instrumental, but always toward God as gift and offering, they permit a tremendous freedom. One would never ask of a eucharist: Was it successful or effective? It simply is. So with the truth of the eucharistic image from *The Mission*. So with all liturgical witness.

Thomas Merton pulls a number of these ideas together in a reflection on Gandhi and the *satyagraha* truth forces:

> In such a view politics had to be understood in the context of service and worship in the ancient sense of *leitourgia* (liturgy, public work). Man's intervention in the active life of society was at the same time by its very nature *svad-harma*, his own personal service (of God and Man) and worship, *yajna*. Political action was therefore not a means to acquire security and strength for one's self and one's

party, but a means of witnessing to the truth and the reality of the cosmic structure by making one's own proper contribution to the order willed by God. One could thus preserve one's integrity and peace, being detached from results (which are in the hands of God) and being free from the inner violence that comes from division and untruth.[43]

Merton concludes that it was this very inner freedom and non-attachment which lent Gandhian politics their extraordinary spiritual force and religious realism. Such politics, in fact, proved enormously effective. The same may be hoped for liturgical action of the sort I have described. Only if it is firstly a faithful activity of prayer and worship may it end by being effective to an extent which appears very nearly shrewd.

The distinction made here is akin to the distinction between nonviolence as a tactic and nonviolence as a way of life deeply rooted in heart and spirit. In the end we are not talking about liturgy as a political tactic, but as life. Our personal life. Our commonlife before the world. This is not the politicization of sacrament, but the sacramentalization of all life.

This point is made dramatically in the Gospel of John. A full chapter of argument and commentary is devoted to "true bread" or "bread from heaven," and to those who "eat my flesh and drink my blood" (Jn 6). The narrative is shot through with eucharistic symbolism and meaning, thinly veiled. Finally we arrive at the Last Supper, toward which it all points, only to find here none of this talk, no words of institution, no eucharist. Instead, in an abrupt literary switch, we find the footwashing labor of service. So simple and humble an act is sacramental. It is his life which is sacrament. Liturgy and life are made one in Christ. Their truth is one and the same.

PART II

THE SEASONS
AT HEART

CHAPTER 6

ADVENT: THE WILDERNESS IN A VERY SMALL ROOM

A voice cries:
"In the wilderness prepare the way of the LORD,
make straight in the desert a highway for our
God.
Every valley shall be lifted up,
and every mountain and hill be made low;
the uneven ground shall become level,
and the rough places a plain.
And the glory of the LORD shall be revealed,
and all flesh shall see it together,
for the mouth of the LORD has spoken."
Isaiah 40:3-5

Now when John heard in prison about the deeds of the Christ,
he sent word by his disciples and said to him, "Are you the
One who is to come, or shall we look for another?" And Jesus
answered them, "Go tell John what you hear and see: the
blind receive their sight and the lame walk, lepers are cleansed
and the deaf hear, and the dead are raised up, and the poor
have good news preached to them. And blessed is the one who
takes no offense at me."

Matthew 11:2-6

In the tradition and history of the church John the Baptist is
associated with Advent. At the turn of the church year, the end

and the beginning he stands, one foot in each, to announce the coming of the Lord. John is the image of Advent par excellence: preeminent personage, spokesperson, figure, and voice. He is the very personification of the season, as seen in these two passages.

The words from Second Isaiah are good news of repentance and return, first commended to a people captive and captivated by Babylon. John, in turn, is captured by the word. There he finds his identity and vocation. Surely he studied this text long and hard, praying from it, and being thereby comforted and provoked. Here is a passage he lives with and so lives in. John finds himself in the word. He fills it with flesh, gives it body and voice, and so becomes the very incarnation of the text.

Who knows? John may have cut his teeth on Isaiah 40, tutored in a desert community with a rigorous manual of discipline like the eschatological purists of Qumran. Luke 1:80 hints that John was raised in the wilderness.

In any event, these words suggest to him a geography of faith. And John, it seems, takes his scripture quite literally; he makes for the desert and sets up spiritual shop.

In the tradition and history of Israel, the wilderness is the time of preparation, the place of testing and repentance. It is the time to travel light, stripped of excess baggage, vulnerable in emptiness. It is the place of powerlessness where we are fully and perpetually at the mercy of God.

Public poverty is part of this package. Not as pretense or gimmick, but as a discipline that flows in and out of the wilderness geography. John's notoriety of diet and dress are part of the proclamation. His lifestyle is a sign. How bitterly ironic it is that the season over which he presides should be so attacked, distorted, and subverted by the principalities of commerce. With a violent twist, they render it the high feast of material consumerism. Their hype and excess would never wash with him. His sign will never suit their festivities, except as a scandal and judgment—and as an ax to their bloody roots.

John's choice of lifestyle is not a private and pious act, but a public and evangelical one. His priestly blood runs prophetic. He's not dropping out for the sake of "number one," or convening a community of isolation that can feel good about itself.

No abstract purity of conscience here. When John sets up his pulpit and initiates his paraliturgical practice, he is inviting others to the scene of radical transformation.

We should be clear about the religious and political geography as well. John isn't running for high priest of the prestigious downtown temple, though Lord knows he could have reached more people. His priestly birthright might have proved sufficient credentials, but his connections were never well-placed.[1] Moreover, he is convinced that things happen "at the edge." When he makes his own exodus, he calls people out of the temple, out of the marketplace, and out of the fallen, unholy city, out to the margin of culture and life. And by all accounts they follow in droves, signing up for the kingdom movement.

"A whole new order is about to take shape, and if you want to be part of it, you'll have to make some radical changes in your lives." That's my own translation of, "Repent, for the kingdom of God is at hand." John spoke it plainly, and his life showed that he was serious. People believed him and believed. They took the dive, immersing themselves in the kingdom movement.

The baptism of John is like nothing so much as induction into a nonviolent army. Recall that eventually the church spoke of baptism as a "sacrament"—Latin for the oath of allegiance sworn to enter the imperial army. All these preparations rankled ominously to the authorities downtown. They saw trouble on the horizon.

Josephus, the Jewish historian who chronicled this period, offers a mouthful on John the Baptist:

> Now, when many others came in crowds about him, for they were greatly moved by hearing his words, Herod, who feared lest the great influence John had over the people might put it into his power and inclination to raise a rebellion (for they seemed ready to do anything he should advise), thought it best, by putting him to death, to prevent any mischief he might cause, and not bring himself into difficulty by sparing a man who might make him repent of it when it should be too late. Accordingly he was sent a

prisoner, out of Herod's suspicious temper, to Macherus,
the castle I before mentioned, and was there put to death.[2]

To my mind such a portrait is not at odds with the various
gospels. Herod's fear of the Baptist, even after John's death, is
well attested. That John should boldly rebuke Herod for mar-
rying his brother's wife, "and for all the other evil things that
Herod had done" (Lk 3:19) is part and parcel of the prophet's
calling. Telling the truth, even to the face of the authorities,
goes with the territory. In the gospel version of events the truth
itself, even more than the crowds who gather to hear it, is threatening to the powers.

The arrest of John the Baptist appears in the gospels as a
decisive event for Jesus' ministry and his sense of the times. He
had gone out to hear John, had been baptized in what by all
accounts was an overwhelming personal and, in some descriptions, public experience. From there he heads straight for the
wilderness. He is driven, as it is put, into forty days of intense
fasting and combat with the powers up close and within. (That,
of course, is meat for another season.) He returns, however, to
find that the "powers without" have been busy at the same
time—John is in jail.

Certain scholars treat this arrest as a convenient literary
maneuver, diminishing John abruptly to clear the way for Jesus'
ministry. But it doesn't read like that. It is more like a clap on
the cheek, a sign of the times that shakes you alert. Jesus must
surely look around, count costs, weigh words, even sense already
his own fate. Herod will mistake him for John the Baptist raised
(Mt 14:2) and will indeed plot his death (Lk 13:31-33). Soon
enough Jesus will be on trial before Herod. He would do well
to be prudent. Instead, he takes John's arrest as a starting signal
for his own ministry. On Herod's Galilean turf, he begins
preaching word for word the Baptist's line: "Repent, for the
kingdom of God is at hand."

John hears of all this, as prisoners do, in piecemeal reports.
Does he not also pace off the dimensions of his cell and brood,
powerless and impatient?

What I propose is that we read our scripture as John read
his. Let us imagine prison as proper, even definitive, Advent

geography. From there let us pray with him for the coming of the Lord.

Late in 1943 Dietrich Bonhoeffer, imprisoned for his faithful resistance to the Nazi war machine, wrote to a friend:

> Life in a prison cell reminds me a great deal of Advent — one waits, and hopes, and potters about, but in the end what we do is of little consequence, for the door is shut and can only be opened from the outside.[3]

There is an awful sense of powerlessness that may beset a person in jail. There is also, of course, a certain systematic intent to that. But even prisoners who land there firm in faith and for the sake of conscience are regularly shaken down. Stripped of possessions and the props of self-identity, prisoners are vulnerable to dreadful emptiness, an absurd vertigo. They may forget where and why they began. Reasons seem small and gratuitous. Futility looms large as the last word.

Prison, to beg from a poet, is the wilderness in a very small space. Simple endurance and fidelity are tested. The demons creep about. Prisoners learn to trust God alone. And that is why so many have discovered it to be a literal scene of transformation.

Another Nazi prisoner, Alfred Delp, wrote a well-known series of Advent meditations from his prison cell. They begin:

> Advent is a time for rousing. Human beings are shaken to the very depths, so that they may wake up to the truth of themselves. The primary condition for a fruitful and rewarding Advent is renunciation, surrender. ... A shattering awakening; that is the necessary preliminary. Life only begins when the whole framework is shaken.[4]

One thinks of Jesus' apocalyptic advice to the disciples, which the church hears as Advent comfort: When everything seems to be crashing down around you, "look up and raise your heads, because your redemption is drawing near" (Lk 21:28).

Father Delp, a Jesuit priest, was charged with treason. He had, in fact, been part of a group who, in the midst of the war, was discussing what a new social order might look like when Nazism collapsed. These imaginings were a refusal of the collective delusion, and they constituted "defeatism" — a crime worthy of the definitive solution: imprisonment and death.

Outwardly things could not have been worse. The only human gesture Delp reports was a jailer kind enough to leave his shackles loose enough to slip one hand free. With cuffs dangling he writes:

> The gospel for the fourth Sunday in Advent evokes history. It refers to the mighty who determine the structure of the small room in which the Light of the World will come into being, bringing salvation. In order to recognize that a moment of historical crisis is implied here, we must clothe these names with the memory of the part they played in history. From the imperial throne to the holy of holies the outlook was hopeless. . . . Hopeless — that is the iron with which history often seeks to fetter healing hands, breaking the hearts of the enlightened few and reducing them to trembling hesitancy or cheap silence or tired resignation.[5]

History closes in like a prison cell. We pace it off in our hearts. John's situation comes to mind. His prospects are hardly optimistic. No thirty-day misdemeanor or six-month rap — his sentence is indefinite. Vaguely terminal. John has been announcing a future; that is his crime. In recompense now his own future is taken from him by force. He'll not walk out the door. Never again breathe desert air. Never wash again in the Jordan. Like Bonhoeffer and Delp, his exit will be by execution — up against the wall.

Perhaps worse, John is cut off, or again so it seems, from Jesus. The wall is between. John cannot see his face. At hand is the arrival for which he's been praying and yearning and preparing, but all he can see are four walls up close. Still we have John's witness in the form of a question, a contraband note kited out between the bars and carried by his disciples like an intercession to Jesus: "Are you the One who is to come?"

This is no vain anxiety about his effectiveness as an evangelist. John is not scrambling for self-vindication: Was I right? Was it worth it? Have I preached it into being? This is not desperation. He discloses no doubt about the steadfast promises of God.

John is not even asking when. He presses his tenses together, and they explode all conventional notions of time. The mingling of present and yet-to-come is quintessential Advent. If anything the question is closer to Paul's on the Damascus Road: "Who are you?" He inquires after the person and identity of Christ. Simply put, the question is a form of faith. And John has uttered it in the closed situation of darkness and despair. The question itself is a sign of hope.

John is blessed with a reply that is really a vision. Imagine! They tell him that the blind see, the lame walk, lepers are cleansed, the deaf hear, the dead are raised up, and the poor have good news preached to them. The bare walls say it is too much to believe. John can't see it. Will he trust it on secondhand testimony?

My wager is that he leaps in recognition, as from in the womb. There is joy here. It may be the joy of prisoners, carefully parcelled out like contraband resources stashed and rationed, shared among cell mates. Or it may be the joy, described by Alfred Delp, "when one is curiously uplifted by a sense of inner exaltation and comfort. Outwardly nothing is changed . . . yet one can face it undismayed. One is content to leave everything in God's hands."[6]

"Rejoice in the Lord always; again I will say, Rejoice." Paul writes this to the Philippians (4:4) in what has become a ringing admonition of Advent. They would seem easy words were they not also written from a prison cell. Such encouragements can be trusted. They are tested in true Advent geography—the word in a very small room.

We wait. And to prisoners the waiting seems forever. But in the meantime, redeem the time: Rejoice. In the end the wall does not avail.

CHRISTMAS: O Holy Nightmare

A great sign appeared in heaven, a woman clothed with the sun, with the moon under her feet, and on her head a crown of twelve stars. Because she was with child, she wailed aloud in pain as she labored to give birth. Then another sign appeared in the heaven: it was a huge dragon, flaming red, with seven heads and ten horns; on his heads were seven diadems. His tail swept a third of the stars from heaven and hurled them down to the earth. Then the dragon stood before the woman about to give birth, ready to devour her child when it should be born. She gave birth to a son — a boy destined to shepherd all the nations with an iron rod. Her child was caught up to God and to his throne. The woman herself fled into the desert, where a special place had been prepared for her by God; there she was taken care of for twelve hundred and sixty days. Then war broke out in heaven; Michael and his angels battled against the dragon. Although the dragon and his angels fought back, they were overpowered and lost their place in heaven. The huge dragon, the ancient serpent known as the devil or Satan, the seducer of the whole world, was driven out; he was hurled down to earth and his minions with him. . . . When the dragon saw that he had been cast down to the earth, he pursued the woman who had given birth to the boy. But the woman was given wings of a gigantic eagle so that she could fly off to her place in the desert, where, far from the serpent, she could be taken care of for a time, and times, and half a time. The serpent, however, spewed a torrent

140

*of water out of his mouth to search out the woman and sweep
her away. The earth then came to the woman's rescue by
opening its mouth and swallowing the flood which the dragon
spewed out of his mouth. Enraged at her escape, the dragon
went off to make war on the rest of her offspring, on those
who keep God's commandments and give witness to Jesus.
He took up his position by the shore of the sea.*

Revelation 12:1-9, 13-17

Some thirty years ago Fritz Eichenberg, the artist associated
for so long with *The Catholic Worker,* published in those pages
a wonderful and disturbing depiction of the nativity. In the center foreground lies the babe on hay and in swaddling clothes.
Nestled round are an adoring donkey and a cow. Through the
crossbeams above a star points down from the heavens. Hall-
mark, you would think, would snatch up the print for a comforting and conventional Christmas card.

But wait. A closer look through the archway reveals a village
nearly off the edge of the frame. However, this is not the cozy
skyline set on a Judean hillside as one might expect, but a
bombed-out city in flames. One has the feeling that it's all coming this way, closing in on the child asleep, holy and innocent.
Look again. Tucked beneath the hay is a soldier's helmet. He is
born in a year of war, and violence is near.

This is a biblically accurate portrait. We suffer much from
the static tableau of Christmas card and crèche. The biblical
images of the incarnation are rendered flat and frozen. A quaint
pastoral idyll is evoked.

Yes, the incarnation of Christ is a still point, a center for
history, the presence of eternity in a moment of time. And the
manger scene may signify well the dominion of Christ in creation, with all creatures gathered (at least by representation) and
bowed down.

Nonetheless, it is a still point at the center of a furiously
turning world, very nearly the eye of a hurricane, which impli-
cates cosmic portents, the powers of history, forces marshalled
and moving, threats and intrigues, journeys and exiles, and raging political violence. In our conventional manger scenes, these
are pushed off the edge of the frame, out of sight and mind.

Chapter 12 of Revelation is not commonly read at Christmas time. The sign of the woman crying out and giving birth to the child with a dragon spitting threats and pursuing is not to be found among the nativity lections. Sometimes I think it should be. It might at least be allowed to inform our reading of the birth narratives in Matthew, Luke, and John.

The neglect of this passage might be laid to any number of causes. One is the general caution about the entire book, which, on account of its versatile and fluid images, is subject to speculative and even ecstatic misrepresentation (let that be a caution to us). Moreover, it is, as we shall see, a politically volatile chapter and not convenient where static and status quo readings are preferred. Lastly, the scholars largely refuse to read it in relation to Christ, either finding its root in more ancient "pagan" mythologies or casting it chronologically as designating some future event, which is thereby assumed to preclude association with the "past" incarnation.

Beside all of that sits the remarkable thesis of Jacques Ellul. He argues that the sections of Revelation are structurally focused inward, like mirrors to a center, and that this center section, the "keystone" (chapters 8-14:5), is about the life of Jesus Christ in history:

> We perceive very clearly, but in silhouette, the person, life, and work of Jesus Christ. . . . While in the other sections Jesus Christ is determinative, here he seems to be absent. Consequently, we must admit, if there is unity and coherence to this ensemble, that Jesus is designated otherwise: here he is not Lord of Lords, the head of the Church, the Master of history. He is the God who is stripped of being God, and consequently here it is no longer possible to speak directly of God.[1]

By this reading God has risked everything to enter into creation and history incognito, in hiddenness. And by this renunciation of absolute power, by this way of humility, the cosmic and worldly powers are overturned much as Paul writes: "God disarmed the principalities and powers and made a public example of them, triumphing over them" (Col 2:15). But essential to this, in the Revelation allegory of the incarnation, is that the powers can smell it; they sense it and go wild with rage. Because of God's chosen powerlessness, they go for a time unchecked and unleashed. They are granted a wide and catastrophic range. Hence, among other things, the woman and the dragon.

Now some see in the image woman as such. Woman with a capital "W." Here, presumably, is another primeval or eschatological encounter with the serpent. And here another outcome entirely.

In some sense she stands for and with all of humanity. The same could be said of Mary, the mother of Jesus, and I prefer to consider the woman firstly and straightforwardly to be her. Here is written in true dimension the momentous character of her decision, her assent to God, the import of her faithfulness. In this view we see no meek and mild mother swept along by events. She has made a very simple choice, taking a stand on the hope of God against all deadly odds.

Liz McAlister, imprisoned for her part in the Griffiss Plowshares action in 1983, had reflected previously and again in jail on this passage:

> The woman of Revelation hoped by looking the dragon in the eye and giving birth. Look it in the eye . . . look death in the eye. At stake for her was her life and the life of the child — and the reign his birth promised. At stake for us is our lives and all of creation.[2]

Mary, in the course of her pregnancy sings a song that looks the dragon in the eye and announces its doom. In this song in Luke 1:51-55, Mary sings:

> Lord, you have shown strength with your arm, you have scattered the proud in the imagination of their hearts, you have put down the mighty from their thrones, and exalted those of low degree; you have filled the hungry with good things, and the rich you have sent empty away. You have helped your servant Israel, in remembrance of your mercy, as you spoke to our ancestors, to Abraham and Sarah and to their posterity forever.

Did she sing that song, commonly called the Magnificat, also as a lullaby of sorts to the babe? If so, perhaps it came back around as seed of certain beatitudes (Lk 6:21,25).

The song and its memory are very ancient. Hannah recited it at the dedication of Samuel (1 Sm 2), and by then it was already a well-worn psalm. When Mary employs it, the hope of Israel courses in her blood. She speaks for the whole people. She is Israel.

In the book of Revelation the woman wears a crown of twelve stars. Can these be any less than the tribes of Israel? In scripture, and notoriously in Revelation, twelve is the number of the community. Here is Mary, here is Israel, crying out for deliverance and struggling to give birth. The Lord hears her cry, but so does the dragon. It waits, ready to devour.

The dragon is a very political creature, though that could hardly be said to exhaust its meaning. The seven heads and the ten horns are a clue in this matter. Not merely a grotesque and terrifying image, they are symbols like the stars in the woman's crown. The horn is a standard symbol of power. The head (I'm following Ellul here) is the sign of direction, of authority and commandment, of consciousness in action. Their multiplication is over time and space and tends toward being pretentious of absolute power.

In the seven and the ten, commentators generally see seven hills and ten emperors as an explicit reference to Rome. The analogies to Imperial Rome are expanded in the famous thirteenth chapter which follows. But, again, we are well advised that this historically specific allusion should not strictly limit the meaning. As chapter 13 makes clear, it is runaway power per se which is addressed and recognized in any given state. Jeremiah saw the image of the devouring dragon in Babylon (Jer 51:34), and Ezekiel saw the dragon slither down the Nile as the Egyptian pharaoh (Ez 29:3, 32:2). Each of these are prototypical imperial powers in the history of Israel.

The dragon appears to be the power behind the powers, the authority within the authorities, the moral reality with a slew of names: destroyer, divider, seducer, confuser, accuser, death.

The woman looks it in the eye. And at the heavenly heart of things, it is already defeated, though not without a bitter fight.

Before the woman, against the incarnation, the dragon takes up a stance that is a twisted parody of Advent. It watches. It is alert and awake, crouched and ready, preparing in its own fashion for the child's arrival.

The powers, it is time to note, are likewise on aggressive watch in the gospel nativities. In Luke's narrative Caesar Augustus stands political watch. By his own decree he claims a station at the outset of the story. By his version of events, he is the story.

Caesar's word goes forth, and history is made. All the world (now there is a totalizing intention!) should be enrolled. The whole of humanity is to be set in motion. Step to and be numbered. He, it goes without saying, is "Number One." This is the business of empire. Caesar's purposes in the registration, as often noted, were several. They come down to the very basis of Roman power: taxation, military induction, and general population control. As to the latter, Rome wants to know the whereabouts and number of able-bodied folks in subject provinces likely to revolt. Perhaps Caesar has heard the words to a popular tune making the rounds about the mighty put down from their thrones. He sits uneasily, crouched and alert, ready to devour the slightest threat to Pax Romana.

Peace on earth will be sung and celebrated, but it is not the oppressive Roman Pax. Glory will be revealed, but it is not the glory that was Rome. The Word is alive and present, but not to be confused with the pompous decrees of the emperor. Among those of lowly estate, Word and glory and peace may be recognized. But for now they will slip the gaze and the grip of the powers.

In Matthew, the dragon's watch is kept by the puppet-king, Herod the Great. He is the representative of Rome. He stands for all the worldly powers. Recall that when Herod gets wind of the child's advent, he is immediately troubled and "all Jerusalem with him." His reaction is entirely in keeping with what the historians tell us of Herod. He had consolidated his power by military ruthlessness and political acumen, employing a series of assassinations against opposition figures and potential claimants to the throne. He had informers and secret police everywhere. In his suspicions of disloyalty, he killed three of his sons, one of his wives, and any number of close advisers.

His response to the prospect of the Messiah's birth is more of the same tired method: to hatch yet another scheme, conceive another assassination plot. His dear hope that he too could come and worship rings a notorious false note. Herod the Great is the one famous for rehabilitation of the Temple in Jerusalem. That too was cynical. It was intended to fortify the city's economy and to effect (very successfully) a public relations campaign, shoring up his reputation with the Jews, who always looked askance at his mixed ancestry. Worship was not the issue in either case. A public lie, a convenience, and pretense — false worship was afoot.

A question on which Matthew's birth narrative turns is this: Will the Wise Men, even unwittingly, be drawn into Herod's scheme? Will they be his agents on the scene? Will they return with names and addresses and physical descriptions? Will they understand the murderous complicity into which they are being drawn?

The wisdom of the Wise Men is that they worship the true king. Their exceeding joy and true worship has as its flip side the discernment of the false. Deep in their psyches, whence dreams come, they discern Herod's lie. They dream, perhaps, of a dragon, crouched to devour.

Therein lies a choice for them. To return another way is of no small consequence. They are foreigners and guests. They travel with permission, their visas stamped with Herod's mark. To go against a king who is not above murder is to risk his fury. Nonetheless, they do not cooperate. By their act of disobedience the child is protected.

In Revelation the child is snatched from the jaws of death abruptly, *deus ex machina*. The woman is lifted from harm's way by an eagle. Is that saving presence of God really another way of speaking about those acts of discernment, conscience, and faithfulness by which the Word of God makes its way in the world? Does Providence weave through history on small choices that end up bearing large consequences?

Herod, let it be said, is furious. He has a new idea: murder again. He strikes at the body of Christ by striking at the body of humanity. He sends in the troops, who are more obedient, and goes for the children. The point of the passage is not that Jesus is exempted from suffering. Indeed, he is barely born, and already he is a refugee and exile. The point of the passage is the opposite: He will share their fate. At Jesus' birth Herod's power is unleashed and exposed nakedly for what it is. He follows and worships the dragon—death. In the end the Lord will walk into the jaws of that power.

At every turn it appears an absurd mismatch: a woman and a dragon, a babe and the kings of this world, a messiah of utter folly and the power of death. But that is precisely the method that God has chosen in the incarnation. God risks everything on the power of powerlessness. The topic of Christmas is whether we have the eyes to see it. And the heart to follow.

It is said in Revelation 12 that the woman and the dragon appear as a great sign. The Greek word is *semeion*. It's the same word the old prophet uses when he announces to Mary, "Behold, this child is set for the fall and rising of many in Israel and for a sign that is spoken against" (Lk 2:34). And it's the same word the angel announces to the shepherds, "And this will be a sign for you: you will find a babe wrapped in swaddling clothes and lying in a manger" (Lk 2:12).

John's preface holds that when the Word became flesh, many didn't recognize it. He was in the world, and the world was made through him, but it didn't know him. He came to his own, and they didn't acknowledge or receive him. But some did. Christmas has to do with seeing the signs, with recognition, with discerning God's presence in the world.

William Stringfellow, a theologian of the incarnation if ever there was one, writes:

> Discerning signs has to do with comprehending the remarkable in common happenings, with perceiving the saga of salvation within the era of the Fall. It has to do with the ability to interpret ordinary events in both apocalyptic and eschatological connotations, to see portents of death where others find progress success but, simultaneously, to behold tokens . . . of hope where others are consigned to confusion or despair. Discerning signs does not seek spectacular proofs or await the miraculous, but,

rather, it means sensitivity to the Word of God indwelling in all Creation and transfiguring common history, while remaining radically realistic about death's vitality in all that happens.[3]

Lord, for such a comprehension in this season and all, grant us the heart.

Epiphany: Light to the Powers

Among the liturgical ironies of Epiphany is that the date of this ancient feast should be rooted in a heresy and then subjected to the interests of Roman imperial manipulation.

There were many gnostic approaches to Jesus, all tending to assault the integrity of his person: He wasn't human, he only "appeared" to be. He floated through life, his feet barely touching ground. Or, as some had it, the divine spirit swooped down on him at a certain point, occupying his body and slipping away just before the agony of the crucifixion. In short, he never died; nor was he ever born. Against such the creeds, indeed the scriptures themselves, avail.

In the second century the Alexandrian followers of one such gnostic, Basilides by name, settled on the baptism of Jesus as the decisive moment of his appearance (*epiphaneia*) and borrowed an Egyptian solstice festival, January 6, to celebrate the moment of divine manifestation.[1] The night before, according to local tradition, the waters of the Nile were reputed to have miraculous qualities. Over against this and the festival of light, they proposed to set the illuminating moment in the Jordan. The heresy failed, but the date and the name stuck.

Before long the orthodox had gotten into the act by bringing the birth narratives along as a lectionary corrective. By early in the fourth century a Christian festival fully regaled both the baptism and the birth of Jesus on January 6.

Yet this was just the beginning of a struggle. About that same time another christological controversy arose, a famous one, pitting Arius's view that Christ was but a creature, albeit a lofty one, versus Athansius's view, which maintained that Christ was eternally begotten, of one substance with God.

Now this was the fourth century, and who should be aghast at the dispute but the newly victorious emperor of Rome! Constantine the Great had just then "converted," casting his lot with Christianity as the religion of choice by which to unify an empire coming apart at the seams. Suddenly, to his dismay, the Christians were at one another's throats, choosing up sides and ousting opponents. His religious project was coming unraveled, and he acted to save it.

He ordered all the leaders of the church, all the disputing parties, into a room and told them to work it all out. Hence the Council of Nicea in 326. The story is long and tangled with reverses aplenty, but in the end Athanasius prevailed and the full-blown doctrine of the Trinity was agreed upon.

The upshot was some urgency in liturgical celebration not to co-mingle the birth with the baptism. Let the incarnation be the incarnation; find it a feast of its own.

Who, moreover, should be found waiting in the wings with an influential preference for a date but Constantine the Great. The chief festival of the Roman sun cult was December 25, also a solstice festival as dated in a realigned calendar. Constantine was a perennial fan of sun worship. Dating before his so-called conversion he had dedicated himself under the tutelage of Apollos, or Helios.[2] Now he pursued a calculated policy of uniting sun worship with homage to Christ, and that furthered the already deep logic of celebrating the birth of Christ, long hailed as the Sun of Righteousness, on the solstice.

Indeed, the emperor continued to employ the image of the sun on his coinage. The imperial cult was ended of course, and officially Constantine renounced his erstwhile divinity, but he nonetheless permitted statues to be made representing him as the sun god, complete with shining rays and such inscriptions as "To Constantine, who brings light like the sun."[3] When he called himself "God's man," he indulged an ambiguity which served his imperial purposes.

Granted, there were those in the church who saw the Christmas solstice as a counter-festival to the Roman pagan doings, and there is a certain compelling logic to that. Still, one wonders whether the massive assault mounted today on Christmas by the commercial powers (that is, the inflation, distortion, and humiliation it suffers) isn't in some sense the revenge of *sol invictus*, the sun god.

In any event the date was accepted, though not without resistance and holdings-out from the Eastern orthodox. As something of a compromise the feast of the incarnation with attendant readings from Luke and John settled on December 25 and the star of the Magi came to rest over January 6, completing Christmastide. The baptism of Jesus is remembered the first Sunday thereafter.

The irony is that both the struggle to discern the truth and the ambiguous or ingenuous homage of the emperor, so typical of the powers, is itself, as we shall see, a suitable parable of the Epiphany feast.

Here's another example, an icon of sorts. One December a few years ago I saw in the newspaper a wirephoto of a downtown, life-size crèche where among the cardboard Magi bringing homage and gifts to the Christchild stood the figure of Uncle Sam. He had come to worship. Was it blasphemy? Was it confusion? Did it sponsor self-righteousness or foster delusions of Christian America? Did it preempt or culturally distort the very image of Christ it pretended to honor? Or might it portray beyond knowing or intention the true vocation of every political power and thereby reveal ironically the meaning of Epiphany? With the icon before us, and the questions in the back of our minds, let us consider the lections of Epiphany.

> For this reason I, Paul, a prisoner for Christ Jesus on behalf of you Gentiles—assuming that you have heard of the stewardship of God's grace that was given to me for you, how the mystery was made known to me by revelation, as I have written briefly. When you read this you can perceive my insight into the mystery of Christ, which was not made known to the children of humanity in other generations as it has now been revealed to God's holy apostles and prophets by the Spirit; that is, how the Gentiles are fellow heirs, members of the same body, and partakers of

the promise in Christ Jesus through the gospel. Of this gospel I was made a minister according to the gift of grace which was given to me by the working of God's power. To me, though I am the very least of all the saints, this grace was given, to preach to the Gentiles the unspeakable riches of Christ, and to make all see what is the plan of the mystery hidden for ages in God who created all things; that through the church the manifold wisdom of God might now be made known to the principalities and powers in high places. This was according to the eternal purposes which God has realized in Christ Jesus our Lord, in whom we have boldness and confidence of access through our faith in him (Eph 3:1-12).

Epiphany is about revelation, the kind of sudden brightness that lights up the landscape of a mind or a community or a whole social order. And what, says Ephesians, is the hidden truth that comes suddenly to light? That the Gentiles are included in the community of faith. Epiphany is a feast of racial reconciliation.

That, of course, was the scandal, rooted in the ministry of Jesus, which remained controversial in the early church and was the topic of that first council in Jerusalem (Acts 15). At concrete issue was table fellowship. When Paul calls the Gentiles partakers in the promise, he uses a word for sharing at table. Should the dividing wall of hostility run down the middle of the table like a legalized apartheid among them? Good news: no.

Clarence Jordan's "cotton-patch" translation of the New Testament, now some twenty years old, spells it out with bald concreteness: "It is for this reason—my own Christian convictions on race—that I, Paul am now in jail. ... The secret is that the Negroes are fellow partners and equal members, co-sharers in the privileges of the gospel of Jesus Christ."[4]

Moreover, this mystery is the key, as Walter Wink has noted,[5] to the otherwise enigmatic assertion, equally central to Epiphany, that "through the church the manifold wisdom of God might now be made known to the principalities and powers in heavenly places." To the powers? Shouldn't it be to the *Gentiles*? Why the switch, and what does it all betoken?

Wink concludes, in a connection momentous for the New

Testament interpretation of the powers, that the reference is to the "angels of the nations." The gist of it being that to address the *ethne* (the nations, the Gentiles) one must first recognize and address the collective spirits which hold them, the angelic guardians who labor to maintain hostile walls.

There is Hebrew background to this strange idea. As traced by the scholars it comes down to this[6]: When the people of Israel came out from under Egypt and found themselves face to face with an array of powerful nations, they were forced to comprehend them in relation to Yahweh. The approach which has become preeminently biblical was to see these other nations and their gods as subordinates under the supreme authority of the Lord.

> God has taken his place in the divine council;
>> in the midst of the gods he holds judgment. . . .
> I say, "You are gods,
>> sons of the Most High, all of you;
> nevertheless you shall die like human beings,
>> and fall like any prince."
> Arise, O God, judge the earth;
>> for to you belong all the nations! (Ps 82:1,6-7)

The title Lord of Hosts, in part features the image of this same heavenly council. And the phrase "host of heaven," while normally naming the sun and moon and stars, may be a studied ambiguity also meaning this heavenly court of angelic guardians. Notice the humor, though. The gods are real, but they are grouped around Yahweh as lackeys, gofers, advisors, and heavenly cheerleaders.

Recall the ancient text found in Deuteronomy: "When the Most High gave to the nations their inheritance, when he separated the sons of men, God fixed the bounds of the peoples according to the number of the sons of God. For the Lord's portion is God's people, Jacob is God's allotted heritage" (32:8-9).

So, the gods were to be granted reality but *not* worship. Herein a further clue to comprehending the principalities. As the Lord commands elsewhere in Deuteronomy, "Beware, lest you lift your eyes to heaven, and when you see the sun and the moon and the stars, the whole host of heaven, you are drawn away to worship and serve them which Yahweh your God has allotted to all the nations under heaven" (4:19).

The temptation recurs incessantly. When Israel was exiled to Babylon in the sixth century B.C.E. the people were once again faced with an overwhelming reality: the success of massive and imperial power. Wasn't this a manifest validation of Marduk and his kin, the Babylonian pantheon? At such time a resource commended itself. The Genesis 1 account of the creation story came into circulation, one might say as an underground political tract. Here is a text which may properly be read, its beauty notwithstanding, as a parody of the Babylonian creation liturgy. By the power of the Word gods of chaos and their subduers, dualistic gods of light and darkness, sun gods, moon gods, the multitude of star deities, indeed the whole "host of heaven" are all named as creatures which owe their being to the one true God and serve Yahweh with their praise.

The nations, meanwhile, remain largely ignorant of the truth, about their own vocation to service and praise, about the divine will which they obstruct, about the manifold wisdom of God now revealed in the life of the witnessing community. That life breaks news in the heavenly places, which is to say (arriving back to the Ephesians text) that Epiphany is the most evangelical of all the liturgical seasons. But ponder: its evangel is addressed explicitly to the principalities of this world.

Will it be a surprise to discover that these same issues, indeed similar images, inhabit the gospel story of the Magi (Mt 2:1-12), which is also read on this day?

Among the host of heaven a light to the nations has appeared. The star is an apocalyptic sign and, as with the nations themselves, an emblem in the heavens of authority upon the earth. On the later day when Jesus says, "The sun will be darkened and the moon will not give its light, and the stars will fall from heaven" we are now well alerted that the fate of nations and powers is the topic.

Who then are the Magi who "have seen his star in the east and have come to worship him"? Their portrayal in popular legend and music as kings is not accurate to the text, but neither is it entirely fanciful and far afield. They are at bare minimum foreigners, Gentiles, representatives of the nations. Drawn to the truth of Christ, they anticipate and prefigure at once both the racially reconciled community which gathers about Christ at table, and, as we shall now see, the submission of all political authority to God in Christ.

If these mysterious Magi were of a priestly class who, originating among the sixth-century Medes, survived the transition of power to the Persian empire,[7] or if they were of the sort mentioned so often in the book of Daniel as attending the king's court in order to function as seers, magicians, interpreters of dreams and the like, then such as these were accustomed to the courtly scene. They would be fully at home in the company of kings. They had time to study the sky, perhaps at the behest and benefaction of a king. Little wonder they make for Herod's palace. And when Herod consults his coterie of priests and scribes, they meet up with their opposite numbers.

With such a natural collusion of class, Herod may rightly expect them to return as he requests. His rage and its consequences are another story told on another feast, but those dark doings hover on the edge, or just below the surface, of the events narrated here. They signify not only the difference between truth and the lie, faith and idolatry, but the manifest consequences of the latter in this world.

By the deepest longings of their hearts, and without the benefit, until now, of the Hebrew scriptures, the Magi have come. Their humility is wondrous, nearly naive. They are foil to Herod, who by the most blatant deception and calculated manipulation expresses the desire to come and worship. His guile is stunning, nearly blasphemous. But ironies abound. Just as the title King of the Jews will be nailed to the cross, mocking but true, so Herod's pretense is also his long-lost deepest yearning, his true vocation.

And what of Constantine or of Uncle Sam, the angelic guardian of America's borders? Their vocations are precisely the same (as are all the powers of this world): to praise God and serve human life under the judgment of Christ. One might even say, to do justice and walk humbly. Yet how great their deceptions and pretensions! And how dark their crimes hovering out of

sight. Such is the crying need of Uncle Sam for the evangel of
Epiphany, the need of light to the powers.

Epiphany is marching orders for the community of faith. It
sends. As much as any other season it sets before us a public
agenda. We ought to be both sobered and encouraged, for by it
our authority to preach to the nations, to speak truth to power,
is spelled out. It is not, however, an abstract truth, but an incarnational one, a truth rooted in Christ which manifestly must first
take form in our own life. Let the light be in us. Let's go tell it
on the mountain and even, irony upon irony, in the heavenly
places.

CHAPTER 9

LENT: A CONFUSION
BEFORE THE CROSS

And Jesus, full of the Holy Spirit, returned from the Jordan, and was led by the Spirit for forty days in the wilderness, tempted by the devil. And he ate nothing in those days; and when they were ended, he was hungry. The devil said to him, "If you are the Son of God, command this stone to become bread." And Jesus answered him, "It is written, 'We shall not live by bread alone.'" And the devil took him up, and showed him all the kingdoms of the world in a moment of time, and said to him, "To you I will give all this authority and their glory; for it has been delivered to me, and I give it to whom I will. If you, then, will worship me, it shall all be yours." And Jesus answered him, "It is written, 'You shall worship the Lord your God and God only shall you serve.'" And he took him to Jerusalem, and set him on the pinnacle of the temple, and said to him, "If you are the Son of God, throw yourself down from here, for it is written, 'God will give angels charge of you, to guard you,' and 'On their hand they will bear you up lest you strike your foot against a stone.'" And Jesus answered him, "It is said, 'You shall not tempt the Lord your God.'" And when the devil had ended every temptation, he departed from him until an opportune time.

Luke 4:1-13

And he came out, and went, as was his custom, to the Mount of Olives; and the disciples followed him. And when he came

*to the place he said to them, "Pray that you may not enter
into temptation." And he withdrew from them about a stone's
throw, and knelt down and prayed, "Father, if thou art willing,
remove this cup from me; nevertheless not my will, but thine
be done." And there appeared to him an angel from heaven,
strengthening him. And being in an agony he prayed more
earnestly; and his sweat became like great drops of blood
falling down upon the ground. And when he rose from prayer,
he came to the disciples and found them sleeping for sorrow,
and he said to them, "Why do you sleep? Rise and pray that
you may not enter into temptation."*

Luke 22:39-46

It can be said fairly that discipleship is the topic of Lent. The
liturgical road from Ash Wednesday leads straight to Passion-
week Jerusalem. To enter wholeheartedly into the season costs
more than tag-along admiration from the margins of a multitude.
A call and a choice are put pointblank: take up your cross and
follow.

Lent was first and still remains a season of baptismal preparation. Before the church year took shape there was only the
unitive feast of Easter, which went on for fifty days until Pentecost.[1] But for those initiates to be baptized into the death and
life of Christ on Easter it was the culmination of a three-year
period of instruction and discipline. In the underground rigors
of pre-Constantinian faith, the scrutiny was serious, the preparation prolonged, and the prayer intense. Those demanding final
days before baptism were marked with a fast. By a simple act
of solidarity and intercession other members, even whole congregations, were drawn instinctively to join the fast and renew
their own sacramental vows come Easter sunrise.

Eventually the association of Easter with Jesus' forty days of
wilderness fasting occasioned by his own baptism gave the season reference and duration. For as long as the church can
remember (or at least from its earliest records) the temptation
narrative (Lk 4:1-13, Mt 4:1-11, Mk 1:12-13) has been the gospel
reading for the first Sunday in Lent.

It's a perfect match. Insofar as the way of the cross is the
theme of Lent, the temptations enumerate an array of potential

deflections, co-optations, repudiations, and misdirections that would refuse the cross. They lead other ways, ways which Jesus, thank God, declines to follow.

Insofar as a theme of Lent is the humanity of Jesus (who-he-is-uttered-in-the-Word-of-God-to-be, as the theologians say), the temptations offer a radical confusion of his identity and vocation. Happily, for our sake, he passes through more fully and freely himself.

Clarence Jordan suggests an unusual etymology for the word *diabolos* ("devil") in this passage. He says

> [*Diabolos*] comes from *dia* meaning "around through" and *bollo* meaning "to throw." Our English word "ball" comes from that. *Diabolos* means "one who throws things about" —one who stirs things up—gets them confused. The work of the devil is just to get us muddled.[2]

The father of lies (who scatters them about), the slanderer, the accuser of the saints, then, is really the Great Confuser. Apropos of Lent, the confusion Jesus suffers is not just over tactics; more than just program or method or means or way is up for grabs. It is Jesus' identity and vocation as such which are being subverted and assaulted.

Jesus' baptism is a moment of divine-human clarity. His identity is made plain as day. It seems to burst from heaven for his own (and in some gospel versions, for everyone's) eyes to see. Luke is not content and compounds all that with a slightly heavy hand by immediately piling on the genealogy of his lineage. But in Matthew and Mark it is a mere two or three verses before that identity is under subtle attack. "If you are the anointed one, the chosen of Israel. . ." A question interposes, packed in the "if." A twisted syllogism follows: ". . . then take power."

The insidiousness of the temptations lies in the integrity of how and who. Power and person are the topic. The one crouched ready to gobble up the other. Power may consume, corrupt, inflate, distort, dissipate, or simply deaden the person. The Confuser's scheme is for Jesus to forget who he is by getting lost in how he'll work, so that the One who is the beginning and end will be swallowed up in the means.

It seems to be more and more widely recognized that each of the temptations is to power: the first is to economic power, the second is to military/political power, and the third is to religious power. In all, we're granted a concise and compact exchange on issues at once very concrete to the life of Jesus and pertinent to our own. Remember that at the conclusion of the encounter the tempter doesn't slink off into oblivion forever defeated; he withdraws "until an opportune time." Such times present themselves repeatedly to Jesus and his followers.

Perhaps we're blinded to the power question by the mundane simplicity of the first invitation: yield to hunger, make stones bread, break fast. In the plainest terms the invitation is to seek first his own needs and appetites—and be ruled by them. To join the "enemies of the cross" whose "god is their belly" (against whom the Philippians were once duly warned).

We need look no further than our own lives and times to comprehend the runaway enormity of the temptation. In consumer culture it is writ large and with a vengeance. Appetites are researched, targeted, hooked, inflated, managed, and manufactured. People are held in bondage by them. Their servitude and silence and single-minded distraction are guaranteed.

To undertake a lenten discipline, to fast or deny an appetite, is not to inflict some perverse self-punishment or to be justified by a religious act. It is a prayer of freedom: to loosen the bonds and to restore a right relation to the created order. It is so politically loaded because it breaks with the culture precisely at its main method of control.

If in his own fast Jesus is exercising a similar kind of freedom, the tempter manages to come back at a more subtle level. The temptation is to power because more than Jesus' own needs are at issue. Can there be any doubt that in his aching need he intercedes for all those who are hungry? He bears all who suffer poverty and want. Can there be doubt that he wants justice so bad he can taste it? He hungers after righteousness.

The sharing of bread is intimately entangled with the ministry of Jesus. It is the great sign and metaphor of the kingdom. I have a friend who says if you can read the gospels without getting hungry then you're not paying attention. The ministry reads like a gigantic floating potluck. From the opening wedding feast to the feeding of the multitudes, by way of banquet parables or eating with the tax collectors and sinners, through the *last* supper and the resurrection meals, Jesus can be seen with bread in his hands — blessing, breaking, offering, partaking.

The temptation, perhaps in all of these, dogs him relentlessly: build a movement of bread alone. Wield it as power. Following John's account of the loaves miracle, Jesus must escape to the hills lest the people "come and take him by force to make him king" (Jn 6:15). A bread messiah. By a simple twist, the same bread offered freely as sacrament or justice may be withheld and granted as a means to power.

Mindful again of ourselves, this temptation has its triumph in the food-as-a-weapon side of our foreign policy. America has nearly the same corner on bread as the OPEC nations do on oil. It appears we do and will exercise that option in concert with the other instruments of global domination, putting on the international squeeze with threat and promise. We beat our ploughshares into swords, targeting nations for slow starvation. This is nothing more than the blunt underside of consumerism's power exposed.

The second temptation is perhaps more straightforward, but nonetheless seductive. It captures my own imagination, so let me draw it freely as though privy to a more extended version of the conversation.

Jesus is taken high above the earth to giddy and dizzying heights with a view from sea to shining sea. One could suggest he's taken for a ride in Air Force One — the presidential jet — but let's be more blunt and make it a flying nuclear command post. The Confuser's argument goes something like this: "Think what influence you could have from a position like this. We need someone here who won't be soft on evil. We're looking for someone who'd put kingdom priorities in the empire budget, someone who'll organize the world for justice and back it up with real muscle. Let's make this place safe for Christian freedom and religious worship. Hell," says the devil, "we could make the whole damn world a Christian nation! You'd ensure that every war was a just war. Think: Commander-in-Chief of Christian Nuclear Forces Worldwide. The thing is, this ultimate power exists. I have it to grant, and I've got to give it to somebody. I'd much prefer you than some reckless megalomaniac with no real moral scruples.[3]

"Of course," his voice dropping ever so slightly, "there are going to be some compromises. Just little ones at first. But after all, we're talking about the real world. This suffering love business is great sermon material. Keep preaching it. That's the way things will be someday, and of course how they are in heaven already. But I'm offering you what works now in this world. If you want to really make a difference, and not just feel good in your conscience, then here's the system and your place in it — at the top. Anything else, this cross business for example, is plain naive foolishness. Go ahead, trust and worship God. But hedge your bets, trust me too."

The offer smells to high heaven of idolatry. Jesus' answer is explicit about that. Whom do we worship? Where do we put our faith, trust, hope?

I would never suggest building a theology of the state on this passage — any more than I would on any other single passage — but I sure would urge that it come under consideration. Jesus doesn't quibble over the tempter's ability to deliver. He doesn't quote Romans 13. Jesus repudiates military/political power by repudiating idolatry and does both at once by taking up the cross.

He faced all this very concretely. Do we not have before us an intensified version of his ongoing conversation with the Zealots, as they eventually came to be called? They were the revolutionary nationalists, the kick-the-Romans-out insurrectionists. They advocated not only noncollaboration, active disobedience, and tax resistance, but also guerilla violence and eventually terrorism. I believe that Jesus had some sympathies for them. There's suggestion in the gospels of a running conversation. Some among his disciples are named as Zealots. Perhaps they hoped he would in the end "come out" for them. He would surely make a fine convert to the movement — a good charismatic king in the Davidic mold to serve the liberated country. Anybody who could gather a crowd in the wilderness and march it into Jerusalem would get their nomination. Someone who had the guts and popular backing to walk into the Temple, turn the tables, and occupy the court, could certainly keep going on to the *praetorium*, to Pilate's house, and really turn some tables. Or, as they might have it, turn some real tables.

Jesus meets this temptation more than once. Peter's judicious advice against the cross at Caesarea Philippi is very tempting, but Jesus responds, "Get behind me, Satan." And if the momentum of Palm Sunday's triumphal entry and the enthusiasm of his disciples carry any weight, then that too was likely a day of confusion, an opportune time.

What is most amazing is not that Jesus says no thanks, but that he sees the implication so clearly. He sees very deep and very far. Behind the insurrection he sees the popular kingship, behind that the military governor, behind that the emperor, the chairman, the president, the führer, premier—as Luke puts it, "all the kingdoms of the world in a moment of time." He comprehends the logic of power. He sees, in effect, all the way to the flying nuclear command post and beyond, which is to say that Jesus is wrestling with our own temptations.

There is something even more amazing. I personally take this to be a real event and not just a schematized literary summary. It was a real trip to the desert, a real fast, emptying out and stripping down. Here in the wilderness, so vulnerable, so frail and human, Jesus is alone with his identity and calling. And here, away from the crowds, away from the collaborators, away from the Romans, away from the Zealots and all their worthy arguments, he runs smack into it all, this is where the voices start echoing around in his head, inflated to their (true?) cosmic proportion.

In one sense it's reasonable to say that the whole battleground for this struggle is in our hearts—the human heart. We're the turf and the wilderness. But it is even more important to me and my own salvation to understand that the battleground is Christ's heart. Yes, Caesar is out there with his bold and blasphemous and tempting claims to be confronted and rebuked, but Caesar is also there—in Christ's heart.

The Pacific Life Community struggling against the Trident submarine has a much repeated saying: "We must face the Tridents which are being built, and we must face the Tridents in our hearts."

None of these are simply messianic temptations suited for

Jesus "in scale with his glory." We want to let ourselves off just so easily, but they are all our own. We, the North American church, the community of disciples, have manifestly yielded to the very temptations which Jesus resisted in himself and on our behalf. By dribs and drabs, by degrees and by silence, we have chosen and chosen again the flying nuclear command post and its derivatives over the cross (or somehow, we think, along with it).

We have lived with a confusion so long that it has grown quite comfortable. It is said most truly that because we have refused the cross, we are in the grip of empire and the bomb.

All of the wilderness temptations conjure up alternatives to the cross, but none is so explicit as the last: not to die.

This one is often called the religious temptation. The view from the Temple, of course, predominates. Scripture is deftly quoted, but in the manner of prooftexting. The Confuser does not counsel faith; he commends mere religion. The freedom of God is not honored, but is instead circumscribed. God is being presumed upon, pinned down, manipulated, if you will. To tempt God is to try to force the divine hand, to leap of your own accord, expecting God will hop to and follow in compliance with your own grand designs.

Certain scholars — including John Howard Yoder — aver that in the moment of this temptation, Jesus envisions surviving a religious form of the death penalty prescribed for blasphemy: to be thrown from a tower on the Temple wall, down into the Kidron valley.[4] That would certainly make detailed sense of an otherwise obscure and peculiar vision.

The devil says to him, "Now take it a step further. Walk to the edge and jump off yourself. Think how your ministry could be furthered. If you land on your feet and hit the ground running, your credentials would be established in an instant: a wonder-working superstar. Give them a sign? You bet, but not the sign of Jonah. Make it a prime-time miracle, a spectacle to remember and proclaim. You'll accrue all the grandstanding benefits of martyrdom, for less than half the cost.

"Your reputation will forever precede you, not to mention carry you through the tough spots. Crowds will hang on your every word, no matter what you say. You will be the idol of the masses, but high above their common fate — you will be safe and immune. If you play it right, the Sanhedrin will fall all over you. Even the Romans will take note, consulting you on key matters of import. That kind of influence is not to be spurned, and you would never need to dirty your hands.

"But mostly, you don't have to die."

Let us not be naive about what it means to find our security in God alone. In the cross, Jesus trusts God completely. That means he is utterly free to die. "Into your hands I commit my spirit."

The temptations against that pursue Jesus nearly to the moment of his arrest. In the garden he is still torn and wrestling, sweating this one out in blood. Yet there, and finally, he freely honors the freedom of God.

In the wilderness he had first engaged the principalities and powers. If Jesus' eye were already on Jerusalem, they, for their part, seemed to see him coming from afar. Aggressive as always, they go out to meet him, not to drive him off like a robber, with blunt threats, swords, and clubs, but to suck him in, to make him one of their own. That is their guile and finesse. The spirit of power would seduce him in one form or another. They would transform him into the very thing against which he strives. He, however, slips their grip.

In Gethsemane he is alone once again. Now they are more straightforward. Hovering at the margins of his prayer, besetting him on every side is the power of death in its most blatant form. The troops are on their way, making their search. "This is your hour and the power of darkness" (Lk 22:53). Power is still trying to have its way with him. Will he not reconsider, take concern for his life, and flee? May it be said that deep in prayer he dies to that fear, dies out from under the rule of the powers, dies finally to his own will, which is their only hook and handle on him. From that prayer he rises, free to die.

To keep Lent is to follow Jesus in the prayer of wilderness and garden.

To keep Lent is to confront the principalities and powers first of all in prayer. With Jesus we face the dark side of ourselves that is so susceptible to capture and control by the powers. If it happens that we keep vigil publicly at the gates of economic, military, political, or religious authority, we do so confessionally, acknowledging the solidarity of sin.

To keep Lent is to discover and remember who in heaven's name we are, as person and community. We pray against all confusers and confusions for our true identity and vocation. We know that means standing before the cross and making some choices.

The grace of this season is that Jesus suffers the choice with us. He's been over the turf and is our brother exactly on that score, with us in the struggle of our hearts. Let the further grace be that we make our choice as disciples, in the mind and heart of Christ.

CHAPTER 10

PALM SUNDAY: PUBLIC CONFRONTATION

O Jerusalem, Jerusalem, killing the prophets and stoning those who are sent to you! How often I would have gathered your children together as a hen gathers her brood under her wings, and you would not! Behold your house is forsaken. And I tell you, you will not see me until you say, "Blessed is he who comes in the name of the Lord!"

Luke 13:34-35

And throwing their garments on the colt they set Jesus upon it. And as he rode along, they spread their garments on the road. As he was now drawing near, at the descent of the Mount of Olives, the whole multitude began to rejoice and praise God with a loud voice for all the mighty works that they had seen, saying, "Blessed is the King who comes in the name of the Lord! Peace in heaven and glory in the highest!" And some of the Pharisees in the multitude said to him, "Teacher, rebuke your disciples." He answered, "I tell you, if these were silent, the very stones would cry out." And when he drew near and saw the city he wept over it, saying, "Would that even today you knew the things that make for peace! But now they are hid from your eyes. For the days shall come upon you, when your enemies will cast a bank about you and surround you, and hem you in on every side, and dash you to the ground, you and your children within you, and they will

*not leave one stone upon another in you; because you did not
know the time [kairos] of your visitation." And he entered the
temple and began to drive out those who sold saying to them,
"It is written, 'My house shall be a house of prayer'; but you
have made it a den of robbers."*

Luke 19:35-46

It is a remarkable turn of biblical events, perhaps the most
astonishing fact of Luke's account, that Jesus should, on more
than one occasion even, address the city of Jerusalem. Coming
down from the Mount of Olives on his notorious march into
town, en route to strong public action in the Temple precincts,
he presumably turns a corner to catch a sweeping view of the
Jerusalem skyline with the gilded tower of the Temple prominent. There he breaks down in tears. And there Jesus speaks to
the city. Going to its heart, he addresses it whole. He treats it
as having a life and integrity of its own.

All of the pronouns in Luke 19 are second person *singular*[1] —
you, you, you. Jesus acts as though a city could see, know, make
a decision affecting its fate in the judgment and mercy of God,
or even kill.

What are we to make of this? A sudden burst of poetic rhetoric? A naive first-century anthropomorphic misconception
Jesus or his gospel writer suffered?

In point of fact, this is a conception deeply rooted in the
Hebraic scheme of things, and subsequently in the New Testament cosmology. It may be found buried etymologically in the
very terms employed.

The city [in Hebrew] is *'iyr* or *'iyr re'em*. Now this word has
several meanings. It is not only the city, but also the Watching Angel, the Vengeance and the Terror. ... We must
admit that the city is not just a collection of houses with
ramparts, but also a spiritual power. I am not saying it is
a being. But like an angel it is a power, and what seems
prodigious is that its power is on a spiritual plane.[2]

If anything is clear from the structure and content of the
synoptic gospels, Jesus experienced the Temple City as a

"power" (simultaneously economic, political, and spiritual). It looms on the horizon. Its influence reaches far into Galilee. He experiences it there as a threat (Lk 13) and as temptation (Lk 4:9-12). Moreover, from a ministry among the poor of Galilee, he knows thoroughly its domination of their life. He makes the connections. And, in part on their behalf, he determines to make the big trip.

Jesus goes to confront Jerusalem as the Occupied Temple City. To comprehend this, we do well to recall certain facts the scholars report which typify each dimension of its power.

Occupied. Since just prior to the birth of Jesus Judea had been a province under direct Roman rule, complete with governor (Pontius Pilate), troops, and officials. Jerusalem had a Roman garrison, namely a cohort under a tribune, backed up by the larger occupying force stationed primarily on the coast at Caesarea.

The local Jerusalem authorities had some leeway, but they were deeply implicated with the empire as well. By this time the Temple high-priesthood had become so entangled with the occupation that it was all but a political patronage job, appointed by Pilate and available to purchase and bribe. A position once solitary and lifelong became temporary, subject to whims and changes in the regime. So it is that the gospels speak of Annas as "high priest that year," or enumerate the names of the high priestly family, including the assorted deposed. The governor's method of control was to keep the priestly vestments under lock and key.[3] In relation to Rome, the position was a hand-in-glove arrangement. (No wonder the first act of the Zealot uprising in 66 C.E. was to kill the reigning high priest and reestablish the Zadokite succession by casting lots!)

The Sanhedrin, the governing council before whom Jesus (and eventually the disciples) would be tried, was made up substantially of the Sadducean party, landed aristocrats whose economic interest in the status quo made them collaborationist backers of military rule, *Pax Romana*.

The Temple. It was being completely redeveloped in a long-standing project begun by the Roman client king, Herod the Great. Crafty, paranoid, and repressive, Herod had ruled as king of the Jews despite his marginal and dubious claim to the title,

simply because he'd proved himself deft at backing the right
Roman horses in their shifting power struggles. His own heavy
taxes won him few friends among the commonfolk, so his development project of the Temple was a shrewd public relations
maneuver to shore up Jewish public opinion.

Herod made the Temple stand out on Jerusalem's signature
skyline. Frankly, it was beautified and rehabbed at the expense
of the poor. It was nonetheless an economic boom for a city
whose main business was the Temple and its pilgrims. The
enlargement went on for decades—it was still in progress when
the Zealots moved in 66—and provided jobs for the skilled
tradesmen and construction workers. Remember the huge influx
of pilgrims at festival time, the city tripling or quadrupling its
population, with attendant sales and services. Recall the big
business of eighteen thousand lambs sacrificed at Passover time.
It was a massive stockyard and slaughterhouse.

The Temple had received a special dispensation from Rome
to collect its own tax. This is the famous half-shekel tax about
which the gospel question and controversy arose concerning
whether or not Jesus pays. Pilate himself was able to dip into
that half-shekel treasury on occasion without objection of the
Temple authorities. Indeed, he financed his aqueduct in part
with just such funds.

Moreover, the Temple functioned as a bank, being not only
a source of loans (for those with proper connections or credit)
but also the place where records of indebtedness were kept. In
the sense that small farmers had lost their land in a squeeze
between incredibly high taxes and runaway interest rates,
thereby forcing them into sharecropping and debt slavery, the
Temple was an instrument in the whole system and cycle of
oppression. (No wonder that in the Great Jewish War of 66, the
second thing the Zealots did was burn the Temple treasury
where the records of indebtedness were kept. It was something
of a first-century "draft board raid.")

There is in Luke a very pointed passage (20:45–21:5) whose
meaning is obscured in part by the "arbitrary" division of chapter breaks. Jesus is teaching in the Temple. In a dangerously
public way he warns the disciples against the Pharisees who
"devour widows' houses and for a pretense make long prayers."

He looks up and sees the rich putting in their gifts and beside them a widow who has, as he notes, "put in all the living she had." The disciples look up and see how beautifully adorned the Temple is. Jesus replies that it's all coming down: "There shall not be left here one stone upon another that will not be thrown down." He makes connections. Built on the backs of the poor, the house of prayer has become a den of robbers, and will come down.

As Luke has it, that reiterates of the vision of destruction which Jesus had set before the city on the day of his entrance march. There, as in chapter 21, his description is embellished with precise details of the siege, details to which Luke would be privy from his hindsight position. Still, did Jesus imagine and foresee this prospect? Did he experience it as a pending judgment?

Jesus was raised as a child in the shadow of a destroyed city, testimony to a failed insurrection.[4] The Galilean headquarters of Herod the Great was just five miles from Nazareth at Sepphoris. Those Galilean peasants under the burden of his taxes and military rule were ripe for revolt when Herod finally died. While his succession hung in the balance, uprisings broke out in every major section of the countryside. The attack on the royal palace and garrison at Sepphoris was led by Judas the Galilean, who raised his army from the nearby villages, including presumably Nazareth. They succeeded for a time in occupying the headquarters, governing Galilee in the name of their messianic king, but were brutally crushed when Roman legions arrived from Syria. To underscore the imperial point they sacked the city, burned it to the ground, and enslaved its people. That should all ring a bell with those who know the details of the Jerusalem events in 66-70 C.E. Luke, himself, recalls the revolt of Judas in Acts 5:37.

One can't help but wonder at how this neighboring city touched Jesus, how it figured in his prayer or broodings, tempting and clarifying his spiritual politics. Jim Douglass puts it plainly:

In the ruins of Sepphoris, a city destroyed by revolutionary and imperial violence (and rebuilt by Herod Antipas when

Jesus was a young man), Jesus would have seen the future
of Jerusalem. In order to save his people in a specific,
historical sense, Jesus set out to realize an alternative,
transforming vision, "the kingdom of God."[5]

Something has to give, and will. Jesus reads the signs of the
times. He can see the suffering and the tension in the air (heavens! he ministers in the thick of it). He can see the general
drift—empire, the sell-out of collaboration, revolt simmering in
the countryside—but the judgment of destruction is not fixed
and final. Between the corruption of the Temple City and the
violence of insurrection lies hidden an alternative, a choice it is
time to make: the city can see, know, choose, and change. It is
a *kairos* moment of spiritual and historical opportunity.[6] He has
come to name the moment, define the choice, and provoke it
with utter clarity. He is the very incarnation of the choice.

Jesus sees what the Temple City could be, what in fact it is
called in the Word of God to be. And he weeps. These are tears
for the victims surely, for those who suffer under the filthy rotten
system now, for those on whom the crumbling structure will fall,
but they are also tears of love for Jerusalem. He longs for it to
praise God and serve human life. He weeps for a house of prayer
that has become a den of thieves, for a city called as a light to
the nations whose light is now covered, for a city of peace which
does not know the things that make for peace.

The name of Jerusalem, according to tradition, means "foundation of peace." Jesus holds the fallen reality of the city up
against its true vocation before God. What makes for peace?
Doing justice and walking humbly with God. Today we say as
commonplace wisdom that if you want peace work for justice.

When and where does one stand to confront the Occupied
Temple City? Jesus walks into town on the eve of a liberation
festival. Deep yearnings and images are in the air. The tension
is his liturgical theater. And he begins his entrance march by
addressing it from the Mount of Olives, the site, says tradition,
for the judgment of Israel's enemies! He ends his walk at the
tables of those who buy and sell in the Temple. That's called
making a public connection.

One can't help but think of certain connectional walks in

more recent nonviolent history: Gandhi's march to the sea declaring the time for salt tax resistance, the San Francisco to Moscow disarmament walk, or such as Selma to Montgomery.

As we have seen, the action at the Temple is more than spontaneous annoyance at the inflated price of doves. It is the completion of naming the power and its moment. Indeed it is an exorcism. Luke's account (as in *every* gospel telling, including John's) uses the formulaic New Testament term for exorcism, *ekballo*. "To cast out" is used nearly forty times in the gospels with reference to the exorcising ministry of Jesus and the disciples.[7]

Between the naming and the exorcising action is the ride on the colt. It may be as Bill Stringfellow once suggested, that this is a day of temptation for Jesus.[8] Luke himself makes clear that following the earlier temptations in the wilderness, in which Jerusalem prominently figures, the tempter departs to await "a more opportune time." Here, the tempter's time may well be ripe. If this thing is built, as we may imagine, in bandwagon fashion with surging and cheering crowds, the option of a sudden Zealot-style revolt—the very thing he's come to avert!—may have its own tempting momentum.

Recent scholarship suggests that the synoptic reporting of this story may be influenced by the Greco-Roman military rite of entrance procession. It was a ritual composed of both the parade into town, and the ruler's ritual of taking possession of the territory, generally by sacrifice at the Temple.[9] (Luke certainly knows his Greco-Roman cultural milieu. It is his forte.) Such a military liturgy as a backdrop would surely suggest the irony and the temptation of the moment. It is, I suppose, a temptation to which the church has succumbed in its own Palm Sunday celebration. The triumphal entry, we call it.

I wager Jesus struggles to keep his balance. And the colt helps. Entering the city on the back of a donkey may be as much for his own sake as for the crowd or the authorities. Yes, it has its own symbolics, messianic meaning from Zechariah which he has consciously appropriated. But it is also *in and of itself* a preeminently nonviolent posture, an act of humility. Here is an announcement and contemplative reminder of spirit and intent. Let's slow this thing down. As linked with the drastic and confrontational action at the Temple, it is perfect preparation. The two actions complement and illuminate one another. Nonviolent humility, and bold strong action. They too connect.

In the synoptic gospels it is the Temple exorcism which precipitates the arrest of Jesus. (The words he utters there are a thoughtful combination of a phrase from a potent discourse of Isaiah, and a line from Jeremiah's fiery Temple sermon. His eyes are wide open to consequences: Jeremiah had been promptly arrested and imprisoned.) While the charges at the trial—inciting revolt, advocating tax resistance, and claiming authority for an alternative government—do not explicitly mention the Temple action, his words about the "destruction of the Temple" are in several accounts brought to bear as evidence against him.

Jesus knows what he's walking into. He was neither ignorant nor naive about the risk, but freely chose it. No one takes his life. Beginning with the announcement at Caesarea Philippi that they were headed for Jerusalem, he spoke openly about the consequences. Little wonder Peter and friends try to talk him out of it. The risk is not incidental to the action. Indeed, it was so integral that in the early church the risk became for some, a thing in itself—to the extent that the active pursuit of martyrdom needed to be declared a heresy! Such temptations linger of course even today. Still the risk was crucial, and it hangs over not only the action but all the events of Jerusalem. For us it hangs over Holy Week. His words about Caesar's coin, all the teaching in the Temple, even the underground contemplative acts of the upper room—everything is against the backdrop of being in trouble. The words are therefore loaded. The disciples listen the harder. For the church, that risk (let's call it the cross) hangs over his whole life and teaching.

The taking of the risk to declare the *kairos* and suffering the consequences are one. The submission of Jesus to death is a faithful public act which is one with the Temple action. In fact, it is in the cross that his confrontation with the powers, in all their depth and range, is finally realized and revealed and resolved. Jesus has come in that faith. Whenever and wherever believers act today, it is under the freedom of that faith. And in proclamation of it.

Good Friday: The Shape of the Scandal

The message of the cross is sheer folly to those on the way to destruction, but to us, who are on the way to salvation, it is the power of God. Scripture says, "I will destroy the wisdom of the wise, and bring to nothing the cleverness of the clever." Where is your wise one now, your person of learning, your subtle debater of this present age? God has made the wisdom of this world look foolish! As God in his wisdom ordained, the world failed to find him by its wisdom, and he chose by the folly of the gospel to save those who have faith. Jews demand signs, Greeks look for wisdom, but we proclaim Christ nailed to the cross; and though it is an offence to Jews and folly to Gentiles, yet to those who are called, Jews and Greeks alike, he is the power of God and the wisdom of God. The folly of God is wiser than human wisdom, and the weakness of God stronger than human strength.

1 Corinthians 1:18-25

We come to the cross. We must. Good Friday sits hard upon the church year, blocking the way forward, a dark day waiting like the worst of bad news.

What is this thing, this sign, this way? The word of the cross — do we have a clue what it is? It ought to be a grace of Good Friday that, at length and in excruciating detail, the story is so concrete. The particulars would seem to militate against abstrac-

175

tion and inflation. From arrest to assorted hearings and trials, from the sufferings of the torture room to the expertise of the nailer's technique, we are invited to look close. Betrayal, denial, abandonment, calculated political maneuverings, and in their midst freedom and grace and fidelity, are all available to the heart's eye.

Yet ever since Constantine got his inspiration and marched into battle with the cross on his standard, it has been a matter of public confusion. The cross itself has suffered under multifarious attack. Its meaning has been ingeniously inverted, trivialized, abstracted, passed over, or ignored. It has been encrusted with jewels and revered as a relic.

In the interest of renewed concreteness, as an act of contemplation at retreats for peacemakers a friend of mine used to set a chair in the center of the circle. "This is an electric chair," he would say. "It is the cross of our day." Then he would read Jesus' invitation to the disciples, "Take up your cross and follow me." It gave pause to say the least. One had to imagine what the North American church would look like if we had empty electric chairs upon the altar. The foolishness and scandal of following an executed Lord would be more upon the table.

Any understanding of the cross must begin in its plainest meaning as the death penalty. It is the ultimate sanction, the last resort to which the powers all too quickly defer in their work of social and political control. How can we contemplate the cross in any full sense apart from the powers that be? The gospels suggest a variety of agencies and rulers at work; which of these bears final responsibility is a matter veiled in ambiguity. If this provides meat for endless scholarly debate, it also suggests a collusion. Are the authorities in conspiracy or conflict? They may jostle and jockey, manipulate and maneuver, but ultimately the principalities and powers act in concert to effect the execution of Jesus. Jewish law and Roman jurisprudence, Temple cops and centurion-led cohorts, informant and spies, Sanhedrin and priestly aristocracy, puppet king and imperial governor (and behind them Caesar and the very spirit of the age)—all are, in the cross, finally arrayed against Jesus and his movement. If the method is notoriously and uniquely Roman, they are nonetheless joined in it. This is their liturgy of death,[1] the true basis of their power.

To say that the crucifixion is the work of the powers is not to imply that Jesus is the passive victim of circumstance. On the contrary, the cross is also his action, freely done. He knows precisely what he's walking into. In John's gospel Jesus is at pains to explain that he lays down his own life as freedom and choice, "No one takes it from me, but I lay it down of my own accord" (Jn 10:18). He is frequently portrayed in gospel accounts slipping their grip, passing through the midst of them, or withdrawing for the moment: Jesus names his own time. Count all those "predictions" on the road—these are not bursts of prophetic omniscience, but self-possessed comprehension of the risks which are part and parcel of "going up to Jerusalem."

The cross, of course, is theologized to death. In North America there is a sophisticated and influential variety of "Christian Realism" which renders it a moment of transcendent passivity. In this view the sinless love of Christ is the *refusal* to participate in the struggles of human life. Jesus does not enter into the claims and counterclaims, the rivalries of human life. He does not impose his will on the situation in any respect. By this account, it all happens to him. And he takes it with head bowed and hands folded. The cross is a transcendent moment in human history because it reveals the possibility of disinterested, selfless love. History is "illuminated" because the sinful self-interest of all human rivalries, no matter how just, is revealed by contrast. Should disciples, in this common political view, take up the cross and follow their Lord? Not really. Or perhaps, but only an isolated few: utopians, anabaptists, and medieval perfectionist-types. According to this theology and its offspring, the cross has no real transforming power in this world. Within history, they say, it is a "bogus promise" to believe otherwise. The cross is revelation alone, not means, or method, or way. Any suggestion that the cross of Christ calls us to a way of life or a hope of social transformation is relegated to the laudable but obscure lifestyles of sectarian purists.

Under such views North American Christians labor.

Lord knows the cross is not a political program, but is there a politics of the cross? It's not to be reduced to principle, but can its form shape our action? And all guarantees aside, can we nevertheless bet our lives on the transforming power of God in history?

Any politics of the cross begins with the heart. At the foot of the cross hearts are touched and pierced. To see the suffering of Jesus is to be wakened, to have our eyes opened to the suffering of all humanity. Put theologically, it is said that in Christ crucified God has entered into every aspect of human life — even suffering and death. That however, is an elaboration of the solidarity of suffering which Jesus has entered into on behalf of the least and the lowliest, the Galilean peasants among whom his ministry began. If he has gone up to Jerusalem to confront the powers under which they suffered, then his own suffering is one with theirs, indeed it is their suffering exposed and made prominent in the public arena.

An African-American spiritual which arose out of the suffering of chattel slavery understood both that solidarity and the import of being present with all your heart, mind, and soul to the sufferings of Christ:

> Were you there when they crucified my Lord? . . .
> Oh! Sometimes it causes me to tremble, tremble,
>   tremble.
> Were you there when they crucified my Lord?

Who in fact was there is a poignant gospel question. In every account, it is prominently if not entirely the women disciples. (No wonder they are first to comprehend the resurrection as well!) The men of name and note are for the most part nowhere to be found. The crucifixion has plied its work of intimidation on them; they scatter for cover. But the women stand by and take it in whole.

What they behold is a method of public torture little improved upon even in our age of covert torture expertise. Because of an archeological discovery outside the wall of Jerusalem a few decades ago, the specifics of this particular art of death are more fully known. The skeletal remains of a young man named John (according to the inscription on the ossuary in which he was buried) settles a longstanding debate on the use of nails in crucifixion. Near the wrist of the forearm bone is a scratch in all likelihood worn by the arm nails; piercing the heel bones is the four and one-half inch spike with a piece of the titular plaque, which announced his crime. At the point of the nail some fragments of the olivewood cross itself survive. The legbones were severed and splintered, probably by a single blow that functioned at once to confirm his death and remove him from the cross. Though subject to several interpretations, the most likely reconstruction suggests that the feet were first nailed to the cross side by side with the single nail, then the arms. The skilled executioners may well have added a *sedicula*, a small crossbar under the buttocks to support the victim's weight and prolong the agony.[2] Crucifixion was a slow and excruciating death, often taking several days; people died of sheer exhaustion. Beatings and scourgings, as recounted in the gospels, were designed to hasten the end. Add to all this the thoroughly public character of nakedness and death. Bodily functions were exposed and loss of control manifest. The powerlessness of the victim was utter and complete. For Jews, the public shame was further compounded by the curse on anyone hanged upon a tree (Dt 21:23; Gal 3:13).

Can anyone doubt that Jesus felt abandoned by God? We should not pass lightly over the sense of ultimate despair which hovers nearby hemming him in and tempting his heart yet again. And yet, according to Luke, it is out of this dark suffering and from it that he says, "Father, forgive them; for they know not what they do." The cross is the love of enemies. It is intimately and inextricably bound up with the Sermon on the Mount (or the Sermon on the Plain, as Luke has it). In a certain sense it is that sermon with its central appeal to active nonviolence[3] and the love of enemies, so out of step with empire and the ethos of occupation, which is the cause of the crucifixion. It makes a certain kind of trouble. It leads somewhere. From another angle the cross is the fulfillment of the Sermon. It is the very embodiment and enactment of the Sermon's truth. To those who say that the Sermon on the Mount is only a "legalized absolute" and an "impossible ideal" against which to measure our own failings, the cross replies, "Nevertheless, it's been done." It can be lived out even unto death. The possible is real.

But who are forgiven and loved? Who are "they"? Here again concreteness proceeds. "They" are enemies and friends. Jesus loves and forgives the executioner, the soldiers who marshal and oversee, the jeering crowd of onlookers and bystanders, the chief priests who scheme, Pilate with clean hands, Judas, Peter, and the disciples who run for cover. And moreover, dear friends, it can then be said that this is how we know God's love for us. We who once were enemies and strangers are now brought close.

The cross breaks down the dividing wall of hostility. And, wherever it takes form in history, it breaks the cycle of violence. Jesus' forgiving love does its work at a decisive moment in a particular history. Theologically it becomes thereby the central moment of history. One thinks in the primeval biblical history of the way violence mushrooms from the fall. The first sin gives way almost immediately to the first murder. By the next "generation" the violence is multiplying exponentially. Says Lemech, "I have killed a man for wounding me, a young man for striking me. If Cain is avenged sevenfold, truly Lemech seventy-sevenfold." Human beings charged to be fruitful and multiply have instead multiplied violence. "Lord, if a brother or sister sin against me, how often shall I forgive? As many as seven times?" Jesus said to him, "Not seven times, but, I tell you, seventy-seven times" (Mt 18:21-22). The cross breaks the cycle of violence in history and in heart. Such is Jesus' prayer.

The cross is indeed passionate prayer, prayer in crisis and under pressure. It is the intercession of engagement stretched to the limit. Those "words" from the cross are almost entirely prayers, generally straight from Psalms, the Hebrew prayer book. Moreover, they are prayers inseparable from the blood-sweating turmoil of Gethsemane, the solitary battle with temptation in the wilderness, the prayer taught at the disciples' request, those abrupt withdrawals to the quiet hills around the Galilee, prayers at table (including the Last Supper)—all of these are gathered up here in the cross. It is one prayer. One voice. One intercession.

The cross is a repudiation of every idolatry. There is probably no better or simpler method for identifying the idols of moment than to ask what people are willing to kill for. Be it the Temple system, the empire, national security, a particular economic order, the energy of oil, follow the killing to the idol's feet. The cross points a different way. Radical grace. The cross has its own scandalous kind of security, that empty-handed variety which trusts in God alone. God alone. "Into your hands I commit my spirit."

The cross of Christ also has about it the spirit and freedom of voluntary poverty. That too is connected to this empty-handed approach to struggle. Neither weapons nor wealth in our hands. (How often they are in both one hand and the other.) There is a famous picture of Gandhi's worldly possessions at the time of his death. Laid out in an order of spare symmetry are two pairs of sandals, his watch, two rice bowls, a funny little statue of the three monkeys (see no evil . . .), his eyeglasses, a copy of the Gita, little more. The snapshot is something of a meditation, the evidence of a life traveling light. We get the same sort of snapshot at the foot of the cross. There the soldiers, as is their booty right in the imperial ritual of execution, cast lots for his garments. They divide all the worldly possessions of Jesus among themselves.

Paul follows the passage above, concerning the foolishness of the cross, with this reminder to the community at Corinth:

> Consider your own call, brothers and sisters: not many of you were wise by human standards, not many were powerful, not many were of noble birth. But God chose what is foolish in the world to shame the wise; God chose what is weak in the world to shame the strong; God chose what is low and despised in the world, things that are not, to reduce to nothing the things that are (1 Cor. 1:26-28).

Here, via the poverty of Corinth, we return to the question: Is this "reduction" of the "things that are" a matter able to be seen only by faith? Or does the cross work at some deep level in the world, in reality?

It is the New Testament claim, cast variously in the gospels, the epistles, and especially Revelation, that the cross of Christ breaks the powers of this world. In the cross God "disarmed the rulers and authorities and made a public example of them, triumphing over them" (Col 2:15).[4] The claim is bold to say the least. It can perhaps be readily understood that pushed to the limit, the powers have been driven into the public arena and their reliance on death as sanction, as their sole moral authority, is exposed. Martin Luther King, Jr., wrote in a similar vein from the Birmingham jail under the public assault of the local liberal pastors who accused him of bringing violence to Birmingham. But the violence was already there day in and day out; he wrote to this effect in his public reply:

> Actually, we who engage in nonviolent direct action are not the creators of tension. We merely bring to the surface the hidden tension that is already alive. We bring it out in the open, where it can be seen and dealt with. Like a boil that can never be cured so long as it is covered up but must be opened with all its ugliness to the natural medicines of air and light, injustice must be exposed, with all the tension its exposure creates, to the light of human conscience and the air of national opinion, before it can be cured.[5]

Exposure, the subtle debaters of this present age might argue in turn, is one thing. Disarming and dethroning is quite another. Where do you see this in present history? We reply, trembling to be tested, in the life and freedom of the community which lives by the cross. Jesus exhibits an astonishing freedom in the cross. He is free from the grip of the powers, free both from their seductions (as summed up in the temptations) and from their intimidations (as encountered in the garden just prior to his arrest, their hour and the power of darkness). He virtually seems free to die, free to stand in this moment's notice before the judgment and mercy of God. Elsewhere Paul calls this justification by faith. In Jerusalem, on trial and before the execution, it might better be called Jesus' freedom of the resurrection.

The cross for Jesus, as for his disciples, is neither desperation nor suicidal despair. He is not throwing himself, a last absurd gesture, like a wooden shoe into the cogs of history's machinery. He goes up in the conviction that God is entering, cracking, turning, and breaking open history. It is an irrepressible act of hope. To his friends at table he says: "Truly I tell you, I will never again drink of the fruit of the vine until the day when I drink it new in the kingdom of God." We could inquire, I suppose, with the scholars as to the consciousness of Jesus regarding time and history. Did he imagine that his own end was tied to the end to history? Did he think his death would usher in the kingdom of God?

The point is that it does. The cross of Christ is quite simply the seed of the kingdom. It is the first and last word in hope and the freedom of God.

All this from beginning to end is denounced and repudiated as naive and foolish by think-tank scholars, worldly-wise politicians, the negotiators and experts, the purveyors of hardware and software wisdom, the subtle debaters of this passing age. But to those who are called to that kingdom, who are prepared to walk its way, it is the power of God and the wisdom of God, the very means of the end.

CHAPTER 12

EASTER: RESURRECTION IS AGAINST THE LAW

The next day, that is, after the day of preparation, the chief priests and the Pharisees gathered before Pilate and said, "Sir, we remember how that imposter said, while he was still alive, 'After three days I will rise again.' Therefore, order the sepulchre to be made secure until the third day, lest his disciples go and steal him away, and tell the people, 'He has risen from the dead,' and the last fraud will be worse than the first." Pilate said, "Take a guard of soldiers; go, and make it secure as you can." So they went and made the sepulchre secure by sealing the stone and setting a guard.

Now after the Sabbath, toward the dawn of the first day of the week, Mary Magdalene and the other Mary went to see the sepulchre. And behold, there was a great earthquake; for an angel of the Lord descended from heaven and came and rolled back the stone, and sat upon it. His appearance was like lightning, and his raiment white as snow. And for fear of him the guards trembled and became like dead men. But the angel said to the women, "Do not be afraid; for I know that you seek Jesus who was crucified. He is not here; for he has risen, as he said. Come, see the place where he lay. Then go quickly and tell his disciples that he is risen from the dead, and behold, he is going before you to Galilee; there you will see him. Lo, I have told you."...

While they were going, behold, some of the guard went into

> *the city and told the chief priests all that had taken place.
> And when they had assembled with the elders and taken coun-
> sel, they gave a sum of money to the soldiers and said, "Tell
> people, 'His disciples came by night and stole him away while
> we were asleep.' And if this comes to the governor's ears, we
> will satisfy him and keep you out of trouble." So they took
> the money and did as they were directed; and this story has
> been spread among the Jews to this day.*
>   *Matthew 27:62-28:7, 28:11-15*

It is among the bittersweet ironies of Matthew's account that
Roman soldiers are among the first witnesses of the resurrection.
Under orders to guard against it, they are granted a front-row
seat. And they are the first to convey, for ill or good, the news
of the truth.

There is, indeed, a whole sequence of ironic twists in Matthew's telling of the story. It begins when the chief priests and
scribes remember so precisely what the disciples have forgotten:
the promise of Jesus that he would be raised. In every gospel
account, however different in person or geography, the friends
of Jesus are surprised utterly by the resurrection. It is as though
everything from his parable hints to the outright and straightforward promises had escaped them. They cower behind closed
doors, resign themselves to fate, head back disappointed to job
and family. The resurrection is neither awaited nor expected. It
catches them entirely off guard.

The authorities and powers of Jerusalem, however, are not
caught off guard. The are, quite literally, on guard. Unless the
gospel writers are paranoid conspiratorial theorists, the crucifixion of Jesus is a carefully arranged event. The scenario has been
planned and thought through. The authorities want to be in
control. They attend to details. And they are not about to blow
it all by miscalculation, even after the accomplished fact. They
attribute to the disciples their own devious means and methods.
So before the body is cold, they sit down for a meeting with
Pilate.

Herewith another irony. After all the quibbling and com-
plaining and righteous indignation about Jesus breaking the Sabbath, they all troop up to the praetorium for a Saturday morning

consultation with the governor. Earlier on, by John's account, they had demurred to enter Pilate's headquarters (18:28) lest they be made unclean to eat the Passover meal. Perhaps that was a more public occasion, because there seem to be no qualms or hesitation now about slipping into the praetorium. They enter not to open eyes or cure the lame (God forbid!) on the Sabbath, but to conspire with profane political authority.

Authority is truly the question of the hour. When the disciples finally meet up with Jesus in Galilee he says, "All authority in heaven has been given me. Go therefore and make disciples . . ." The chief priests and Pharisees, however, look in a different direction and bow to a different lord. They ask Pilate for some troops to guard the tomb. It is, in short, an appeal to the authority of death, to the one who sits enthroned by virtue of wielding the sword and condemning to the cross. Pilate authorizes them and sets the seal.

The sealing of the tomb is, I believe, notoriously misunderstood. I grew up with a Sunday School notion that to seal the tomb was a matter of hefting the big stone and cementing it tight. The seal, in my mind's eye, was something like first-century caulking—puttying up the cracks to keep the stink in. Not so. This is a legal seal. Cords would be strung across the rock and anchored at each end with clay. To move the stone would break the seal and indicate tampering.

The event conspicuously echoes the story of Daniel sealed in the den of lions. "And a stone was brought and laid upon the mouth of the den, and the king sealed it with his own signet and with the signet of his lords, that nothing might be changed concerning Daniel" (Dn 6:18). As there, this is a legal lock on the tomb door—not air tight, but politically tight. To move the stone and break the seal is a civil crime. The resurrection is against the law.

The seal is also a recurring theme in the book of Revelation. Remember the scroll of history sealed with seven seals? Only One is worthy to break them and look upon or unveil the truth: that One is the Lamb who was slain. The seal is a claim of ownership and authority. Its meaning in Revelation is at least that God in Christ reigns sovereign over all history and in all events.

Caesar in Pilate, on the other hand, violently disputes the claim. He has set his seal of approval on Jesus' death, and now he guarantees it with troops. Secured by security forces. When the seal is broken in the resurrection, it stands among the signs that the power of the powers (death in all its forms) has been broken. The dominion of political authority, especially inflated, aggressive, and imperial authority has been cut to the heart.

Well, some will say, that's a lovely statement of faith, but you needn't look far afield to cast a shadow of doubt across that doctrine. From Auschwitz to Hiroshima to Beijing to San Salvador, the authorities seem not to have caught on that their imperial power has been cracked. They brutally deny the fact. Exactly so. And Matthew himself may well be making a similar point.

Here we come to yet another perhaps more bitter irony. The chief priests, privy to the eyewitness reports of the Roman watch, are neither astonished nor converted by the glad news. I guess we are naive to expect otherwise. They simply hatch another phase of the program. The truth is a matter of indifference to them; it is merely a factor to be controlled in the battle for people's minds. They are not misinformed; they deny what they know. These friends of the law manage a coverup. Official sources will have a censored and carefully worded version of events. Confusion will be encouraged. The credibility of the women and the other disciples will be impugned.

It is implied that the Roman soldiers are concerned what Pilate will make of their night on guard duty. They worry perhaps for their jobs, their records, and their military careers. They are a vulnerable and easy mark for the Temple crew. No sweat, say the planners, we can cover your backsides with the governor. Moreover, as the King James version puts it, there is "large money" available. They are bought off. Now the seal is on their lips. In counterpoint to the Great Commission, they are paid handsomely to advertise a lie, to publish abroad the anti-Word, to bury again the truth.

This simply says that violent imperial rule, be it in San Salvador or Moscow or Washington, is founded and sustained by a Big Lie: the resurrection never was. We are not freed, we are not reconciled, we are not justified. Indeed, there is no freedom, there is no reconciliation, there is no justice. There is only power.

That, however, is not the last word, either in Matthew's gospel or in our common history. Maybe we need to confess that we have acted as if it were. Have we swallowed the official line and lived as though the resurrection were merely a pleasant lie betrayed by the facts? Have we proved to be one of the facts? Perhaps (surprise!) the very ground we stand on will be shaken. No doubt we would tremble with that odd combination of joy and fear. For such an Easter let us pray: an ironic twist of faith.

CHAPTER 13

EASTERTIDE: THE POLITICS of HEALING

This was now the third time that Jesus was revealed to the disciples after he was raised from the dead. When they had finished breakfast, Jesus said to Simon Peter, "Simon, son of John, do you love me more than these?" He said to him, "Yes Lord; you know that I love you." He said to him, "Feed my lambs." A second time he said to him, "Simon, son of John, do you love me?" He said to him, "Yes, Lord; you know that I love you." He said to him, "Tend my sheep." He said to him a third time, "Simon, son of John, do you love me?" Peter was grieved because he said to him a third time, "Do you love me?" And he said to him, "Lord, you know everything; you know that I love you." Jesus said to him, "Feed my sheep. Truly, truly I say to you, when you were young, you girded yourself and walked where you would; but when you are old, you will stretch out your hands, and another will gird you and carry you where you do not wish to go." (This he said to show by what death he was to glorify God.) And after this he said to him, "Follow me."

John 21:14-19

Then Peter, filled with the Holy Spirit, said to them, "rulers of the people and elders, if we are being examined today concerning a good deed done to a cripple, by what means this man has been healed, be it known to you all, and to all the

people of Israel, that by the name of Jesus Christ of Nazareth,
whom you crucified, whom God raised from the dead, by him
this man is standing before you well.

                                        Acts 4:1-10

According to the most ancient and reliable manuscripts the
last words of the earliest gospel (Mark) form a curious conclusion to a resurrection testimony: "And then the women disciples
went out and fled from the tomb; for trembling and astonish-
ment had come upon them; and they said nothing to anyone for
they were afraid." (Verses 9-20 are appended by a later author.)

It is so remarkable an ending that scholars speculate about
what mishap might have befallen the original manuscript. Perhaps the evangelist was arrested, executed, or met an otherwise
untimely death just as he came to the most interesting part of
the story. Perhaps there is a lost ending, a last page which some
first-century Christian scribe misplaced on his or her disordered
desk. (From where I sit that theory has a certain compelling
feasibility.) Maybe an aggrieved party to an early apostolic dispute took scissors to the scroll. Some commentators go so far as
to speculate on the contents of the "missing page."

From another angle it is argued that the spare, abrupt, and
unexpected ending can't be original because it's too original, too
unprecedented, too literate, too sophisticated, too brilliant even,
too inspired.

Inspired indeed.

What if the true ending hangs like a pointed and personal
question mark? What if it trails off into the reader's own life
searching for a conclusion? What would you be afraid of? An
ending which bleeds into a beginning? What if the unsettling,
unfinished air of the conclusion is a call to decision and discipleship?

It appears that a number of the resurrection experiences,
beginning with Mary and the women, then variously for the
other disciples, have this character of restating the call to discipleship. "Behold, he is going before you. . . ." "Go, therefore,
and make disciples of all nations. . . ." None, however, is more
explicit than the passage from John's epilogue where the Risen
Christ says straight out to Peter, "Follow me."

The scene in chapter 21 is the Sea of Galilee. Peter and the sons of Zebedee, among others, are at their nets fishing. Sound familiar?

There was a temptation, the gospels suggest, following the crucifixion for the disciples to head home, back to Emmaus, say, back to normal, back to the comforting ritual of business as usual. There may be some hint of that here.

If so, or in any event, Peter meets up exactly there with his original call. All the trappings are present. The smell of the sea. His own boat. Even, as in Luke 5, the overloaded nets of a miraculous catch: "Do not be afraid, from now on you will be catching people." The echoes are strong and haunting.

It is often said, and rightly, that in the original call of the disciples there is stark simplicity. Jesus says, "Follow me." They drop everything and go. There is no record that they had previously heard him preach, mulled over the message, and finally met him by the sea ripe for an invitation. Nor does Jesus lay out the details of what they might expect: "You'll join a vagabond community and live by begging. Eventually we'll go up to Jerusalem to confront the authorities. You will betray me and deny me and scatter. I'll be arrested, tried, and executed. Come, follow me." No such thing. It's all simpler, if no less surprising, in that first go-round. He offers neither program nor predictions, but himself. Jesus calls them, and they follow, in Bonhoeffer's phrase, as an act of single-minded obedience.

Now, however, there is a little more water under the bridge. When Peter is called to follow in the resurrection he knows a good deal more about what that means, and where it leads, and even who he is himself. There is room for neither naivete nor bravado, though a touch of fear might reasonably slip in. After all, Peter has just been confronted by the Risen Lord with the very prospect of his own martyrdom: "You will stretch out your hands, and another will gird you and carry you where you do not wish to go."

To meet Jesus, crucified and risen, is at least to face your own death. It is perhaps as well to understand your relation to the powers. Jacques Ellul writes that "for the first prolonged Christian generation . . . the authentic Witness, the Martyr upon which all else depends, was Jesus Christ and it was enough so

to consider him in order to comprehend what the political power
was and the true situation of the Church in the world."[1]

So what's new? "If the world hates you, know that it has hated
me before it hated you. ... If they persecuted me, they will
persecute you" (Jn 15). "If any one would come after me, let
them deny themselves, take up their cross, and follow me" (Mk
8:34).

What's new about the resurrection call to follow is that before
the risen Lord Peter becomes utterly vulnerable and transpar-
ent. Heretofore he has talked tough in the face of risk, making
big claims with a puff of macho. By various gospel accounts Peter
pledges never to fall away; he avows he's ready for prison and
death; he offers to lay down his life for Jesus. But in the hour
of darkness when push comes to shove, he's running on ego and
comes up empty. He caves in, lies, and denies.

The resurrection means that Peter cannot deny the truth
about himself. Oh, perhaps he could turn away and refuse to
see, but to look in the eyes of the risen Christ, is in that moment
to face himself. Looking there, Peter must surely die. Three
questions for three denials. Simon, son of John, do you love me?
And three replies, each more anguished than the last: Lord, you
know everything, you know my weakness, you know my love.
Jesus sees him through and through, and Peter knows it. Peter,
in point of fact, is the one who is loved in this encounter. Love
is what it is about. It surrounds the moment of confrontation
and makes it possible. Nothing, even death, can separate Peter
from that love. By it he is forgiven and freed and called again.
By the love of Christ, Peter is healed for discipleship.

If he is thereby commissioned with pastoral authority, it is
predicated *on his very weakness*. The issue here is grace and the
freedom to follow Christ, even in death. Peter's pastoral work
begins and ends there.

In the early weeks of the Eastertide lectionary, there appear
a series of texts from the third and fourth chapters of Acts which
address these same issues. It is a shame we get it patchwork and
piecemeal, for the consequential chain of events have an amazing coherence. They deserve to be read as a single story.

Peter and John, on their way to Temple prayers, heal a man
begging at the Beautiful Gate. His joy begets a sermon from

Peter on the resurrection, at the close of which the disciples are arrested and spend the night in jail. Next day in court they testify boldly again, refuse to comply with the court's order, and are released after calculated threats from the authorities. Their release prompts prayers of thanksgiving in the community whose common life is then described.

It shouldn't be, but always is, a surprise that healing in the New Testament is cause for political trouble. It is for Jesus. His healings are carefully surveilled; they are the topic of elaborate "grand jury" investigations (Jn 9). More than eyebrows are raised. They conjure conflict and plottings against him. In John, remember, it is the raising of Lazarus, the ultimate in healing miracles, which finally precipitates Jesus' arrest.

Why so? You'd almost be led to suspect that political authority rules by brokenness, infirmity, blindness, division — by death itself. Authority over death would be an affront to any such rule.

Peter and John exercise that authority spontaneously, almost offhandedly. It begins with a moment of electrifying eye contact. Something is already going on. Three verses (3:3-5) are packed with an intense visual connection. "Seeing Peter and John about to go to the temple, he asked for alms. And Peter directed his gaze at him, with John, and said, 'Look at us.' And he fixed his attention upon them." What's happening?

Perhaps no one ever looks at the man, an invisible fixture at the Temple gate to be hurried past. Even those who give him alms may avert their eyes and never really see him. Perhaps he is accustomed to averting his own eyes from theirs, the downcast and demeaned self-image of someone born lame, the inevitable topic for theological debate: "Who sinned, this man or his parents?" (see Jn 9 again).

But now their eyes are fixed and fastened. They connect. Love is not mentioned, but I'll bet it's there. Tears even? They see him broken and know him. They see him whole and claim that in the name of the Risen One.

Actually we know more about this man and his situation than we commonly imagine. We know some things from his daily position at the Beautiful Gate. The station was more than a little shrewd. Beside the expensive splendor of the gate (Josephus mentions some Corinthian bronze doors of exquisite workmanship) his need was set in high relief. Of course, you still have to have an eye for such contradictions. Compare Jesus sighting the widow with her mite among the lavish givers, even as the disciples comment on the bejeweled wealth of the temple architecture (Lk 20:45ff).

In any event, the beggar has surmised that people going up to prayers may be momentarily sensitized to the cry of the poor, especially in this place. Torah obligations included almsgiving, moreover, and he may have something of a franchise on this spot. He has a "place," albeit a lowly one in the Temple system.

But more. This gate marked the passage into the Court of the Women, where the treasury was (site of the widow's mite incident), and the Court of the Gentiles, where the moneychangers and sellers of doves had set up shop.[2] There certainly was a lot of money changing hands around this beggar. The gift of healing, the authority of Christ, is set over against silver and gold; it is in contrast to all the money and wealth in sight.

More yet. If Luke's chronology is accurate and if his friends also brought this man *daily* to his station as the text carefully insists, then he has only last month witnessed a dramatic event in the Court of the Gentiles. This beggar had a front-row seat for the cleansing of the Temple.[3] He witnessed all those Roman coins spilling out the front door. When Peter and John say, "In the name of Jesus," he knows exactly whom they're talking about. In that place they might just as well say, "In the name of the Troublemaker, rise and walk."

It's a miracle that he doesn't take a look around the room, pause to think it over just a minute, and say, "Thanks, but no thanks." That would be the safer path. Instead, he jumps up and runs from table to table, spouting the news, praising God, calling attention, and gathering a crowd. Peter has no alternative but to preach—and nothing to preach but the resurrection of Christ. Given the time and place, that word is every bit as strong and inflammatory as the original Temple action. It is in fact one with that action, in continuity and solidarity with it. No wonder the authorities are "annoyed"; the disciples are arrested to cool their heels in jail.

Notice something about their court appearance next day before the Sanhedrin: the beggar is with them (4:14). How does he come to be there? Was he also arrested, spending the night at hymns and prayers with Peter and John in jail? Has he been subpoenaed? I think not. The authorities don't want him there. He is the living evidence and testimony they want suppressed. They wish him lame again. Apparently he has simply walked in and presented himself. He has come to stand beside the disciples. These officials must know him from his daily station at the gate. Some perhaps are friendly regulars with alms. Some are condescending, the averted eyes. Some hustle by pretending not to see, and others, worst of all, mark him truly invisible.

They see him now. It must take incredible nerve to stand before them. This is a real transformation. It is a complete healing, body and soul and social relationship. The real miracle is not just that he's standing, but that he's standing there.

Did the Sanhedrin know Peter? It is said they recognized him as having been with Jesus. Peter has previously, as already mentioned, been recognized at a session of the Sanhedrin. It was an irregular meeting convened late at night, and he was warming himself by a fire, listening at the door for the outcome of certain deliberations. Perhaps he even overheard how Jesus comported himself before this self-same crew.

Then when he was recognized he denied his identity, repudiated his association, and shuffled off in tears. The Sanhedrin would like nothing better than more of the same now. They intend public intimidation issuing in denial, apology, and the promise not to do it again. Case dismissed. (Endless courts would ask the same of countless Christians until the Constantinian conversion of the church, and even beyond.[4])

Peter, in turn, recognizes them. They are the rich (landholding Sadducees, in the main, from the wealthy collaborationist classes), the scholarly elite (scribes, Pharisees and experts in the Law), and the ecclesiastical leadership (chief priests and Temple rulers who served in part at the behest of the Roman governor). Together they exercised both a legislative and judicial function. It was every bit like standing before a corporation board, a university faculty, a house of bishops, congress and the supreme court—all rolled into one. But mostly he would know that this was the body that condemned Jesus and demanded his execution. They were precisely, in Paul's turn of the phrase, among the rulers of this age who crucified the Lord of Glory. Peter makes it his business to tell them exactly who they are in relation to Christ. He pulls no punches.

And the man born lame has come to stand beside him. Beyond being nervous Peter must be incredibly moved by the beggar's presence. Maybe he savors the irony and smiles. Certainly he recalls his own denial.

Two healings have come together. The healing of the beggar was in fact his call to discipleship in the resurrection. He is already faithful to that. Peter's call to discipleship in the resurrection was also his own deep healing. Now, side by side, the resurrection is verified in this moment of community under pressure. The love of Christ sustains them.

They do not back down. In the face of threats, some carefully spoken, others veiled and implied, they make no promise to go away and shut up. They evince a complete freedom. It is not merely that they preach another resurrection sermon, they demonstrate it. They're the living evidence!

Under threats they reply: "Whether it is right in the sight of God to listen to you rather than God, you must judge" (the authorities are offered a choice) "for we cannot speak of what we have seen and heard" (4:19-20).

Released, the disciples return home to report all these events to their friends. Their reporting, slightly stunned, turns quickly to prayers of praise and thanksgiving. The topic of their prayers is the sovereignty of God in history. They pray cogently from Psalm 2: "Why do the nations conspire and the peoples plot in vain? The kings of the earth set themselves, and the rulers take counsel together, against the Lord and God's anointed. . . . The One who sits in heaven laughs; the Lord has them in derision."

Their prayer is to the point and informed by their experience. The rulers lay out big claims, they set schemes in motion, call shots, make threats, execute plans. They set themselves against the Lord; hence the crucifixion. But God sets the limits, undoes their plan, exercises the final freedom in history. God laughs; hence the resurrection.

The disciples have met that healing freedom face to face, in their hearts and in their bones. Now they are exercising that freedom publicly, which is to say, politically. They laugh out loud with God.

The prayer of Acts 4 makes clear their surmise that this is no obscure and isolated encounter with authority. (We know it was just the beginning.) Yet they give thanks, welling up and spilling over with joy—rejoicing, even, to be counted worthy to suffer with Christ.

The public work (liturgy) of Easter is to celebrate all such things. Eastertide marks the renewal of discipleship. We are healed in it. Unflinching honesty about our weakness and frailty gives way to our rehabilitation in the call. We follow and follow again.

To keep the season is to embrace and proclaim the sovereign freedom of God in history. In spite of, and against the overwhelming claims of power, disciples announce and enact that freedom. There is no shortage of opportunity on that score.

To keep Easter is to rejoice—all the way to jail and (for the time being) home again. Our celebration is neither flip, for we know the cost and the long haul, nor morose, because we're in on the joke. We rejoice, even suffering, in our own healing, in our freedom, and for the presence of God in Christ.

The powers have had their day.

CHAPTER 14

PENTECOST: TAKING IT TO THE STREETS

When the day of Pentecost was fully come, they were all together in one place. And suddenly a sound came from heaven like the rush of a mighty wind, and it filled all the house where they were sitting. And there appeared to them tongues as of fire, distributed and resting on each one of them. And they were all filled with the Holy Spirit and began to speak in other tongues, as the Spirit gave them utterance.

Now there were dwelling in Jerusalem Jews, devout people from every nation under heaven. And at this sound the multitude came together, and they were bewildered, because each one heard them speaking in their own language. And they were amazed and wondered, saying, "Are not all these who are speaking Galileans? And how is it that we hear, each of us in our own native language? Parthians and Medes and Elamites and residents of Mesopotamia, Judea and Cappadocia, Pontus and Asia, Phrygia and Pamphylia, Egypt and part of Libya belonging to Cyrene, and visitors from Rome, both Jews and proselytes, Cretans and Arabians, we hear them telling in our own tongues the mighty works of God."

And all were amazed and perplexed, saying to one another, "What does this mean?" But others mocking said, "They are filled with new wine."

But Peter, standing with the eleven, lifted up his voice and addressed them, "People of Judea and all who dwell in Jeru-

salem, let this be known to you and give ear to my words. For these are not drunk, as you suppose, since it is only the third hour of the day . . .

Hear these words: Jesus of Nazareth, a man attested to you by God with mighty works and wonders and signs which God did through him in your midst as you yourselves know — this Jesus, delivered up according to the definite plan and foreknowledge of God, you crucified and killed by the hands of lawless men. But God raised him up, having loosed the pangs of death, because it was not possible for him to be held by it.". . .

Now when they heard this they were cut to the heart, and said to Peter and the rest of the apostles, "Brothers and sisters, what shall we do?" And Peter said to them, "Repent, and be baptized every one of you in the name of Jesus Christ for the forgiveness of your sins; and you shall receive the gift of the Holy Spirit. For the promise is to you and to your children and to all that are far off, every one whom the Lord our God calls." And he testified with many other words and exhorted them, saying, "Save yourselves from this crooked generation." So those who received his word were baptized, and there were added that day about three thousand souls. And they devoted themselves to the apostle's teaching and fellowship, to the breaking of bread and the prayers.

And fear came upon every soul; and many wonders and signs were done through the apostles. And all who believed were together and had all things in common; and they sold their possessions and goods and distributed them to all, as any had need. And day by day attending the temple together and breaking bread in their homes, they partook of food with glad and generous hearts, praising God and having favor with all the people.

Acts 2:1-15, 22-24, 37-47

William Stringfellow once remarked that Pentecost is the most political feast of the church year. Trouble was, he said much the same, in their own season, for the events of Holy Week, Easter, or even Epiphany. He wasn't being imprecise. The festival was at hand, the text was open, and he was simply alive to the Spirit's militant implication in common history.

By now it ought to be clear that Stringfellow was right on several counts. With the possible qualification of the Passion Week events in Jerusalem, Pentecost marks the most open, direct, and public encounter with the powers celebrated in the liturgical year.

Pentecost, of course, is not a season as such, but a feast that culminates the Great Fifty Days of Eastertide. It was, and is, connected inseparably to the previous events of the passion and resurrection, by way of completion.

The discovery of Pentecost, in recent years, as suitable for "political" witness is not, as some believers and non-believers alike must think, either curious or weird. It is liturgically fitting and theologically to the point.

Pentecost signifies freedom. Freedom now. Public freedom. Freedom from fear. It's no coincidence that various of the resurrection occurrences transpire behind closed doors. This has less to do with the teleportive properties of the resurrection body than with the locked-door mentality of the disciples. If I read properly the story immediately preceding Pentecost, there are 120 disciples packed into one dark room. They have been regathered in the Easter event, but they're still lying low, skulking about, looking over their shoulders, and whispering the glad news.

They have good reason to be afraid. The authorities want them exactly so. Remember that when Peter denies Jesus and slinks off, he's playing out the political script they have written. The gospels make their logic very clear. Caiaphas says: It would be better for one man to die than for this thing to get out of hand and bring the Roman heel down upon us all. There is a fragile framework, a tenuous political arrangement which they can't afford to upset. They do away with Jesus in order to crush a budding movement. Strike the shepherd, and the sheep will run for cover.

The question (to which Pentecost comes as bold answer) is this: Will the movement be ruled by fear? Will they be contained and confined? Rendered timid and silent? Pentecost says no.

The story in Acts 2 begins presumably in the upper room and ends in the streets of Jerusalem. How did they get there? Carried by the big wind? It's as if the walls dissolve. Or in a reversal of the resurrected Christ's passage into their midst, they pass through and out. The disciples take the resurrection to the streets. They go public.

To the authorities it must appear as political madness, an acute and hopefully isolated case of sanctified anarchism. Some people say they have had too much to drink. Granted this refers in part to the inspired and ecstatic utterances, but I wager even more so to their reckless courage. After what's been done to Jesus, you'd have to be either crazy or drunk to be shouting his name in the streets and pointing accusing fingers at the executioners.

Heretofore the disciples have beheld Christ; now they experience the concrete and practical freedom of the resurrection. No political authority any place or any time can shut that down. Pentecost means speaking without confusion.

I don't pretend to understand precisely what happened in the speeches that day. The marvelous utterance is a mystery guarded much like the gospels veil the particulars of resurrection. (There's only an empty tomb.) What's clear to me, however, is that they spoke clearly. What I'm able to understand is that they were understood.

These were just plain Galileans. There wasn't a seminary degree among them. No studied rhetoricians. They couldn't call a hermeneutic by name to save their souls. They spoke rough, fisherman's-wharf, down-to-earth Aramaic. But on Pentecost they speak the truth with eloquent simplicity.

In 1948 Albert Camus addressed a group of Christians at a Dominican monastery. He had a complaint and a yearning. It seemed to him that as the preparations for World War II were undertaken, as the bloody toll of victims grew, as fear spread, the church remained unconscionably silent or spoke only in an abstract and obtuse style. He, by turn, was candid and blunt:

> For a long time during those frightful years I waited for a great voice to speak up in [the Church]. I, an unbeliever? Precisely. For I knew that the spirit would be lost if it did not utter a cry of condemnation when faced with force. . . . What the world expects of Christians is that Christians

should speak out, loud and clear, and that they should
voice their condemnation in such a way that never a doubt,
never a slightest doubt, could arise in the heart of the
simplest person. That they should get away from abstraction and confront the blood-stained face history has taken
on today. The grouping we need is a grouping of people
resolved to speak out clearly and to pay up personally.[1]

That is the sort of clarity the Spirit compels and grants when
the day of Pentecost is fully come. The disciples spoke with a
voice so loud and clear that never a doubt could arise in the
heart of the simplest person. They were understood. Moreover,
they spoke under the aforementioned pressure, with the authorities watching and listening hard from the window. They too
understand.

The chief priests, let it be said, keep their cool. They exercise,
at first, a prudent and calculated restraint. It is argued among
them that perhaps the big wind of a movement will blow itself
out (Acts 5:38). The boldness of the disciples is relentless however. They are back day after day in the Temple (the scene,
remember, of Jesus' notorious money tables action) proclaiming
the resurrection. In the end, as the book of Acts attests, the
consequences of Pentecost are arrest and imprisonment.

Look it up. The promise of the Holy Spirit in the gospels is
almost invariably associated with conflict, controversy, and persecution—and notably with the ability to speak coherently in
court or before the thrones of power. "And when they bring you
before the synagogues and the rulers and the authorities, do not
be anxious how or what you are to answer or what you are to
say; for the Holy Spirit will teach you in that very hour what you
ought to say" (Lk 12:11-12, cf. Mt 10:17-20, Mk 13:9-10, even
Jn 15).

It may seem a small thing, but in the course of that first
sermon on Pentecost, Peter employs a telling phrase. He says,
"let me speak freely unto you" (Acts 2:29, *KJV*). The decisive
Greek work in the text is *parrhesia*. It is a word which appears
only once in Luke (and the other synoptics) but then suddenly
flourishes in Acts from the day of Pentecost on. Most often

translated as "boldness," or "speaking openly," it seems a mini-Pentecost is packed into the word.

Here is another term cunningly lifted from the political vocabulary of the Greek city-states. Originally it signified the rights of the full citizen to speak fully and freely in the public assembly. It means literally "the freedom to say all."

However, when exercised by the disciples, that freedom has categorically nothing to do with constitutional guarantees, official sanction, or the good graces of the state. It is the evangelical freedom of speech granted to them by the experience of the resurrection. It is the freedom of another kingdom. It is endowed by the Holy Spirit.

Perhaps it is not too far afield to mention that when the Septuagint (the Greek translation of the Hebrew scriptures) renders the line, "Wisdom cries aloud in the street; in the market she raises her voice" (Prv 1:20), *parrhesia* is employed. Boldness is an attribute there of the Wisdom of God.

Or further, note that in the Johannine letters *parrhesia* repeatedly signals "the confidence we have *before God*" (1 Jn 3:21), as though it were another name for justification itself: the freedom to stand before God in prayer and in judgment. These and other themes are explored in *Speaking the Word Fearlessly* by Stanley Marrow.[2]

Suffice it to say that in Acts nearly every instance of this boldness is attended by risk and threat. As often as not the exercise of *parrhesia* creates the situation of danger. Consider Peter and John before the Sanhedrin (4:13,29,31), or Paul in Damascus (9:27) where they plotted to kill him, as they did again in Jerusalem (9:29). Paul and Barnabas speak boldly in Antioch (13:46) where "the leading men of the city stirred up persecution against them and drove them out of the district." Likewise in Iconium (14:3) and Ephesus (19:8). Before King Agrippa, after a two-year prison bit, under cross-examination by Festus, Paul speaks freely. In the concluding verse of Acts (28:32), under house arrest in Rome, Paul is still going on about the gospel, talking away unhindered and unintimidated. Nothing, it seems, can shut him up.

It is no surprise that when Paul himself writes from jail he invokes *parrhesia* as courage and boldness to speak even in chains (Eph 6:19-20, Phil 1:12-26, Phlm 8-9).

The word and the gift it names may be exercised up close, in community, as frankness, plain speaking, and candid openness (that is by no means beside the point!), but for the moment we are concerned with boldness as a public and political term. It is in this connection that when Colossians recounts how God "disarmed the principalities and powers and made a public example of them, triumphing over them" (Col 2:15) *en parrhesia* is used to underline the spectacle of that conspicuous exposure and publicity.

Notice that in Pentecost the nations are gathered and openly judged.

When the second chapter of Acts is read liturgically, the list of nations represented that day in Jerusalem is often omitted, perforce to spare the lector any tongue-tangled embarrassment. The omission is unfortunate, for the table is something of a political geography lesson. It reads like a page from the contents of an Empire Atlas. Common representatives from "every nation under heaven" hear the word, are convicted and gathered (against all babel) into community.

The Holy Spirit is a very political bird—one which doesn't stop for border guards. The authoritative lines are crossed. Indeed in Pentecost those lines are blown right off the spiritual map.

Admittedly there were still details to be worked out. The "Gentile question," which occupies much the remainder of Acts, revolves around this same very concrete and hotly contested issue. Plainly put from one angle: Would the community keep a kosher table? Or another way: Would the lines of nation, race, and culture set the limits of the movement? Would they render the fellowship divided? In sum, would they rule even at the table of the Lord? Not if the Pentecostal tongues could be heard.

There is much to be said about the table fellowship of the early community. It was, of course, a direct, concrete, immediate, and explicit consequence of the Pentecost event (2:46). The common life in the Spirit which forms up that day is characterized by economic sharing, worship, and breaking bread together (the latter being sign and seal of the other two).

This does not come exactly out of the blue. The table fellowship Jesus kept was not simply with the mendicant inner circle of the disciples. Their mealtime circle never seemed complete until it crossed conventional boundaries to take in a diverse collection of Samaritans, women, tax collectors, lepers, assorted uncleans, outcasts, and of course the poor. Only when these took their honored places at the banquet was the kingdom in session.

In the wake of Pentecost, the first "ordinations" confer on Stephen and six other deacons authority to "wait on tables," as most translations put it. The picture is one of service at a potluck agape or ladling out soup at the common meal, though certain commentators stress that the service was broader, involving the day-to-day economic distribution to poorer church members from the communal pot. The distinction is small, however, because for the Pentecostal fellowship, common table, and common purse are spiritual correlatives of one another. In any event, the "ordinations" are prompted by an in-house controversy: the Hellenists are up in arms with the Hebrews because their widows (which is to say the poor) are being neglected in the daily distribution. The apostles move quickly to settle the matter, to reestablish equity, and to restore the unity of table and economic fellowship.

Paul attends to a similar crisis by apostolic correspondence with the church in Corinth (1 Cor 11: 17-33). The place is factionalized to death. For one thing, the church members are organized into parties, including some which take a divisive position on the Gentile question. The letter is addressed on all sorts of issues to the unity of the body. However, the news that most scandalizes and outrages Paul is word that the Lord's table is itself violated. "When you come together it is not for the better but for the worse. For, in the first place, when you assemble as a church, I hear that there are divisions among you. . . . When you meet together, it is not the Lord's supper that you eat. For in eating, each one goes ahead with their own meat, and one is hungry and another is drunk." The Supper of the Lord is, plain and simple, not the Supper of the Lord if the bread is not fully and freely shared. Only when there is "one loaf" do those who are many become one body. If the table is divided, the meal becomes a pretense and a lie. If the poor go hungry among the fellowship, then the body is not discerned. Those who eat the bread or drink the cup of the Lord, says Paul, in such an unworthy manner are not just missing the point, they are eating and drinking judgment upon themselves. That should make us all swallow hard.

Pastoral ministrations such as these mainly point up the normative unity of the fellowship against all incursion of the standard worldly divisions. Nation, race, class, and sex hold no sway at the table. Neither Jew nor Greek, slave nor free, male nor female . . . a community in the Spirit of Christ is a new creation. The old order is passing away, behold! the new is come.

The interior life of the new community is as much an affront to the powers as the public freedom evinced in the streets. The one nourishes the other, flowing in and out. In the chapters following the outpouring of Pentecost, Luke portrays their life as a rhythm of street presence, jail, preaching in court to the authorities, home for prayer and breaking of the bread, back to the streets.

And the movement grows. Fellowship and risk draw folks in, against all reasonable expectation. Under the shadow of crucifixion, in the face of unspoken threat, people are attracted to the intoxicating crazy truth the disciples proclaim and the invitation they lay out. Three thousand people, it is reported, sign up that very day, jumping ship from this crooked age going under. The Holy Spirit has neglected proper church growth sociology. Her formula is all wrong. It breaks the rules of homogeneity and comfortable security. Indeed!

Any liturgical celebration which comprehends Pentecost will likely break those rules as well. It will be a duly public affair. The streets are the proper geography for Pentecost prayer and preaching. We honor the Holy Spirit when we do not shrink from risk, but exercise the gifts of freedom. Bold imagination, bold speaking, and bold action are all appropriate to the day.

Pentecost liturgy ought be expressly communal, speaking to and through the pernicious divisions between us which only serve the powers and schemes of this world. Peoples and communities and diverse gifts will be celebrated in their connection to one another. They might all listen attentively and speak and act and, needless to say, break bread together.

The Spirit moves when and where it will. No one can crank up the rush of the wind. But we can certainly gather together in one place. And for such a movement we can always pray.

NOTES

INTRODUCTION

1. Jack and Felice Cohen-Joppa, "Nuclear Resistance, 1989," *The Nuclear Resister*, no. 67 & 68 (January 25, 1990), p. 1. During the 1980s they count upwards of thirty-seven thousand anti-nuclear arrests.

CHAPTER 1: CONFESSION AND COMBAT

1. William Stringfellow's *An Ethic for Christians and Other Aliens in a Strange Land* (Waco, Texas: Word Books, 1973) begins with exactly this insight (pp. 25f).

2. Daniel Berrigan, *The Nightmare of God* (Portland, Oregon: Sunburst Press, 1983), p. 53.

3. The *St. Louis Post-Dispatch*, December 27, 1985, cited in Walter Brueggemann, *Israel's Praise: Doxology Against Ideology* (Philadelphia: Fortress Press, 1988), p. 171, n. 27.

4. Ibid., p. ix.

5. Sigmund Mowinckel, *Psalmstudien*, vol. 2 (Amsterdam: Schippers, 1961). Unavailable in English. Brueggemann's summary and analysis appear in Brueggemann, pp. 4-10.

6. In Brueggemann, p. 8.

7. Peter L. Berger and Thomas Luckmann, *The Social Construction of Reality* (New York: Doubleday & Company, 1966).

8. Ibid. p. 89.

9. Brueggemann, pp. 41-42.

10. Norman Gottwald dates it from the late twelfth century B.C.E. Norman Gottwald, *The Tribes of Yahweh* (Maryknoll, New York: Orbis Books, 1979), p. 508.

11. George V. Pixley, *On Exodus* (Maryknoll, New York: Orbis Books, 1983), p. 97.

12. Brueggemann, pp. 58-59.

13. Ibid. p. 89.

14. Ibid. pp. 90f.

15. Ibid. pp. 96f.

16. Ibid. p. 105.

17. He, in fact, offers a series of prophetic signs and symbolic actions: burying and despoiling a loincloth (13:1-11), becoming celibate (16:1-9), confronting ambassadors by wearing first a wooden and then an iron yoke upon his neck (27-28), purchasing a field when Babylonian conquest was imminent (32:1-15), burying large stones in front of an Egyptian government building as a throne site for Nebuchadnezzar (43:8-13), and casting into the river an oracle of doom against Babylon (51:59-64).

18. It is commonly understood that the Pentateuch (the first five books of the Hebrew Bible) represent an interweaving of several source documents stemming from different periods or communities. They are the Yahwist (J), the Elohist (E), the Deuteronomic (D), and the Priestly (P). Each has a unique theology reflecting the issues at the time and place of its production.

19. See Chapter 3 for more on the creation liturgy. When the strands of the exodus tradition are sorted out, this Priestly or sacerdotal source may be seen to have an inherently conservative bent reflecting elements of the promissory royal tradition and pointing, now back at home, to the world of the Temple-cult. However, in the imperial context it urges a variety of cultural resistance and so preserves memory in "religious" form.

20. See Chapter 4.

21. Brueggemann, p. 31.

22. Ibid. p. 49.

23. Peter Berger, *Invitation to Sociology* (Garden City, New York: Doubleday & Company, 1963), p. 128.

24. Ibid. p. 130.

25. Thomas Merton, *Seasons of Celebration* (New York: Farrar, Straus and Giroux, 1965), p. 3.

26. Richard K. Fenn, *Liturgies and Trials* (New York: The Pilgrim Press, 1982), p. 28.

27. Pliny the Younger, Book 10:xcvi.

28. The correspondence between Pliny and Trajan was submitted as legal exhibit in an Amicus Brief to the Supreme Court of the State of Michigan by Bishops Judith Craig, Coleman McGehee, and Thomas Gumbleton. The case (No. 77337 and 77338), in which I had some personal involvement, concerned the use of open-ended civil contempt against resisters. In effect the lower court was holding us in jail until such time as we would bind our consciences, promising not to return

to the property of Williams International, the local cruise missile engine manufacturer, as ordered by the court. The brief was filed in support of arguments brought by those who appealed this interpretation of contempt. Whether the witness and intransigence of Pliny's subjects carried any weight with the court, I do not know. The lower court ruling, howsoever, was overturned.

29. The reigning interpretation, typified by H. Cadbury and H. Conzelmann, has been that Luke/Acts is "political apologetic," designed to exonerate Rome and demonstrate the virtual *compatibility* of Roman and Christian allegiances.

30. In contrast to the theory of "political apologetic," Cassidy names this the "allegiance-conduct-witness" theory of Luke's purpose in writing. Richard J. Cassidy, *Society and Politics in the Acts of the Apostles* (Maryknoll, New York: Orbis Books, 1987), pp. 158-70.

31. Walter Wink, *Naming the Powers* (Philadelphia: Fortress Press, 1984), p. 111. Wink's work will be discussed more fully in Chapter 4.

32. Ibid.

33. Tertullian, *De Idolatria*.

34. The table of Roman army feast days is detailed in the *ferial* discovered at Dura Europas on the Euphrates. Cited in F. F. Bruce, *The Book of Acts* (Grand Rapids, Michigan: William B. Eerdmans Publishing Company, 1988), p. 203, n. 9.

35. Quoted in Marion J. Hatchett, *Sanctifying Life, Time, and Space* (New York: The Seabury Press, 1976), pp. 32-33.

36. Ched Myers, *Binding the Strong Man* (Maryknoll, New York: Orbis Books, 1988), p. 384.

37. Ibid. pp. 384-85. In *Wars*, VII, v, 4-7. Josephus describes to considerable effect the "magnificence" of this procession in full: its pomp and prayers, images of the gods and an excessive show of wealth, detailed battle portraits of the war, its trophies (especially those taken from the Temple), and the feasting which followed.

38. Wink, p. 56, n. 46.

39. See Wink, pp. 55-60.

40. Wayne Meeks, cited in David Rensberger, *Johannine Faith and Liberating Community* (Philadelphia: The Westminster Press, 1988), p. 96.

41. John may be the most developed in this respect, as illustrated long ago by Oscar Cullmann's classic study, *Early Christian Worship* (London: SCM Press Ltd., 1953).

42. I will continue to use the concept of a war of myths. I am indebted to Ched Myers for urging the political import of the term. It has been popularized by Amos Wilder, who pioneered literary criticism

in its application to the New Testament. In *Jesus Parables and the War of Myths* (Philadelphia: Fortress Press, 1982), he identifies the struggle of early Christianity (by way of naming, writing, speech, and witness) against the dominant symbol systems of both Palestinian Judaism and Roman Imperialism as a war of myths, or "as one of liturgy against liturgy or liturgies, with the understanding that liturgy involves a whole life style, action and ethic as well as recital" (p. 37).

43. Hans Ruedi Weber, cited in Myers, p. 389.

44. William Stringfellow, *A Simplicity of Faith* (Nashville: Abingdon Press, 1982), pp. 112-13. His meditation on the psalm (pp. 105-13) has prompted my attention to the liturgical content of Jesus' cry.

45. J. Massynbaerde Ford, *My Enemy Is My Guest* (Maryknoll, New York: Orbis Books, 1984), p. 130.

46. Josephus, *Antiquities* XVIII, v, 2.

47. For an illuminating reading of this passage, see Myers, pp. 154-55.

48. Hannah Arendt, cited in Walter Brueggemann, *The Prophetic Imagination* (Philadelphia: Fortress Press, 1978), p. 83. This subsequently became a decisive issue in the early church as well, namely, the third-century conflict over who had the authority to forgive sins, readmitting the separated back into fellowship—the "confessors" and "martyrs" who had suffered faithfully under Roman persecution, or the bishops? Cyprian effectively broke the power of the charismatic ministry of the confessors by asserting that bishops alone had this authority. See Rosemary Radford Ruether, *Women-Church* (San Francisco: Harper & Row, 1986), p. 13.

49. For a discussion of the debt and purity codes, see Myers, pp. 73-80.

50. See Richard A. Horsley and John S. Hanson, *Bandits, Prophets, and Messiahs* (Minneapolis: Winston Press, 1985), pp. 178-79.

51. Myers, pp. 142-43. "Exorcism is one of the central characteristics of the messianic mission of Jesus (1:39; 3:11), and he will pass this vocation on to his main followers (3:15; 6:7). It is the main vehicle for articulating the apocalyptic combat myth between the powers (and their earthly minion) and Jesus (as envoy of the kingdom). . . . Mark thus establishes the political character of exorcism as a political action" (p. 143). Subsequent exorcisms in Mark concern the Roman military occupation ("Legion" 5:1-20), the deep rift between Gentile and Jew (7:24-30), the struggle to believe in the new order of the kingdom (9:14-29), and the "casting out" in the temple action (11:15-19). We will discuss politically informed exorcisms in Chapter 5.

52. See also Ex 21:2-6, Lv 26:34-38; Dt 15:1-18; 2 Chr 36-20-21; Ez 46:16-18; and Jer 34:8-17.

53. Andre Trocme, *Jesus and the Nonviolent Revolution* (Scottdale, Pennsylvania: Herald Press, 1973), pp. 27-76. John Howard Yoder drew on Trocme's 1961 original French version in popularizing the same ideas in *The Politics of Jesus* (Grand Rapids, Michigan: William B. Eerdmans Publishing Company, 1972), pp. 64-77.

54. Richard Horsley, *Jesus and the Spiral of Violence* (San Francisco: Harper & Row, 1987), pp. 50f.

55. Ibid. p. 34.

56. Joachim Jeremias, *Jerusalem in the Time of Jesus* (Philadelphia: Fortress Press, 1969), pp. 158-59.

57. Ibid. pp. 148-49.

58. Ibid. p. 192.

59. Ibid. pp. 51-57.

60. Ibid. pp. 77-84.

61. Even John's gospel, which locates the Temple action early in the ministry of Jesus, casts it within the feast of Passover (Jn 2:13-25).

62. I am not unmindful of either the liturgical overlay from the history of subsequent ritual church practice inevitable in this passage, or the scholarly debate as to whether the Last Supper was indeed a Passover meal. Joachim Jeremias's *The Eucharistic Words of Jesus* (Oxford: Basil Blackwell, 1955) remains the classic treatment of these issues.

63. The latter is Jeremias's argument. Ibid. pp. 57-60.

64. Myers, pp. 445-46.

65. Passover: 2:13-25; 6:1-71; 13-19; Tabernacles: 7:1-8:59; Dedication: 10:22-39. Sabbath might also be included: 5:1-47; 7:14-24; 9:1-41. There is no mention of the Feast of Weeks/Pentecost unless it is the unnamed feast of 5:1.

66. See Cullmann, one of the first thorough studies.

67. Rensberger, p. 27.

68. One of the most important books of the pseudepigrapha, Jubilees was known by a variety of names: The Little Genesis, The Apocalypse of Moses, The Testament of Moses, The Book of Adam's Daughters, and The Life of Adam.

69. By the complicated reckoning of the Book of Jubilees, not only the Mosaic covenant, but also Noah's, Abraham's and even Isaac's births occurred on the Feast of Weeks!

70. Bent Noacle, "The Day of Pentecost in Jubilees, Qumran, and Acts," *Annual of the Swedish Theological Institute* 1 (1962), pp. 72-95.

CHAPTER 2: A QUESTION OF CONFESSIONAL POLITICS

1. Myers's *Binding the Strong Man* places it so. Myers applies a socio-literary hermeneutic to the gospel and provides a political reading

of Mark's time and work compatible with and supportive of the reading of our own times that I am attempting here.

2. Quoted in Eberhard Bethge, *Dietrich Bonhoeffer* (New York: Harper & Row, 1970), p. 191.

3. Quoted in Robert P. Ericksen, "The Barmen Synod and Its Declaration: A Historical Synopsis," in *The Church Confronts the Nazis: Barmen Then and Now*, ed. Hubert G. Locke (New York: The Edwin Mellen Press, 1984), p. 27.

4. Dietrich Bonhoeffer, letter to Barth, September 9, 1933, in Dietrich Bonhoeffer, *No Rusty Swords* (London: Collins, 1970), p. 227.

5. Arthur Cochrane, "Barmen Revisited," *Christianity and Crisis* 33:22 (December 24, 1973), p. 267.

6. Arthur C. Cochrane, *The Church's Confession Under Hitler* (Pittsburgh: The Pickwick Press, 1976), p. 239.

7. Cited in Cochrane, "Barmen Revisited," p. 271.

8. "Ansbacher Ratschlag," drafted by Paul Althaus on behalf of the theological faculty at Erlangen University. Cited in Ericksen, p. 73.

9. A translation of the Stuttgart Confession appears in Franklin H. Littell, "From Barmen (1934) to Stuttgart (1945): The Path of the Confessing Church in Germany," *Journal of Church and State* 3 (1961), pp. 41-52.

10. See John Howard Yoder, "Appendix: The Continuing Church Struggle," in *Karl Barth and the Problem of War* (Nashville: Abingdon Press, 1970), pp. 133-37.

11. John DeGruchy, *Bonhoeffer and South Africa* (Grand Rapids, Michigan: William B. Eerdmans Publishing Company, 1984), p. 133.

12. Among these are the Cottesloe Statement (1961), "The Message to the People of South Africa" (1968), Statement on Confessional Integrity, Lutheran World Federation Meeting at Dar-es-Salaam (1977), the Charter of the Alliance of Black Reformed Christians in South Africa (1981), The Confession of the Dutch Reformed Mission Church (1982), and the Kairos Document (1985).

13. Allan Boesak, *Black and Reformed* (Maryknoll, New York: Orbis Books, 1984), p. 109.

14. See John DeGruchy, "Towards a Confessing Church," in *Apartheid Is a Heresy*, ed. John DeGruchy and Charles Villa-Vicencio (Capetown: David Phillip, 1983), pp. 75-93.

15. Jim Wallis, "Into the Crucible of Fire: The Church Steps Forward in South Africa," *Sojourners* 17:8 (August/September 1988), pp. 12-18.

16. Charles Villa-Vicencio, "An All-Pervading Heresy: Racism in the 'English-Speaking Churches,'" in DeGruchy and Villa-Vicencio, p. 70.

17. *The Kairos Document: Challenge to the Church* (Grand Rapids, Michigan: William B. Eerdmans Publishing Company, 1986), p. 23.

18. Charles Villa-Vicencio, "South Africa: A Church Within the Church,"*Christianity and Crisis* (January 9, 1989), pp. 462-64.

19. "The Central American Kairos," *LADOC* 19:2 (November/December 1988), pp. 1-19.

20. The 500th anniversary of the arrival of Columbus is at hand in 1992. It looks as if the meaning of the anniversary—as either the celebration of a "great discovery" or a time of repentance for this long era of conquest, slavery, and genocide—will be hotly contended. Liturgical events will surely abound, clearly exposing or declaring these aspects of the *kairos*.

21. "The Central American Kairos," p. 10.

22. *The Road to Damascus: Kairos and Conversion*, drafted and signed by third-world Christians from El Salvador, Guatemala, Korea, Namibia, Nicaragua, Philippines, and South Africa (Washington, D.C.: Center of Concern, 1989). Excerpted in *Sojourners* (January 1990), pp. 26-28.

23. Ibid. pp. 25-26.

24. Ibid. pp. 12, 8.

25. Ibid. p. 16.

26. Ibid. p. 18.

27. Ibid. p. 22.

28. Since the completion of this chapter all three *kairos* documents have been compiled with reflection and a study guide by Robert McAfee Brown in *Kairos: Three Prophetic Challenges to the Church* (Grand Rapids, Michigan: Willim B. Eerdmans, 1990).

29. The fiftieth anniversary in 1984 saw numerous conferences and forums, but none so thoughtful and lucid as the essay of George Hunsinger, "Barth, Barmen, and the Confessing Church Today," *Katallegate* 9:2 (Summer 1985) and its subsequent responses in *Katallegate* 10:1-3 (Fall 1987).

30. Will D. Campbell, *Brother to a Dragonfly* (New York: The Seabury Press, 1977), p. 230.

31. Robert Jay Lifton, *The Broken Connection: On Death and the Continuity of Life* (New York: Simon and Shuster, 1979), p. 369.

32. Jürgen Moltmann, in G. Clarke Chapman, *Facing the Nuclear Heresy* (Elgin, Illinois: Brethren Press, 1986), p. xi.

33. Ulrich Duchrow, *Global Economy: A Confessional Issue for the Churches?* (Geneva, Switzerland: WCC Publications, 1987).

34. For an excellent account of low-intensity warfare, including its consideration in a confessional context, see Jack Nelson-Pallmeyer, *War*

Against the Poor (Maryknoll, New York: Orbis Books, 1989).

35. DeGruchy, *Bonhoeffer and South Africa*, p. 138.

CHAPTER 3: THE ENGINE OF HISTORY

1. Arthur J. Laffin and Anne Montgomery, eds., *Swords Into Plow-shares* (San Francisco: Harper & Row, 1987), pp. 177-85.

2. Elizabeth McAlister presented the oral arguments on behalf of the seven. Her remarks may be found in Philip Berrigan and Elizabeth McAlister, *The Time's Discipline* (Baltimore, Maryland: Fortkamp Publishing Company, 1989), pp. 132-44.

3. For a definitive and practical survey of these arguments, see Francis Anthony Boyle, *Defending Civil Resistance* (Dobbs Ferry, New York: Transnational Publishers, 1987).

4. The Griffiss Seven cite in combination Deuteronomy 5:6-7; Exodus 34:13-14; Deuteronomy 5:8-9; and Exodus 34:17.

5. Laffin and Montgomery, p. 179.

6. Robert Jay Lifton and Richard Falk, *Indefensible Weapons* (New York: Basic Books, 1982), pp. 38-56, 100-110.

7. Ibid. pp. 66-79.

8. Ibid. p. 87.

9. Thomas Farrell, quoted in Lifton and Falk, pp. 88-89.

10. Andrew Lawrence, quoted in Lifton and Falk, pp. 89-90.

11. See Gar Alperovitz, *Atomic Diplomacy* (New York: Viking Penguin, 1965, 1985).

12. There were a few voices who did. Dorothy Day's immediate editorial in *The Catholic Worker* (September 1945) comes to mind. That she recognized so readily the blasphemous significance is remarkable. For the text see Robert Ellsberg, ed., *By Little and By Little: The Selected Writings of Dorothy Day* (New York: Alfred A. Knopf, 1983), pp. 266-69.

13. I refer to the unilateral ultimatum delivered to the Soviet Union in March of 1946, forcing Soviet troop removal from Iran. Michio Kaku and Daniel Axelrod, *To Win a Nuclear War* (Boston: South End Press, 1987), p. 32.

14. Paul Ricoeur, *The Symbolism of Evil* (Boston: Beacon Press, 1967), p. 172.

15. Ibid. p. 192.

16. Judge Gordon Havey, 41st District Court, "The People of the State of Michigan *vs.* Kathleen Bowlin Meyer, et al.," May 13, 1980.

17. Ira Chernus, *Dr. Strangegod: On the Symbolic Meaning of Nuclear Weapons* (Columbia, South Carolina: University of South Carolina Press, 1986), pp. 49, 135.

18. Jacques Ellul, *The New Demons* (New York: The Seabury Press, 1975); idem, *The Technological Society* (New York: Vintage Books, 1964), pp. 141-46.

19. Ibid. pp. 55-56.

20. Lifton and Falk, p. 52.

21. Chernus, p. 134.

22. Chapman, p. 71.

23. Chernus, p. 15.

24. Lifton and Falk, p. 26.

25. Ibid.

26. Robert Oppenheimer, cited in Sissela Bok, *Secrets: On the Ethics of Concealment and Revelation* (New York: Vantage Books, 1984), p. 199.

27. See Howard Zinn, *Postwar America: 1945-1971* (New York: The Bobbs Merrill Company, 1973), pp. 158-63.

28. Daniel Ellsberg, "Call to Mutiny," in *Protest and Survive,* ed. E. P. Thompson and Dan Smith (New York: Monthly Review Press, 1981), pp. v-vi.

29. Ibid. p. i.

30. Kaku and Axelrod, op. cit.

31. Chernus, pp. 154-55.

32. Chapman, p. 13.

33. *In Defense of Creation: The Nuclear Crisis and a Just Peace* (Nashville: Graded Press, 1986), p. 92.

34. Dana Wilbanks and Ronald Stone, *Presbyterians and Peacemaking,* study document published by the Advisory Council on Church and Society (December 31, 1985).

CHAPTER 4: PRINCIPALITIES AND THE POWERS THAT BE

1. Stringfellow, *An Ethic for Christians and Other Aliens in a Strange Land*, p. 17.

2. Wink, p. 113.

3. S.G.F. Brandon, *The Trial of Jesus* (London: Paladin, 1971), p. 19.

4. Yoder, *The Politics of Jesus*, p. 141.

5. For a brief summary see Hendrik Berkof, *Christ and the Powers* (Scottdale, Pennsylvania: Herald Press, 1962), p. 73, n. 3.

6. Carl Jung, "Wotan," in Jim Garrison, *The Darkness of God* (Grand Rapids, Michigan: William B. Eerdmans Publishing Company, 1982), p. 154.

7. Carl Jung, "Terry Lectures at Yale, 1937," cited in Garrison, p. 158.

8. There is a resurgence of powers and demon talk across the theological spectrum. At this writing it is the rage in fundamentalist circles. There are conferences on spiritual warfare. Novels parading as spiritual thrillers are in their twenty-second printing. For a summary covering this broad range, see Thomas McAlpine, *Rediscovering "the Powers,"* in *Mission* (MARC Innovations in Mission Series, forthcoming). While this heavily spiritualized version makes no reference to the historical crises, they may form the social background for the revived interest.

9. William Stringfellow, *Free in Obedience* (New York: The Seabury Press, 1964). The pertinent chapter is "Christ and the Powers of Death," pp. 49-73. In essence, it is the talk at the Harvard Business School mentioned at the beginning of this chapter.

10. Walter Wink, *Unmasking the Powers* (Philadelphia: Fortress Press, 1987).

11. Wink, *Naming the Powers*, p. 8.

12. Ibid., p. 5.

13. Ibid., p. 84.

14. In what follows I am tracing the earlier work of G. B. Caird more than Wink's, which is also much commended. See G. B. Caird, *Principalities and Powers* (London: Oxford University Press, 1956), pp. 1-30.

15. Caird points out the *ben* in these titles does not signify a filial relationship but a classification. So, the expression "sons of the prophets" denotes a professional guild, not the offspring of prophets. "Son of man" is a human being, "son of a quiver" is an arrow, "sons of death" are those condemned, and so on. Caird, p. 2.

16. Ibid. p. 3.

17. James Sanders, "God Is God," *Foundations* 6 (October 1963), pp. 349f.

18. Wink, *Naming the Powers*, p. 91.

19. Caird, pp. 31-39.

20. Ibid. p. 37.

21. Wink, *Naming the Powers*, p. 136.

22. Stringfellow, *An Ethic for Christians and Other Aliens in a Strange Land*, p. 93.

23. Jacques Ellul, *The Presence of the Kingdom* (New York: The Seabury Press, 1967), p. 25.

24. Ibid. p. 69.

25. Ibid. pp. 71-72.

26. Jacques Ellul, *The Technological System* (New York: Continuum, 1980), p. 232.

27. Ellul, *The Technological Society*, p. 89.

28. Ibid. pp. 92-93.

29. Ellul, *The Technological System*, p. 130.

30. Ibid. p. 147.

31. Ibid. p. 152.

32. I am aware that I am less inclined to observe strictly this methodological caution. In much of the foregoing, and again in what is to follow, I move freely back and forth between the two tracks.

33. Ellul, *The Technological System*, p. 335, n. 2.

34. Jacques Ellul, *The Ethics of Freedom*, trans. and ed. Geoffrey W. Bromiley (Grand Rapids, Michigan: William B. Eerdmans Publishing Company, 1976), pp. 153-54.

35. Zinn, p. 13.

36. Ibid. p. 17. Specifically, Admiral William Leahy, Truman's chief of staff; General Henry Arnold, commanding general of the Air Force; General Carl Spaatz, commander of the Strategic Air Force; General Douglas MacArthur, commander of the Pacific theater; and General Dwight Eisenhower did not think the use of the bomb was necessary.

37. The most careful reading of the sources on this point is found in Alperovitz.

38. Cited in Thomas Merton, "Original Child Bomb," in *The Nonviolent Alternative*, ed. Gordon C. Zahn (New York: Farrar, Straus, Giroux , 1980), p. 11.

39. Ellul, *The Technological Society*, pp. 224-25.

40. Kaku and Axelrod, pp. 266-71. For more on cruise missile technology see Robert Aldridge, *First Strike!* (Boston: South End Press, 1983), pp. 141-59.

41. Escalation dominance is the ability to threaten or coerce other nations by being capable of dominating the next level of violence. Borrowed from the strategies of conventional warfare, it has been used with respect to nuclear weapons virtually since 1945. Kaku and Axelrod, pp. 4-5.

42. The story of his awakening and conversion is told briefly in Janet and Robert Aldridge, "A Nuclear Engineer's Family," in *Peacemakers*, ed. Jim Wallis (San Francisco: Harper & Row, Publishers, 1983), pp. 7-13.

43. Zinn, pp. 10-13.

44. For more on the place of SDI in the American political discourse, see Edward Tabor Linenthal, *Symbolic Defense* (Urbana: University of Illinois Press, 1989).

45. Oppenheimer was one of four scientists who served on Truman's Interim Committee. Their recommendation for immediate use of the

bomb was important in its public and historical justification. In later testimony before the Atomic Energy Commission Oppenheimer indicated that they had been kept in the dark as to the real military situation. His subsequent opposition to development of the hydrogen bomb led to his loss of security clearance under McCarthyism. Zinn, pp. 9-10, 200.

46. Lifton, *Indefensible Weapons*, p. 96.

47. The stories of McMichael and McGehee are recounted, among others, in Melissa Everett, *Breaking Ranks* (Philadelphia: New Society Publishers, 1989), pp. 47-86.

48. Dwight D. Eisenhower, quoted in Lifton, *Indefensible Weapons*, p. 96.

49. Stringfellow, *An Ethic for Christians and Other Aliens in a Strange Land*, pp. 88-89.

CHAPTER 5: LITURGICAL DIRECT ACTION

1. Stringfellow, *An Ethic for Christians and Other Aliens in a Strange Land*, p. 150.

2. Patrick Coy, "The One-Person Revolution of Ammon Hennacy," in *A Revolution of the Heart*, ed. Patrick Coy (Philadelphia: Temple University Press, 1988), p. 163.

3. Dorothy Day, quoted in Ann Klejment, "War Resistance and Property Destruction," in Coy, p. 285.

4. Stringfellow, *An Ethic for Christians and Other Aliens in a Strange Land*, p. 151.

5. Daniel Berrigan, *The Trial of the Catonsville Nine* (Boston: Beacon Press, 1970). The complete text is reprinted in *Daniel Berrigan: Poetry, Drama, Prose*, ed. Michael True (Maryknoll, New York: Orbis Books, 1988).

6. Francis McNutt, "Social Exorcism," in *Radical Grace*, published by the Center for Action and Contemplation, Albuquerque, New Mexico (Aug-Sept 1990), p. 8. Also recounted in Wink, *Unmasking the Powers*, p. 190, n. 65.

7. The ritual is described in detail in John Seed, Joanna Macy, Pat Fleming, Arne Naess, *Thinking Like a Mountain* (Philadelphia: New Society Publishers, 1988).

8. See Wink, "The Angels of Nature," *Unmasking the Powers*, pp. 153-71.

9. There are thoughtful and politically informed commentators, such as the feminist witch Starhawk, within the related movements of neo-paganism and eco-feminism. See Starhawk, "Ritual as Bonding,

Action as Ritual," in *Dreaming the Dark* (Boston: Beacon Press, 1982), pp. 154-80.

10. Jacques Ellul, *Money and Power* (Downers Grove, Illinois: InterVarsity Press, 1984). This is a translation of a work first published in 1954 as *L'Homme et l'argent*.

11. Ellul, *Money and Power*, p. 110.

12. Ibid. p. 113. Emphasis added.

13. H. Hamburger, "Money, Coins," in *The Interpreter's Dictionary of the Bible*, vol. 3 (Nashville: Abingdon, 1962), p. 433. Not figuring in the debate, but underscoring the liturgical character of the tribute, was the image on the coin's reverse; that is, Pax seated and holding a branch with the inscription *Pontif Maxim* ("High Priest").

14. See S. Kennard, *Render to God* (New York: Oxford University Press, 1950).

15. Ruether, p. 3.

16. Ibid. p. 61.

17. Dorothy Day noted the significance of this irony immediately. See "We Go on Record" (September 1945), in Robert Ellsberg, pp. 266-69.

18. For an excellent social commentary on the seasons, see Dieter T. Hessel, ed., *Social Themes of the Christian Year* (Philadelphia: The Geneva Press, 1983).

19. For a positive assessment of the magical intention of imagination and symbolic action, one which actually does fit with the liturgical reflections here, see Rubem Alves, *Tomorrow's Child* (San Francisco: Harper & Row, 1972), especially chap. 5.

20. Their separate origins are suggested in part by the ancient festival lists. In Exodus 34 they are separated. In Exodus 23:14-17, Unleavened Bread appears along in the list of pilgrim harvest festivals. Within the exodus narrative the statutes establishing them are distinct in the early literary strand, such as J: Exodus 12:21-27 and 13:3-10. It is not until the exile, represented by the P source, that they are merged: Exodus 12:1-20.

21. Hans-Joachim Kraus, *Worship in Israel* (Oxford: Basil Blackwell, 1966), p. 46.

22. This, of course, is part of the appeal of neo-paganism in the circles of radical environmental activism.

23. Roland DeVaux, *Ancient Israel* (New York: McGraw-Hill, 1961), p. 492. For example, Unleavened Bread—Ex 23:15 (E), 34:18 (J), Dt 16:3; Passover—Ex 12:21-27 (J), Dt 16:1,6; Both—Ex 12:1-20 (P).

24. "Worship does not depoliticize the event. On the contrary, it enhances the political implications of the event. . . . For this reason I

am not in agreement with the 'cultists' who attempt to minimize the political character of the exodus by insisting that the goal of the exodus was to celebrate a liturgical rite. ... From these and other texts they have attempted to support the position that the finality of the exodus was the cult—that is, an act essentially religious and not political." Rafael Avila, *Worship and Politics* (Maryknoll, New York: Orbis Books, 1977), pp. 14-15.

25. This would be reflected in Deuteronomy 16:1-17, though it is argued that this text is not a literary unity. DeVaux, p. 485.

26. Kraus, p. 54.

27. Avila, pp. 55-58; and Tissa Balasuriya, *The Eucharist and Human Liberation* (Maryknoll, New York: Orbis Books, 1977).

28. Jürgen Moltmann, *The Power of the Powerless* (San Francisco: Harper & Row, 1983), pp. 122-26.

29. The fullest description of the baptismal process of examination and ritual in this period is found in the *Apostolic Tradition* (16-23) of Hippolytus, which probably originated in Rome about 215 C.E.

30. Hatchett, p. 48.

31. Ibid.

32. In the liturgical meditations of the next section, there is a brief historical reflection on this very theological and political irony. See Chapter 8, pp. 149-56.

33. This is typified in a later era by the working out and provision of the Gregorian calendar, named after Pope Gregory XIII in 1582, which replaced the Julian calendar introduced under Julius Caesar. Until recently it was common usage to number years in the "secular" calendar A.D., that is, *Anno Domini*, "the year of the Lord."

34. Mowinckel's theory of the enthronement of Yahweh placed it at Tabernacles, the ancient beginning of the year. Jean Danielou, *The Bible and Liturgy* (Notre Dame, Indiana: University of Notre Dame Press, 1956), p. 335.

35. In the Constantinian period Gregory of Nazianzus even connected Christmas with Tabernacles: God coming to tabernacle among us with human flesh! Danielou, p. 344.

36. Ruether, pp. 103-4.

37. Thomas Merton, "Time and Liturgy," *Seasons of Celebration*, p. 47.

38. Paul Neuenzeit, "Time," *Sacramentum Verbi III* (New York: Herder & Herder, 1970), p. 914.

39. Karl Barth, *The Church and the Political Problem of Our Day* (New York: Charles Scribner's Sons, 1939), pp. 82, 84.

40. Avila, p. 27.

41. Ibid.

42. A similar story is told about St. Rose of Lima. She is reported to have gone out in solitary march to greet invading conquistadors with elements of the eucharist in hand. She offered; they, in this account, departed. I heard this story from my Peruvian friend Pio Celestino.

43. Thomas Merton, "A Tribute to Gandhi," in Zahn, p. 181.

CHAPTER 6: ADVENT

1. See pp. 23-25.

2. Josephus, *Antiquities* XVIII, v, 2.

3. "Letter to Eberhard Bethge," Dietrich Bonhoeffer, *Letters and Papers from Prison* (New York: The Macmillan Company, 1953, 1967) p. 96.

4. Alfred Delp, *The Prison Meditations of Alfred Delp* (New York: The Macmillan Company, 1966), p. 17.

5. Ibid. p. 45.

6. Ibid, p. 29.

CHAPTER 7: CHRISTMAS

1. Jacques Ellul, *Apocalypse* (New York: The Seabury Press, 1977), p. 67.

2. Elizabeth McAlister, "Bringing Forth in Hope," *Year One*, mimeographed newsletter of Jonah House, Baltimore, Maryland (January 1984). For more on the Griffiss Plowshares, see pp. 53-55.

3. Stringfellow, *An Ethic for Christians and Other Aliens in a Strange Land*, pp. 138-39.

CHAPTER 8: EPIPHANY

1. I am relying on Oscar Cullmann, "The Origin of Christmas," *The Early Church* (Philadelphia: Westminster Press, 1956), p. 25f.

2. For a readable account of the ambiguities of Constantine's conversion, see Roland Baintain, *The Horizon History of Christianity* (New York: Avon Books, 1966), p. 92.

3. Cullmann, *The Early Church*, p. 31.

4. Clarence Jordan, *The Cotton Patch Version of Paul's Epistles* (Chicago: Follett, 1968).

5. Wink, *Naming the Powers*, p. 93f.

6. Ibid. pp. 26-35. Also Caird, especially pp. 1-22. See above pp. 77-81.

7. Herodotus, cited by Raymond Brown, *The Birth of the Messiah* (Garden City, New York: Doubleday, 1977), p. 167.

CHAPTER 9: LENT

1. See above, "The Turning World: A Biblical Reprise," pp. 115-17.

2. Clarence Jordan, *The Substance of Faith and Other Cotton Patch Sermons* (New York: Association Press, 1972), p. 56.

3. See above, Chapter 3, and "A Case of Possession," pp. 99-102.

4. Yoder, *The Politics of Jesus*, pp. 32-33.

CHAPTER 10: PALM SUNDAY

1. Walter Wink, who has been working these passages for the third volume of his trilogy, *Engaging the Powers* (Philadelphia: Fortress Press, forthcoming), has pointed out the significance of this for a biblical understanding of the principalities.

2. Jacques Ellul, *The Meaning of the City* (Grand Rapids, Michigan: William B. Eerdmans Publishing Company, 1970), p. 9. Needless to say, this is also a view consistent with Wink's view of the powers as developed in Chapter 4 above.

3. See above, pp. 28-29.

4. This observation has been made by Jim Douglass in "Transformation," *Ground Zero* (Spring 1990), pp. 6-8. He suggests it in the context of reporting a delegation to Gaza and the West Bank, though it also figures prominently in *The Nonviolent Coming of God* (Maryknoll, New York: Orbis Books, forthcoming).

5. Douglass, "Transformation," p. 6.

6. See above, "A Biblical Word for the Times," especially p. 42.

7. See Wink, *Unmasking the Powers*, p. 65, and p. 190, n. 63.

8. Stringfellow, *Free in Obedience*, pp. 35-37.

9. Paul Brooks Duff, " 'Fools Rush In': The Disciples and Jesus' Entry Into Jerusalem in the Gospel of Mark," The College of St. Thomas, St. Paul, Minnesota, unpublished.

CHAPTER 11: GOOD FRIDAY

1. See "Jesus and Liturgical Action," pp. 18-25 above. The Jews would have experienced crucifixion not only under Roman rule, but in all likelihood under Persian and Greek rule as well. Josephus recounts the crucifixion of resistance leaders under the Selucid rule of Antiochus

Epiphanes (175-163 B.C.E.) for refusal to abandon their religion (*Antiquities* XII, 256). Around the time of Jesus' birth, following the uprising prompted by Herod the Great's death, some two thousand Jews were crucified by the Romans outside of Jerusalem as a deterrent to further revolt (*Antiquities* XVII, 295; *War* II, 75).

2. J. F. Strange, "Method of Crucifixion," *The Interpreter's Dictionary of the Bible*, supp. vol. (Nashville: Abingdon Press, 1976), pp. 199-200.

3. See Walter Wink, *Violence and Nonviolence in South Africa* (Philadelphia: New Society Publishers, 1987), pp. 12-34, for a wonderfully uppity reading of the Sermon.

4. See "Jesus and Liturgical Action," pp. 18-25 above.

5. Martin Luther King, Jr., "Letter From a Birmingham Jail," April 16, 1963 (Philadelphia: American Friends Service Committee, 1963).

CHAPTER 13: EASTERTIDE

1. Ellul, *Apocalypse*, pp. 16-17.

2. Vincent and Steve, *Jerusalem de l'Ancien Testament*, cited in W. F. Stinespring, "Temple, Jerusalem," in *Interpreter's Dictionary of the Bible*, vol. 4 (Nashville: Abingdon Press, 1962), p. 556.

3. Regardless of chronological accuracy, this point is structured into the narrative continuity of Luke/Acts.

4. See above, "Liturgy and Allegiance," pp. 14-17.

CHAPTER 14: PENTECOST

1. Albert Camus, "The Unbeliever and the Christians," fragments of a statement made at the Dominican Monastery of Latour-Maubourg in 1948, in *Resistance, Rebellion and Death* (New York: Vantage Books, 1960), p. 71.

2. Stanley B. Marrow, *Speaking the Word Fearlessly* (New York: Paulist Press, 1982). See also Cassidy, pp. 45-46.

Index